THE POLITICS OF REAPPRAISAL 1918–1939

THE POLITICS OF REAPPRAISAL 1918–1939

edited by

GILLIAN PEELE
Fellow and Tutor in Politics
Lady Margaret Hall, Oxford

and

CHRIS COOK
Senior Research Officer
London School of Economics

Selection and editorial matter
© Gillian Peele and Chris Cook 1975

Introduction and Chapter 9 © Max Beloff 1975
Chapter 1 © John Stubbs 1975
Chapter 2 © David Harkness 1975
Chapter 3 © Geoffrey McDonald 1975
Chapter 4 © John Campbell 1975
Chapter 5 © Gillian Peele 1975
Chapter 6 © John Stevenson 1975
Chapter 7 © Chris Cook 1975
Chapter 8 © Paul Addison 1975
Chapter 10 © Colin Seymour-Ure 1975

First published 1975 by
THE MACMILLAN PRESS LTD
London and Basingstoke
Associated companies in New York
Dublin Melbourne Johannesburg and Madras

SBN 333 16653 1

Photoset, printed and bound
in Great Britain by
REDWOOD BURN LIMITED
Trowbridge & Esher

Contents

Acknowledgements

This book owes a considerable debt to a variety of persons and organisations. Both editors were for a time students of Nuffield College, Oxford, and a special debt is owed to the Warden and Fellows of the College. An individual debt is owed by the editors to the Warden and Fellows of St Antony's College, Oxford, and to colleagues and friends at the London School of Economics. Max Beloff gave generously of his time and knowledge in the production of this volume. The index for the book was compiled by Mrs L. V. Peele.

We are indebted to the family of the late Collin Brooks for permission to quote from Brooks's diary, to the *Nation* for permission to quote from D. Lloyd George's 'The Statesman's Task', and to H.M.S.O. and Cambridge University Press for permission to use tables from *Report of the Royal Commission on the Press, 1949* and Kaldor and Silverman's *A Statistical Analysis of Advertising Expenditure and of the Revenue of the Press*, respectively. In addition, we have used or referred to material in the Bonar Law, Austen Chamberlain, Salisbury, Quickswood, Balfour, Steel-Maitland, Hewins, Bull, Crewe, Asquith, Carson, Bridgeman and Conservative Central Office papers.

The publishers have made every effort to trace the copyright-holders but if they have inadvertently overlooked any, they will be pleased to make the necessary arrangement at the first opportunity.

Notes on Contributors

PAUL ADDISON. b. 1943. Educated at Pembroke and Nuffield College, Oxford. Lecturer in History, Pembroke College, Oxford, 1966–7; formerly Research Assistant to the late Randolph S. Churchill; Lecturer in Modern History, University of Edinburgh since 1967. He has contributed to *Lloyd George: Twelve Essays*, ed. A. J. P. Taylor, and to *By-Elections in British Politics*, ed. Chris Cook and John Ramsden.

MAX BELOFF. b. 1913. F.B.A., D. Litt. Principal, the University College at Buckingham; formerly Gladstone Professor of Government and Public Administration at Oxford and Fellow of All Souls College.

JOHN CAMPBELL. b. 1947. Educated at Edinburgh University. His first book, *Lloyd George: The Goat in the Wilderness* is to be published in 1976. He is currently writing a biography of Lord Birkenhead.

CHRIS COOK. b. 1945. Educated at St Catharine's College, Cambridge; Oriel and Nuffield College, Oxford. Lecturer in Politics, Magdalen College, Oxford, 1969–70; since 1970 Senior Research Officer at the London School of Economics. His previous published books include *The Age of Alignment: Electoral Politics in Britain, 1922–1929* and (with co-authors) *By-Elections in British Politics, European Political Facts, 1918–1973, Sources in British Political History, 1900–1951, The Decade of Disillusion* and *British Historical Facts, 1830–1900*.

DAVID HARKNESS. b. 1937. Educated at Campbell College, Belfast, and Corpus Christi College, Cambridge. Professor of Irish History, Queen's University, Belfast, and Deputy Editor of the *Journal of Imperial and Commonwealth History*. Formerly Senior Lecturer in History at the University of Kent and Visiting Lecturer at the University of Ibadan. His previous published works include *The Restless Dominion: the Irish Free State and the British Commonwealth of Nations* and 'Mr. de Valera's Dominion: Irish Relations with Britain and the Commonwealth', *Journal of Commonwealth Political Studies*, Vol. VIII, No. 3 (1970).

GEOFFREY MCDONALD. b. 1945. Educated at the University of Queensland and Wolfson College, Cambridge. Formerly archivist to the Confederation of British Industry.

GILLIAN PEELE. b. 1949. Educated at the University of Durham and at St Anne's and Nuffield College, Oxford. Formerly Research Fellow, St Antony's College, Oxford, she is currently official Fellow and Tutor in Politics at Lady Margaret Hall, Oxford. Her previous publications include 'St. George's Westminster and the Empire Crusade', in *By-Elections in British Politics*. She is currently working on a study of the Conservative Party and imperial questions in the 1930s as well as a textbook on British Government.

COLIN SEYMOUR-URE. b. 1938. Educated at Magdalen College, Oxford, Carleton University and Nuffield College, Oxford. Currently Senior Lecturer in Politics at the University of Kent. His previous publications include *The Press, Politics and the Public* and *The Political Impact of Mass Media*, as well as contributions to successive Nuffield election studies.

JOHN STEVENSON. b. 1946. Educated Worcester College and Nuffield College, Oxford. Lecturer in History, Oriel College, Oxford, since 1971. His previous publications include *Popular Protest and Public Order*, ed. with R. Quinault.

JOHN STUBBS. b. 1943. Educated at the University of Toronto, the London School of Economics and St Catherine's College, Oxford. Lecturer in Politics, Trent University, 1967–9; currently Assistant Professor of History at the University of Waterloo. His previous publications include 'Lord Milner and Patriotic Labour, 1914–18', *English Historical Review*, Vol. LXXXVII (Oct 1972).

Introduction

MAX BELOFF

All ages are ages of reappraisal; social and political institutions must readjust to changes in the environment. If we use the term to describe the state of British politics between the two world wars, it is, however, with some quite specific features of the period in mind. The First World War – the Great War as it was called then – affected the position of Britain in the world and altered the internal balance of her economy and society more than any single experience for a very long time. So great were the strains upon traditional institutions, that there was even serious talk of the possibility of a revolutionary solution to the problems of the day. In fact in retrospect all these problems did receive some kind of solution; all the institutions that had been challenged underwent a sufficient degree of adjustment to make them viable once more. In this volume of essays our concern is with the constitutional, political and administrative aspects of the general theme.

The history of the twenty years that separate the two world wars of this century has, from the narrowly British point of view, been studied in different ways in the subsequent decades. The accent at first was very largely on foreign policy centring on the question of 'appeasement' and the responsibility for the outbreak of the second great conflict. It was material on this subject, whether from the archives or in the form of memoirs or apologias that was the first to appear. For more domestic aspects of the story it was still necessary to rely largely on what could be followed by studying through the published sources, and by attention to what attracted attention in the light of the events of the immediately

1

post-1945 period – the rise of Labour, the further development of the 'welfare state', the curse of mass unemployment and its social consequences. The accent was either on the basic continuity of British institutions or on the failures to grapple with certain problems as seen in the light of the new triumphant Keynesian collectivism to which the major elements in all parties gave their adherence.

In the 1970s there is an apparent change of some importance. The historians writing on the interwar years have no first-hand memory of them; 'Munich' is as remote to all the contributors to this volume (except the present writer) as was 'Fashoda' to him at their age. They are writing in a world in which the achievements of Britain in recovery after the Second World War are no longer seen as a prelude to an unending era of peace, prosperity and massive economic growth. They can no longer take for granted either the achievement of social harmony or the institutions that depend upon it. They are therefore driven to asking rather different questions about the preceding period and to giving greater weight to some aspects of it than would have been the case some years ago.

They are liable to see British parliamentary government – the whole heritage of nineteenth-century liberalism – as having been much more at risk, as having had a more precarious existence than one would be led to expect by the standard histories of the time. And this would be still more true of the world system – Empire turning into Commonwealth – of which Britain was then the acknowledged centre. The idea that the system could peacefully evolve through the operation of British parliamentarianism into a series of successful exponents of the Westminster model still linked by material and moral ties to the Crown and the Mother of Parliaments now appears very difficult to grasp as a serious vision of the future, seriously though it was taken at the time.[1]

What now seems significant is something of which contemporaries were perhaps less fully aware than their successors, namely the impact upon Britain not just of the First World War but of the movement towards democracy in the broadest sense to which the war for a number of reasons gave an added impetus. The period with which we are dealing was the first in which legitimacy was conferred upon British government by the operation of universal adult suffrage – the only major bar to the franchise was removed when the voting age for women was made the same as that for men by the Act of 1928. At the same time the operation of the educational changes of the late nineteenth century was having its effect. Some degree of literacy became normal, and this made organisation outside the confines of the traditional upper and middle classes much easier to effect and at the same time helped to alter the ways in which political interest was stimulated or directed.

The passage from a society based upon distinctions largely of property to a mass society in which privilege could fight at best only a rearguard action is something which whenever it occurs is likely to subject the society in question to very great strains. In some it has led to catastrophe. But at the very least it is bound to alter the way in which things are perceived and the way in which things are done. The historian of the interwar years is today likely to be curious as to the structure of politics in the period, as to the operation not only of the machinery of government or the political parties but of all the variety of groups from organised interests to those on the fringe offering utopian or extremist solutions to the problems of the time. How did people define what they wanted out of politics and how did they set about getting it? How far were things ostensibly the same – Parliament, the civil service, the parties, the press – in fact very different from their pre-1914 exemplars?[2]

It is clear that from the point of view of the 1970s questions of this kind must bulk large and that historians of politics are now more sensitive to what goes on outside the Westminster–Whitehall circuit. No doubt some of this change of viewpoint has been due to the new availability of materials. Some of this material is new in kind; the public opinion poll was only beginning its career at the very end of the period; and it is the availability of polling material as well as of other evidence capable of statistical analysis that has produced such things as the Nuffield College election studies. It will be seen that a number of contributors to the present work have had connections with Nuffield College. Indeed it is interesting to note that it is now for the first time that we have studies devoted to earlier general elections or to the by-elections of the interwar period (and after) to which, again, a number of the writers in the present volume have contributed.[3]

But these studies in so far as they deal with relations between politicians and the electorate still leave one with the task of discovering what the politicians themselves were doing, and here of course we now have what the previous generation did not, a good deal of documentary material. The new rules for dealing with official archives (and these rightly or wrongly affect the conduct of private collections) mean that they are now open for the whole period with which the present volume is concerned. But public papers have their limitations – even if the extent of these is not always appreciated by enthusiastic graduate students staggered by the riches open to them. Often it is private papers that need to be consulted to get closer to the truth.

It is of course true that large collections of the private papers of politicians have been a prominent feather of the environment of British historians, particularly of the nineteenth century; in that sense they are the envy of their continental *confrères*, since in countries such as France similar collections either do not exist at all or are jealously guarded by the families of the individuals in question. To a limited extent this is true for more recent British history as well. The Churchill papers will not be fully in the public domain until Mr Martin Gilbert finishes his authorised biography and the companion volumes of documents. Much work on the other side of politics has been held up for Mr David Marquand to produce his life of Ramsay MacDonald. But even so the historian cannot reasonably complain.

Two particular points are worth noting here. In the first place there is a more conscious effort under way to house and catalogue documents of this kind whether at the London School of Economics, the Bodleian Library, the Cambridge University Library, Churchill College, the House of Lords Record Office, or other lesser repositories. In the second place it may be true that one result of the democratisation of British politics – one of the principal themes of current study – is that there may be no more collections of this kind. The telephone is bound to have been a substitute to some extent for written communications – imagine a modern governmental crisis without one, and think of the legions of footmen carrying handwritten notes around the West End and clubland during nineteenth-century crises of this kind. But even when people write the conditions under which they live no longer conduce to the retention of archives. If you are a Cecil and part of a family with four centuries of involvement in public affairs and houses to match, keeping papers may be routine. If like Herbert Morrison you have made your own way and find it necessary to move to something smaller, the papers go.

What all this means is that the period here under consideration may prove to be unique, the first and last in which in a basically democratic system one can not only document the strivings of the masses and of particular groups but also deal with what Mr Maurice Cowling has called high politics, the kind of decision-making that in all systems remains the prerogative of the few.

One other feature of the present volume perhaps demands emphasis – it gives a good deal more space to the 'right' in British 'politics' as against the left. There are some reasons for this apart from the preferences of particular writers. It is partly a question of redressing the balance. On the whole historians have been interested in 'progress' – the Labour Party appeared to be the progressive party of the age and to American scholars whose work has not been unimportant, there was a certain thrill in dealing with socialists and socialism as central subjects while in their own country they would have had to be treated as elements on the fringe. It is therefore the case that so far the 'Whig dogs' have had the best of it. And for the nostalgic the decline of the Liberal Party has also had an appeal, which has had little to do with the Party's more recent 'revival'. (It may be hazarded that Mr Jeremy Thorpe's legions have not much more to do with Gladstone's or Asquith's than Gerald Ford's Republicans with those who voted Abraham Lincoln into office.)

Another reason for the partial concentration on the right is that it also means concentrating as far as the period is concerned on government rather than on opposition. After all, for all but about three years the Conservatives with or without allies were the governing party of interwar Britain. It is now thought remarkable that a party of the 'right' should thus entrench itself in a regime of universal suffrage, and reasons for its success are rightly sought. In addition, with governments that increasingly find it hard to exert their authority at all, government itself as one finds it in earlier periods becomes at once a more attractive and more mysterious subject.

A series of essays such as those collected here is neither a substitute for a general history of the period nor an exhaustive introduction to those aspects of it which the writers feel are neglected; chance must, as always, come into the picture. What it can do, and what no doubt the editors hope it will do, is give an impetus to further studies of the period both by pointing to questions which still require much more work to be done upon them and by indicating ways in which the material now at our disposal can most effectively be used. The remaining task of this brief introduction is to illustrate in a little more detail the nature of the contributions of the different authors and their essays.

In form, John Stubbs's chapter on the Conservative Party during the First World War deals with a period prior to that with which this volume is in general concerned. In reality, however, as he conclusively demonstrates, the experience of the war years are essential in order to understand some of the features of the Conservative Party in the interwar period, with which some of the later chapters deal. For understandable reasons much of the writing about the politics of the war years has concentrated on the conflicts within Asquith's government and their solution in the elevation to power of David Lloyd George. The Conservatives have played mainly the role of an off-stage chorus. But there was in fact a good deal more to it than that.

In respect of policy, some of the issues that still convulsed politics on the eve of the war – Ireland, the Welsh Church, the House of Lords, 'drink' – were to prove on their way to resolution or simply abandoned as no longer in the forefront of people's minds. For a time issues arising out of the war itself – conscription in particular, but also the demands made upon property-owners, landlords for instance, in the name of the war effort, provide a substitute.

But these issues in their turn only pointed to broader ones to which the Conservative Party had increasingly to turn its attention as the problems of reconstruction loomed on the political horizon; the role of government in respect of the economy which involved a clash between the paternalist traditions of one aspect of Toryism and the inheritance from a section of *laissez-faire* Liberalism of another. It involved both attitudes towards the 'welfare state', which in some of its aspects had clearly come to stay, and towards the old question of protection versus free trade that had wrecked the party's unity during its most recent period of independent power. But even these important questions, together with the imperial problems (with which the question of protection was so closely linked), might be thought of as less important than the acceptance of universal suffrage, and so of democracy, as the environment within which the party would have to operate in future.

John Stubbs's chapter, ending as it does in 1918, does not enable one to follow the effects of this change in the electorate upon the party in the country, the changes in candidatures and ultimately in the political leadership which progressively diminished the aristocratic element in the highest councils of the party in favour of its more middle-class components; though Stubbs does mention one abortive attempt on the margin of official Conservatism to win a section of the working class over to a patriotic and imperialist standpoint by contrast with the growing pacifism of official Labour. What he does also show is the way in which the constraints first of patriotic opposition and then of coalition brought about a movement towards organisation among backbenchers, first in the Business Committee and then in the War Committee which were in their turn the forerunners of the '1922 committee' which was to play so important a part in the affairs of the party in later times.

The replacement of the Liberal Party by the Labour Party as the alternative party of government has, as has been noted, been a more frequent preoccupation of recent historians. In looking into the matter in more detail they have on the whole produced a picture in which the element of inevitability owing to long-term social changes has tended to diminish in the face of considerations arising from the tactics of leadership and the impact of fortuitous circumstances. It may be that greater familiarity with American history of the same period that is characteristic of so many of the younger generation helps to direct attention towards the very different development there and results in people asking why the British Liberal Party did not manage to perform the same metamorphosis into the normal party of labour, as did the Democrats in the United States.

Two essays deal with aspects of this problem. Chris Cook directs attention to an aspect of the Liberal–Labour question that has been largely overlooked, namely what happened at the level of local government. How did the Liberals let themselves get ousted from the Town Halls just at a time when local government was increasingly important as the executive arm of new social policies themselves largely deriving from the legislation of previous Liberal governments? How far, for instance, did fear of 'socialism' in the postwar period drive Liberal councillors into alliances with the Conservatives that were to prove an ultimate source of weakness at the local and the parliamentary level?

Chris Cook's conclusions are challenging. In the 1920s, when fear of socialism was most trumpeted, the Liberal decline at local level, though marked, was not yet catastrophic. It was in the 1930s that any serious challenge by the Liberals as an independent force faded away even in the Midlands industrial cities and towns where they had been a major force. Does the loss then of the citadels of nonconformity suggest some other and deeper reason why

Liberal councillors succumbed to the Tory embrace while their old following among the electorate largely drifted into the Labour camp? Have we not here one clue to the Labour landslide victory of 1945 with which modern British electoral politics begins?

John Campbell directs our attention to quite a different aspect of the problem, namely the way in which the Liberal Party, though weakened at the grass-roots, retained an important following among intellectuals and was the vehicle for the consideration and enunciation of policies that found increasing echo outside the Liberals' own ranks. This situation was true both in respect of international affairs (the League of Nations, disarmament), of imperial affairs (the kind of gradual devolution of power in India recommended in the Simon Report and taken a stage further by the Government of India Act, as well as the formalising of the independent status of the old Dominions), but above all in domestic affairs.

Keynesian economics did not receive their full public theoretical exposition until the appearance of the *General Theory of Employment, Interest and Money* in 1936; its general approach underlay the Liberal 'Yellow Book' of 1928 and Lloyd George's claim in the 1929 general election that the party could 'conquer unemployment'. But in all aspects of policy taken up and promoted by the Liberal Party it could be argued that other, by now more powerful parties, were in a better position to put them into effect. Liberalism did not apparently need Liberals; 'we are all Liberals now' meant that no one need proclaim himself a Liberal in particular. And after the very narrow failure of 1929, when the working of the electoral system destroyed Lloyd George's hopes, an increasing number of people (including intellectuals) behaved as though this were true.

Two other essays touch on an aspect of politics that has largely been overlooked by historians who have concentrated on the parliamentary scene, and that was the degree to which fear of revolution or an out-and-out challenge to the political system itself was a reality. It arose partly from reaction to the Russian revolution and to the subsequent challenges to the existing order elsewhere in continental Europe and partly from the reaction to the widespread industrial unrest of the immediate postwar years. In his chapter on the defeat of the General Strike of 1926 Geoffrey McDonald throws new light upon the extent to which government had been prepared since 1921 to meet such an all-out threat to economic life. But he also shows the extent to which the realisation by the T.U.C. that strike action of the classical kind was turning out to be inadequate to force the government's hand, and the way in which its leaders came to accept surrender rather than see the movement develop into a revolutionary one that might have got out of their control.

As a result of the failure of the General Strike, leadership in the trade union movement came to rest firmly in the hands of the right, so that it was largely the trade union wing of the Labour movement that prevented the Labour Party from undergoing a strong leftward shift that might otherwise have been the response to the debacle of 1931.

In the 1930s the situation was altered by the high rate of unemployment and the apparent inability of government to make much impact upon it. It was further the case that this unemployment, being largely in the older staple trades, was also geographically concentrated, so that the unemployed themselves seemed to inhabit a different world from the more prosperous South and Midlands. In 1931–2 this situation gave scope to the Communist-led – though not wholly Communist-dominated – National Unemployed Workers Movement which pursued its agitation in respect of relief scales and their administration through marches and demonstrations which brought about a number of violent clashes with the police. This activity culminated in the hunger march of the autumn of 1932, which the authorities viewed with considerable apprehension, and which did indeed lead to some degree of disorder, particularly in London when the marchers converged upon the capital. Yet as John Stevenson points out in his chapter on this subject, what remains remarkable is not the extent of the violence but how little of it there was in view of the hardship and hopelessness that prolonged unemployment was bringing about in many communities.

Stevenson examines some of the reasons that have been adduced for this fact and adds some of his own, including the failure of the N.U.W.M. to involve the traditional labour organisations, the trade unions and the Labour Party in its struggle. It would seem in the light of what is now known that the N.U.W.M. got the worst of both worlds. It was not in fact prepared to use violent means in order to get its way, but it was sufficiently under suspicion of being an instrument of international Communism for it to have no hope of overcoming the prejudices felt against it throughout the range of the normal political spectrum. The disorders provoked by Fascism later in the decade, leading to the

Public Order Act of 1936, were also a pale simulacrum of what was happening in continental Europe. In so far as British politicians gave serious weight to the possibility of revolutionary violence from any quarter affecting politics in the Britain of the interwar years, they were clearly wrong. Stevenson's comparison with the fate of Chartism in 1848 is a particularly apt one.

It has been suggested that the Irish Treaty of 1921 ended the Irish question in the form in which it had affected the British political scene for almost a century and in particular removed the principal factor for cohesiveness in the Conservative and Unionist Party. The Union as far as the twenty-six counties of the Free State were concerned was now at an end. Yet as we in the 1970s have had ample reason to know, this was not to be the end of the Irish impact on Britain itself. While no major issues of conflict arose between the two countries and while, largely because of the closeness of economic and personal ties, total separation seemed unthinkable, there was enough friction on a variety of issues to prevent the question from ever becoming wholly dormant. The so-called 'partition' of Ireland, that is to say Ulster's separate status under the Treaty, was thrust into renewed prominence by the boundary settlement of 1926; disputes over financial questions arising out of the Treaty spilled over into the economic field; the rights retained by Britain in the Irish ports intended for the common defence were treated as though they represented a continuation of alien control, until surrendered by the Chamberlain government as part of the policy of 'appeasement'. And, as David Harkness has shown in his other writings, there was the underlying difference over Dominion status, seen by Britain as the culmination of a process, by the Irish as a stepping-stone towards republican independence on the road towards which they contributed mightily to a general loosening of the ties of the Commonwealth.

In the immediately postwar period, the 'die-hards' had opposed and deplored the concessions made to Ireland by Lloyd George, and the 'betrayal' of southern Unionism was no doubt one of the factors that contributed to his downfall. Thereafter much of the die-hard spirit was concentrated on the question of constitutional change in India. This subject has latterly been treated largely in terms of the Indian nationalist movement itself as a part of the history of the Indian sub-continent, in respect of which the period of British rule increasingly takes on the appearance of an interlude less important than other and more

permanent factors in the making of a socially Indian consciousness. In Gillian Peele's essay the question is looked at from
quite a different point of view. What she is seeking to show is the
impact of the debate over the direction and pace of constitutional
change in India upon British party politics and in particular upon
the unity of the Conservative Party.

The struggle within the party in the period between the Irwin
declaration in favour of ultimate Dominion status (made in 1929)
and the passage of the Government of India Act, is very illumi-
nating as to the structure of the party at that time, since the issue
was fought out at both the parliamentary and the constituency
level. It was also involved for a time with the challenge to
Baldwin's leadership mounted by the press lords in 1930. It also
suggests the possibilities of action by pressure groups and the
limitations upon such action in the British system, whether the
pressure groups be motivated by general ideological predilections
or by more direct material interests. Since one result of the argument was to alienate Winston Churchill from the bulk of the Conservative Party with the result that he could not be brought back
into office by a Conservative prime minister in peace-time – his
conduct at the time of the abdication crisis widened but did not
cause the breach – the whole question is one of very considerable
importance and deserves the extensive treatment given to it here.

Of Baldwin's two opponents among the press lords, Beaverbrook was never interested in India, but for Rothermere the importance of the issue was at least equal to those of empire free
trade and imperial preference which were more congenial to his
partner and rival. Paul Addison's treatment of Rothermere's role
as a die-hard in the 1930s raises other and interesting issues. The
principal one – and one of the few in this volume that touches
directly on foreign policy – is the impact on British politics of the
rise of Nazi Germany.

The connection between support for appeasement and hostility
to Bolshevism has perhaps been over-stressed by some writers in
respect of the Conservative Party as a whole. But in Rothermere's
case it certainly holds good. Indeed in 1934 he went so far as to
approve the return to Germany of all her former colonies. Yet at
the same time, as a die-hard, Rothermere was bound to be a sup-
porter of rearmament. It was the air arm that most attracted his
attention. But the air arm was of much greater significance in relation to a presumed threat from Germany than against any
Russian menace. So at the same time as Rothermere advocated

friendship with the Nazis he was pressing for defence policy to be based on the presumption of a sudden and overwhelming German attack from the air.

But the contradictions in Rothermere's attitude to foreign and defence questions were as nothing compared to his random and idiosyncratic approach to home politics. Setting up a party of his own, supporting Oswald Mosley and the British Union of Fascists, seeking an understanding with Churchill – the main impression left is that of an irresponsible and almost directionless dabbler.

Addison's essay on Rothermere is in one sense a footnote to the analytical study of the British press as a whole during the twenties and thirties, which is Colin Seymour-Ure's subject. He is interested not in what the press lords wanted in politics but in the conditions in the press that gave them their short-lived illusion of power. In a sense the presslords of this period had their forerunner in Northcliffe, but the world in which they were operating was a different one – it was the new literate working class and no longer the lower middle-class of the original *Daily Mail* readership that was now to be wooed and won. With the decline of the traditional ruling class and the change in social habit that went with it, the importance of clubland and the evening newspapers that fed its appetite for gossip both declined. On the other hand, further improvements in communications and the disappearance of the self-sustaining economies and cultures of some provincial centres meant a corresponding downgrading of the provincial press in favour of the national dailies and the 'chains'. Money could still be made out of newspapers but competition was deadly; politicians no longer controlled or much influenced newspapers, but the power of the press lords to equate the circulation of their papers with the command of their readers' votes was by no means to be taken for granted. The age of the 'platform' was over – radio gave it a fitful new lease of life – the age of the 'box' lay ahead. No wonder that the touch of the politicians was so uncertain when it came to dealing with the public.

If the control of the media is a subject that must be attended to in order to understand the structure of politics, it is the contention of my own essay that the same is true of the civil service. The civil service was also something designed to suit other conditions and now put to work for what was becoming a democracy. As a corporate entity and through individuals who carried great authority, it played a major part in the history of the interwar years and once again it is a part which we are only now in a position to assess.

Notes

1. For the outlook as seen at the beginning of the period see Max Beloff, *Imperial Sunset*, vol. I: *The Liberal Empire* (London, 1969).

2. I hope to explore these themes in the volume on the period 1915–51 which I am contributing to Arnold's *History of Modern Britain*, ed. A. G. Dickens and Norman Gash.

3. See *By-Elections in British Politics*, ed. Chris Cook and John Ramsden (London, 1973).

1 The Impact of the Great War on the Conservative Party

JOHN STUBBS

Those few historians who have written about the modern Conservative Party have not devoted a great deal of attention to the period of the 1914–18 war. Yet an understanding of this period is essential to any study of both the modern Conservative Party and modern Conservativism. Fundamental principles of Conservativism and the *modus vivendi* of the parliamentary party were reshaped by the war. And, as a result, the interwar politics of the Conservative Party were profoundly influenced by the politics of the war.

That reactionary and totally negative mood which had gripped the Unionist Party since 1910, and which had been most visibly evident in the excesses of opposition to Home Rule, was apparently calmed and refined by a national dedication to the war. By 1918 the combination of Bonar Law's successful education of his supporters to the necessity of a wartime coalition and the dynamic appeal of Lloyd George's leadership fused to produce an almost unchallenged continuation of that coalition into the period of the peace. To an observer schooled only in the harsh realities of pre-war politics such a dramatic change in the nature of the Conservative Party would have seemed totally incomprehensible. In fact, the change was ultimately incomprehensible and unacceptable to many Conservatives. It was not an accurate reflection of .the collective experience of the party during the wartime years. Only in October 1922 did the Conservatives regain the political freedom of the pre-war years. Law's schooling of his party had been so successful that he finally became

the only symbolically acceptable figure to smash the very coalition that he had so painstakingly sought to create.

The war years were critical for the evolution of the modern
party. During the period of Bonar Law's leadership (1911–21;
1922–3) the party passed through five distinct phases of development. Three of those phases occurred during the war. From 1906,
and more particularly from 1911 to 1914, the Unionists were tied
to a posture of blind and unrewarding negativism. The outbreak
of war abruptly stilled political passions and the party passed into
a period of patriotic opposition which lasted until the reconstruction of the Asquith government in May 1915. For the next eighteen months the Conservatives were the junior members of an
uneasy party coalition which finally collapsed at the end of 1916.
At that point, with the more than willing acquiescence of the Conservatives, Lloyd George established a national coalition which
was to survive through the Coupon Election of 1918 until the
autumn of 1922. But for the Conservatives the years 1918–22 can
be identified as a time of mounting debate about the future of the
party – debate which led ultimately to the Carlton Club meeting
of 19 October 1922.

The period of the war saw the emergence of a new form of relationship between the Conservative leadership and its rank and
file supporters in the House of Commons. Unionist backbenchers
became organised in a manner that was unknown in the pre-war
years. The roots of this experience proved strong enough to ensure
that it was carried forward to the postwar period to culminate in
the establishment of the 1922 Committee. The traditional relationship between the leaders and the led changed because of the
pressures of the politics of war. Within the Conservative Party the
permanent emergence of backbench politics was one of the most
important changes to be brought on by the war and was carried
over to the politics of the interwar years.

In the 1906 election a massive Liberal victory ended nearly
twenty years of Unionist rule under Salisbury and Balfour. Buf-
feted by Chamberlain's tariff reform challenge, humiliated by two
electoral failures in 1910 and constitutionally crippled by the Parliament Act of the following year, Balfour resigned as leader of the
party in November 1911. His successor was Andrew Bonar Law.
The style of Conservative politics in the years preceding the war
was set by him. He did much to harden relations between government and opposition. Gone was the ease of social and political in-
tercourse that had smoothed relations between Asquith and

Balfour in spite of the great issues of principle that had divided them. But Law's leadership clearly delighted the bulk of his parliamentary followers and his supporters in the country at large. Fifteen by-election gains and the loss of only two seats were recorded in the period from 1911 to the outbreak of war, thereby strengthening that leadership. After the unhappy last years of Balfour's compromising direction, the party had a new and cutting edge. The aggressiveness of Law's 'new style' – as Asquith dubbed it – ensured that between 1912 and 1914 the relationship between leader and followers was mutually supportive. Law satisfied F. S. Oliver's maxim for the successful politician: 'The approval of his adherents is the breath of his nostrils, the wind in his sails; without it he can do nothing.'[1]

The timing of Law's accession to the leadership was fortuitous. Unionist fortunes were at their nadir. The passage of the Parliament Act marked the complete and final defeat of the Unionist political strategy that had been followed since 1906. But the passage of that Act meant that, in one sense, a revival of Conservative fortunes was inevitable. There was now no longer any reason to delay the introduction of a Home Rule Bill which had been promised by the Liberals to the Nationalists at the end of 1909. Home Rule was an issue that Law and the Unionist Party could oppose with wholehearted unanimity. It was an issue that could be fought not only in Parliament but in the country at large. From 1912 to 1914 the Irish question was the supreme political issue of the moment for the Unionist Party. It was an important, perhaps the most important, catalyst for the unification and regeneration of the party after the shambles of the period 1906 to 1911. This apparent unity was of immense psychological importance to the party at Westminster and the party in the country.

But although the period before the war was one of visible recovery for Unionism, it was by no means an entirely healthy recovery. Unionism had become rooted in negativism and ritualistic opposition. The party had little that was positive to offer. Those few younger supporters of the party, such as Steel-Maitland, who concerned themselves with social questions and worked together as members of the Unionist Social Reform Committee,[2] were given little encouragement by Bonar Law. On the whole he considered social reform to be an 'unprofitable line' to pursue.[3] All Unionist energy was subordinated to the cause of destroying the government's Irish policy. Yet the opposition's Irish policy was ultimately a lost cause. It rallied the troops but was doomed to failure. Either there would be Home Rule with an excluded Ulster or there would be civil war in Ireland. The real legacy of those pre-war years was a united and cohesive party with partisan politics embedded in its soul.

With the outbreak of war in August 1914 the Unionists were faced with the necessity of redefining their role in the political system. The guidelines for the parliamentary truce were established by Asquith and Bonar Law in the House of Commons on 30 July. Government business would be confined 'to necessary matters and [would] not be of a controversial nature'.[4] However, two highly controversial and intensely partisan matters had first to be dealt with. The resolution of these issues put an immense strain on the fragile unity of the political truce and also severely tested the pre-war unity of the Conservative Party itself.

The European crisis broke just at the moment when the Home Rule (and to a lesser degree the decision to disestablish and disendow the Welsh Church) issue was reaching its political climax. The constitutional position was simple: 'Members were freely speculating in the lobby', wrote the parliamentary correspondent of *The Times* on 31 July, 'as to whether the closing Session would be prorogued or adjourned. When prorogued, the Parliament Act Bills [Home Rule and Welsh Church Disestablishment] will automatically be presented for the Royal assent. An adjournment would merely hang them up till a more convenient season.' Should the European crisis continue and the reopening of 'party controversy' be prevented, the Unionists assumed that the government would 'fulfil an honourable obligation in the spirit by agreeing to an adjournment', while the Nationalists were talking in terms of an early prorogation with Home Rule on the statute book and an [Home Rule] Amending Bill in the next session.[5] Politically, the government was trapped. To end the parliamentary session by prorogation would, by automatically ensuring the passage of Home Rule and Welsh Disestablishment without the necessary safeguards, invite the wrath of the Unionists. A widely canvassed Amending Bill which would have suspended the implementation of the Home Rule Act for an agreed period of time, or until the end of the war, would then be lost to the Conservatives. However, merely to adjourn the session and adhere to the letter of the truce, would prevent Home Rule, under the Parliament Act, reaching the statute book and would inevitably lead the increasingly beleaguered Redmond to pressure the Asquith government, dependent, ultimately, on the Nationalists for parliamentary survival.

For six weeks the government and the opposition struggled to find a way out of the political and constitutional dilemma. Law received a variety of conflicting opinions from his colleagues and supporters as to how to proceed. For example, Walter Long, though as patriotic as any Englishman with regard to the war, suggested a kind of parliamentary filibuster as a means of preventing prorogation.[6] More ingenious and more alarming were the proposals for constitutional obstruction that emanated from the House of Cecil where, certainly in the case of Lord Robert Cecil, the alarm over Welsh disestablishment was as great if not greater than over Ireland. On 18 August Lord Robert consulted with Sir Henry Graham, Clerk of the Parliaments, and reported that Graham was 'very confident [that] the government cannot put either Bill on the Statute Book if the Lords choose to fight. He agreed that it would be improper for him to hand over either Bill to the Speaker without the express authority of the Lords'.[7] From Scotland, Sir George Younger, the Scottish Unionist Whip, advised Law that opinion there was strongly against raising further controversy. 'A strong and dignified protest from yourself and perhaps from Carson and a firm adherence to our position should suffice.'[8] This advice was reiterated in the plea of the Unionist M.P. for Durham, John W. Hills, that the duty of Unionists to Ulster and the Unionist pledge to the North had to be 'swallowed up by our higher duty to our country' in a time of national crisis.[9] This appeal concisely reflected the Conservative dilemma: the need to choose between country and party. Ultimately for the Conservatives, as the government well knew, the choice would be for country. To act otherwise would have destroyed all claims on the allegiance of the country and would be to fly in the face of the historical development of the party. As patriots par excellence the Conservatives had to steer clear of domestic controversy in time of war.

Although Asquith was briefly and tantalisingly to tempt the Unionists with a proposal involving Home Rule with a provision for Ulster exclusion,[10] the final solution involved putting both Bills on the Statute Book with their operation suspended for a year or longer if the war continued.[11] This was not achieved before the Conservatives had staged an emotional and well reported protest meeting at the Carlton Club,[12] followed by a mass withdrawal from the House of Commons on 15 September when the government presented its proposals. Even the Cecil scheme of using the

House of Lords to block the two Bills was not dead. On 16 September the Unionist leaders considered the idea again. The weight, though not the numerical majority, of the shadow cabinet was opposed to such action. Bonar Law, Lansdowne, Balfour, Curzon and George Cave objected to a challenge on such technical and obscure grounds which would not be understood by the public at large and which would weaken the position of the party. The majority, consisting of Austen Chamberlain, Carson, Lord Midleton, Lord Robert Cecil, Walter Long, Lord Selborne and Lord Halsbury wanted to use the weapon, and rejected a compromise suggesting that the existence of this power should be advertised but not used. In the end it was agreed that no action would be taken since, as Selborne noted, 'for the majority to have insisted on their way would have made the position of the leaders impossible, so we submitted to be overruled.'[13]

Both Lord Beaverbrook, who wrote the most well known contemporary account of the politics of the period,[14] and Lord Blake, who is the leading historian of the Conservative Party in the years of Bonar Law's leadership,[15] have concluded that Bonar Law and the Conservative leadership had lost all sense of proportion about the Irish question in the midst of a major war. But, in terms of government-opposition relations, this judgement fails to take full account of the creation of a deep seated atmosphere of distrust at the very beginning of the war which remained the legacy of this resolution of what was the major domestic issue of the pre-war years. In terms of his own party Bonar Law could ill afford to deal with the Irish issue simply in terms of a national crisis. Unrelenting opposition to Home Rule had been one of the main props of a newly-achieved party unity; as one of his supporters bluntly reminded him, he was the leader of the Unionist Party – 'that is we exist to oppose Home Rule.'[16] After mid-September 1914 the Irish prop, if not altogether gone, was at least severely weakened. It was not to be the only occasion that the politics of war ensnared the Unionists in their own historical evolution and rhetoric. That ambiguity of role was neatly expressed on 6 August when the Executive Committee of the National Union agreed because of the war to come to 'an arrangement for closing down political activity . . . conditional on the policy of the Government with regard to the Home Rule Bill and Welsh Church Bill and other matters being settled with the approval of our leaders'.[17]

As a result of the double electoral defeats of 1910, Balfour had initiated a series of major changes in Unionist Party organisation.

This revamped party machinery, under new personnel, carried the Unionists through the war and beyond. The creation of the position of chairman of the party organisation and Balfour's appointment of Arthur Steel-Maitland to that office in June 1911 was the most important single new change. As party manager Steel-Maitland (and his successor Sir George Younger) was directly responsible to Balfour (and then to Law) for the entire operation of the party machinery outside Westminster. Functions that had previously been the responsibility of the chief whip and the principal agent were now consolidated into this one office. This included not only the party's central office but also its extra-parliamentary organisation by virtue of the fact that the party chairman now also became chairman of the Executive Committee of the National Union. In early 1912 the Liberal Unionist and Conservative Parties formally merged as part of the policy of general reorganisation. Acland-Hood departed as chief whip in 1911 and, after a brief interregnum under Balcarres, Lord Edmund Talbot became chief whip. Talbot, freed of many organisational responsibilities under the new reforms, readily proved to be an effective Unionist whip. Also in 1911 Percival Hughes retired as principal agent; his successor was John Boraston.[18] In terms of personnel the war brought few alterations to the party apparatus. Younger, the Scottish Unionist whip, succeeded Steel-Maitland as party chairman at the end of 1916. William Jenkins joined Boraston as joint principal agent in 1915 and a woman's branch of the party organisation emerged by 1918 to deal with the problems and opportunities presented by newly enfranchised women.

Party organisations were primarily concerned with elections. However, on 28 August 1914 representatives of the Liberal, Unionist and Labour Parties signed an agreement which provided 'that in the event of any Parliamentary vacancies occuring, there shall be no contested elections.' Over the next twenty-six months this agreement was renewed ten times. After December 1916 the truce was not renewed *de jure* but was observed *de facto* by both the Liberals and the Unionists until the election in 1918.[19] But, as in the case of so much that was political in the war years, the difference between appearance and reality was considerable. That this was so can be seen, for example, in a note by Steel-Maitland concerning the first renewal of the truce in December 1914. He pressed for the loosest possible arrangements in case it suddenly became necessary for the Unionists to contest by-elections: 'the present agreement should be renewed in the most informal manner possible till the date at present settled for the next meeting of Parliament and thereafter from month to month.' In addition, 'so far as any point of this kind can influence Government with regard to making it difficult for them to carry essential legislation such as the Plural Voting Bill, the above suggestion is quite suitable from this standpoint.'[20] Perhaps not unexpectedly, party managers still found themselves thinking, from time to time, as party managers.

The war had a profound effect on the functions of the party organisation. The machinery of all the political parties was put to work in the national interest. On 6 August 1914 the Executive Committee of the National Union accepted Steel-Maitland's recommendation to join with their Liberal counterparts in closing down publication of party leaflets, paying off some of the party speakers, and stopping all partisan public speaking.[21] Some local organisations acted even in advance of Westminster. In Guildford, for example, with the coming of the war the party associations announced in the local press the abandonment of all political gatherings for the duration of the struggle.[22] At both the national and the constituency level the party machinery, particularly the party agents, took on a host of new activities. Distribution of war literature, collection for the various war funds and war savings schemes and, in the latter and more depressing stages of the struggle, the National War Aims campaign became important concerns for party officials. Even more impressive was the work done by the party personnel in recruiting for military and civilian (munitions, shipbuilding and agricultural) service. Through a progression from the Parliamentary Recruiting Committee, the National Register, the Derby Scheme, the Military Service Acts and finally to the National Service schemes, the Unionist Party machine played a vital role.[23]

As a result of this almost exclusive concentration on non-partisan activity, coupled with the diminution in the number of experienced agents (over 125 Unionist agents saw active service in the British forces), the overall political efficiency of the Unionist party organisation (in common with other party organisations) was greatly reduced by the end of the war. Accordingly, when the decision to appeal to the nation as part of a continuing and apparently unbeatable national coalition led by Lloyd George was finally taken in the autumn of 1918, it was a decision that was welcome to most leading Unionist officials who were well aware of how badly run down the party machinery was and who were also uneasy about the electoral implications of the new Representation of the People Act. A flurry of memoranda by Sir George Younger to Law at the end of September 1918 revealed the thinking of Central Office. On the one hand, Law was warned of the 'atrophied' nature of many local Unionist organisations while, on the other hand, Younger pushed hard for a generous allocation of seats to the Lloyd George Liberals.[24] By then Lloyd George had become indispensable for the Unionist party.

If history in 1914 dictated the role of patriotic opposition for the Conservatives, it offered few guidelines as to how that role should be fulfilled. At Westminster, as in the constituencies, Unionist M.P.s joined enthusiastically in the work of the Parliamentary Recruiting Committee, in a propaganda campaign to explain the war to the people and in the deliberations of a host of new governmental committees. Austen Chamberlain briefly assisted Lloyd George in private Treasury discussions about the Budget until the question of higher taxation on beer became a matter of contention between them. Balfour became a member of Asquith's war council. This activity on behalf of the national cause camouflaged a series of unco-ordinated and often unconscious attempts to discover a working definition of patriotic opposition. The opposition had to find a political mean that would fall between the traditional role whereby, as Lord Robert Cecil had explained to the Select Committee on Procedure in 1914, 'much of the tactics of an opposition are devoted, not to obtaining any result in the House itself, but to producing some effect among the electorate,'[25] and becoming nothing more than mute observers of the events of both the home front and the battlefields. A party that suddenly ceased to have a positive or even a negative role in the political life of the country, that acted as a mere rubber stamp in the legislative process, and that seemed doomed to silence through patriotism not unnaturally found some release of tension in internal stress and strain. A political vacuum, all the more powerful due to the unity that had been forged over the Irish question in the years 1912 to 1914, suddenly developed. As Lord Crewe, the government leader in the House of Lords observed, a 'dangerous energy' was building up in the leading Unionists. He wrote to Lord Hardinge in January 1915: 'It is partly from the curiosity which in these days of reticence is shared by the public generally, and partly from a sort of sub-conscious resentment felt by the opposition leaders that fate has denied them the posts of prominence and (I freely admit) usefulness during this crisis.'[26] At the end of that month

Law was faced with an overt challenge to his political strategy for patriotic opposition by Lord Curzon and Walter Long and implicitly therefore to his authority as leader of the party in the House of Commons. The challenge was unsuccessful. Party strategy would not be changed.[27] But, as Law admitted privately to Balfour: 'The real difficulty will be to keep criticism within proper limits, and I think we shall find it pretty difficult as the session goes on.'[28] F. S. Oliver summed up the situation with his usual verve in a letter to Austen Chamberlain:

> A government accustomed to work on party lines is just like a child leaning over a balcony with one of its elders (you or me) holding on to the back of a pinafore. If you let it go it tumbles over the balcony rail and breaks its little head. If the opposition stops criticising it is just like letting go ahold of the child's pinafore. Our political arrangements do not contemplate and are not prepared for an opposition which doesn't find fault, and which is not even on watch to point out back-slidings.[29]

The emergence of the Unionist Business Committee, as the first organised expression of Conservative backbench opinion during the war, was an important milestone in the evolution of the modern party. The exact origins of the Business Committee[30] are difficult to determine but there appears to have been a pre-war predecessor concerned about 'Treaties with Foreign Powers, Tariffs and any legislation that affected shipping and British industries'.[31] The first wartime meeting of either this old committee or, more probably, a new one, was convened on 27 January 1915 by two Unionist backbenchers – Ernest Pollock and Basil Peto. If Peto and Pollock were the *de facto* founders of the Business Committee, its moving spirit was W. A. S. Hewins – Unionist M.P. for Hereford since 1912, Director of the London School of Economics from 1895 to 1903 and since 1903 the Secretary of the Tariff Commission – the research and propaganda arm of Joseph Chamberlain's tariff reform campaign. The Business Committee functioned for the duration of the war. Generally it devoted itself to economic questions relating to 'the effective prosecution of the war'. Included under this rubric were tariffs, contraband, shipping, war financing, aliens, trading with the enemy, contracts and the rationalisation of industrial resources. Munitions production was a regular preoccupation. Membership, in spite of a canvass of all Unionist M.P.s with the exception of ex-ministers and whips,[32] was rather low (although Hewins claimed otherwise in his biography) and attendance at general meetings of the Committee never exceeded forty.[33] A rough examination of their occupations reveals that nearly all the active members were either retired soldiers, manufacturers, barristers or solicitors while only a handful regarded themselves as landowners. That backbench activism was centred in such an essentially non-landed element of the Conservative Party tends to confirm the view that the party's centre of gravity was increasingly urbanised, commercialised and industrialised. The war accelerated an already well advanced pre-war trend.[34]

Initially the links between the Business Committee and the Unionist leadership were extremely close. In his memoirs Walter Long, who was the first chairman of the Committee, asserted that Bonar Law asked him to head the Committee.[35] In retrospect this was an astute move by Law to harness a restless Long to the development and channelling of constructive criticism. At the second meeting of the Executive of the Committee, Lord Edmund Talbot, the Unionist chief whip, was in attendance.[36] A few days later Hewins recorded that he had drafted a resolution for the Business Committee 'which was approved by Bonar Law and according to present arrangements I am to move it . . . Our official party organization has virtually abdicated and Bull was told yesterday that it was desired that we should manage the debates.'[37] The circular letter canvassing for membership referred to 'the approval of our leaders' in its appeal for support.[38] The Business Committee proved to be at least a limited success in providing a release for the pent-up energies of some of the backbenchers and in easing the strain between Unionist leaders and their followers until about the end of March.

In the spring of 1915 the stability of the political truce was seriously threatened by a complicated series of reactions to Lloyd George's proposals to deal with the question of 'drink'. The government's and particularly Lloyd George's handling of the drink question revealed to the Unionist party in Parliament – especially to the more activist members of the Unionist Business Committee – that the truce was vulnerable and that the Unionist leaders could be effectively threatened by backbench revolt. The limits on criticism were seen to have been unduly narrow; the political situation was less rigid than had been imagined. To the traditional short-term explanations of the first coalition (the munitions scandal and Fisher's abrupt departure from the Admiralty) a third might be considered – the inept handling of the liquor question in April and May 1915.

Lloyd George believed excessive drinking to be a grave hindrance to the production of munitions. 'Drink', he asserted in a major speech at Bangor on 28 February, 'is doing more damage in the War than all the German submarines put together.'[39] However, by hitting out at the drink question in the context of munitions, Lloyd George widened and blurred the debate further than was politically sound. 'From the morrow of the [Bangor] speech,' noted Henry Carter, 'for nearly three months, the drink question was a main subject of debate in the Press and in private circles.'[40] Munitions and the general production of war material were the issues of that spring; too often, and too precipitately, the debate found itself on the emotive byeways of drink alone. The teetotallers, the temperance advocates, and the proponents of the trade, aided and abetted by the politicians, refought many of the battles of 1904 and 1908 at a time when the country could ill afford such rancour.

Initially Lloyd George appears to have flirted with the idea of total prohibition but then settled on a scheme of state purchase of the trade at an estimated £250,000,000.[41] The Unionist leadership readily accepted the idea. Law, pleased at the prospect of his cutting his party's ties with the trade,[42] informed Lloyd George that if 'it is necessary for the successful prosecution of the war that the State should take over the production and distribution of alcohol with adequate compensation to the existing interests we shall not as a party oppose the proposal.'[43] The views of the leadership were not shared by the Unionist rank and file who were more receptive to the pressures of the well organised trade lobby at Westminster. Nineteen of the twenty-three M.P.s listed as having connections with the trade by *The Brewers' Almanack* in 1915 were Unionists. Of these nineteen, at least five were active in the Unionist Business Committee. Their acknowledged spokesman, Sir George Younger, was Scottish Unionist whip, and also may have been Bonar Law's link to the Unionist Business Committee.

The intense public and private debate on the drink issue lasted until mid-May. Apparently prohibitive costs and lack of support from his cabinet colleagues led Lloyd George to abandon the state purchase scheme by mid-April but the Unionist leadership was not informed of this fact.[44] Meanwhile, the trade lobby was exceedingly active. The Business Committee delivered a blistering attack on the government proposals (as then understood) in the House of Commons on 21 April.[45] A fortnight later the Business

Committee, in conjunction with the Irish Nationalists and in defiance of Bonar Law's expressed views, engineered a parliamentary deadlock over Lloyd George's proposed scheme of heavily increased taxes on the trade.[46] *The Times* observed: 'The scene reminded one of other days. It was an old time Parliamentary crisis.' To talk only in terms of an Irish revolt, as the traditional account has come down in a variety of sources,[47] is to miss the important significance of the discontent on the backbenches and, in particular, on the Unionist side where the leadership's accommodation with the government on the subject of drink had passed the limit of patriotism. As Hewins recorded in his diary of the day's events: 'Bonar Law sent back a message that we should take no part [in the debate] to which I replied we were competent to form our own judgment on the position'.[48]

According to Lord Beaverbrook the friendly atmosphere over the question of drink 'smoothed the way towards Coalition'.[49] Just the reverse was the case. Drink was a political issue on its own. It forms a neglected, and necessarily partisan, background to the events which led to the formation of the coalition government at the end of May. When drink was thus isolated, it necessarily became a question of partisan politics. Here the Unionist rank and file stood squarely on the side of the trade. The party leadership came close to losing the confidence of its supporters. In May, when the explosive implications of Fisher's resignation from the Admiralty in protest against what he considered to be the folly of the major British military exercise to force the Dardanelles and thus defeat the Turks, were added to the pressures of the Business Committee on the Unionist leadership to bring the question of the crippling effects of the munitions shortage in France out into the open, Law realised that he had to move his party towards the proffered coalition. Not to have done so would have destroyed his credibility as leader. This was one of the lessons learned from the partisan struggle over drink. The May crisis provided a clear illustration of the changing relationship, generated by the politics of war, between the Unionist leadership and its parliamentary supporters. To see the Unionist Parliamentary Party as a docile and deferential group of well-drilled backbenchers working in close harmony with their leaders is most misleading.

Asquith wanted the May 1915 coalition to be 'as much like a normal party government as possible, with no unusual position for the leader of the minority party'.[50] The first coalition functioned not as a national coalition of equals but as a party coalition of unequal and often mutually suspicious rivals. Coalition brought with it a further diminution of the role of both the individual Member of Parliament and of Parliament itself. In addition, as Sir Henry Lucy, the veteran observer of·the political scene, commented in April 1916: 'It is the inherent weakness of a Coalition Government that it has no devoted friends . . . [and] party loyalty is non-existent.' As a result, 'not since the days of Mr. Gladstone's prime as leader of the House of Commons has there been such activity in the creation of what were known as Tea Room Cabals. Now they are called Ginger Committees, their avowed patriotic purpose being to keep the Government on the hop.'[51]

That the Asquith coalition survived as long as it did was due in no small measure to the selfless leadership of a dissatisfied Unionist Party by Bonar Law.[52] Inevitably this meant a further challenge to his leadership. The resignation of Sir Edward Carson from the government in October 1915 raised the distinct possibility of an active parliamentary opposition under the leadership of a figure of national stature. Abroad the war continued to yield no successes for Britain. At home the parliamentary and press clamour for the introduction of military conscription mounted steadily. Discontent was most evident in the Conservative Party; as a result the Unionist War Committee emerged at the beginning of January 1916 for 'the purpose of supporting a vigorous prosecution of the war'.[53] It appears that the initial impetus in actually forming the Committee came from two men – Sir Frederick Banbury, an acknowledged master of parliamentary obstruction, and Ronald McNeill, an Ulsterman and intimate adviser to Carson, the chairman of the Committee. Membership of the Unionist War Committee grew rapidly; by the end of March the Committee was 'a body of 150 members, and includes practically all the unofficial Unionists who are in regular attendance at the sittings of the House'.[54] Unlike the Business Committee, the War Committee courted publicity as a means of bringing pressure to bear on the government. It met regularly once a week during the parliamentary session and its discussions were normally reported in some detail in *The Times* the following day. From its inception the Unionist War Committee worked with varying degrees of coordination and co-operation with the much smaller Liberal War Committee which also emerged in January 1916. Indeed, according to *The Times*, the organisers of the Liberal War Committee were unwilling to accept members who were not prepared to co-operate with the Unionist Committee.[55] The extreme Tory press looked forward to the two War Committees forming the basis of a new National Party to function as a coalition opposition.[56]

Conscription was one of the crucial political issues of the war years. By the beginning of 1916, due largely to Unionist pressure and the timely support offered by Lloyd George, the government had grudgingly adopted a scheme of conscription for unmarried men. In the early months of 1916 the two War Committees ran a vigorous campaign for universal conscription. So intense was the pressure exerted by the Unionist War Committee that, when combined with the opinion of the Army Council in mid-April, it forced Bonar Law to conclude that he could no longer object to conscription for married men. He wrote to Asquith: 'to ask the Unionist Members [of the House of Commons] to oppose a motion [from Carson for equality of sacrifice] of which on its merits they approve . . . would be to place an impossible strain upon the confidence in and loyalty to their leaders.'[57] By early May universal conscription had been accepted. Carson had used the threat of the Unionist War Committee with considerable skill. By doing so in a way that did not create a situation which made Law's resignation inevitable or even a serious possibility, Carson got Law to become an advocate of general compulsion. The War Committee also forced the government to acknowledge the existence of Parliament. As Carson told his devoted followers at a victory luncheon, 'the Unionist War Committee was the outcome of the dissatisfaction that was felt by many, and of what we conceived to be to a large extent the studied contempt by the Government of the House of Commons . . . we wanted action, immediate and decisive.'[58]

On at least two other occasions the Unionist War Committee made important incursions into wartime politics. The first of these was the celebrated Nigerian debate of November 1916 which has come to be portrayed as the long expected 'trial of strength' between Bonar Law and Sir Edward Carson over who should command the allegiance of the Unionist rank and file in Parliament.[59] But, contrary to what both Beaverbrook and Blake have written, the Nigerian palm-kernel question was not 'a topic as remote from war as can well be conceived'. The combined effects of the blockade and military success in West Africa meant that the British suddenly inherited the lucrative German trade in palm kernels and palm oils after having been driven out of the trade some thirty years earlier by high German tariffs against

British manufactured oils. A revitalised British industry clamoured for tariff protection behind which to modernise its antiquated plant and machinery.[60] The palm-kernel question was, and had been, a symbolically important issue of economic warfare throughout 1916. Working through the War Committee, Liverpool mercantile interests were asserting their desire to maintain a recently gained monopoly position in West African trade. The Colonial Office was out to break the monopoly which this Merseyside 'ring' had inherited from the Germans.[61] The Nigerian debate was not a resounding success as a parliamentary 'trial of strength' for the War Committee. Almost one-third (thirty out of ninety-five) of those members of the Committee who voted accepted the government's argument that the sale of the Nigerian properties was indeed part of tariff reform orthodoxy (Beaverbrook to the contrary), and voted against Carson.[62] In fact, the Nigerian division was something of a minor triumph for Bonar Law; in the previous parliamentary division on 26 October 1916, sixty-eight Unionists had voted against Law and the government while only nineteen had supported their leader.[63] The Nigerian division gave Law a Unionist majority of seven (72–65); he had gone over to the offensive against his critics.

In the early months of 1918 the Unionist War Committee again played an active role in wartime politics. By then the political context had changed considerably from the 1914–16 period. When the political crisis of December 1916 arose, it was inevitable that the Conservatives would accept Lloyd George as Prime Minister. Bonar Law, putting national unity ahead of party and personal ambition, stood aside for Lloyd George who symbolised 'the effective prosecution of the war' – something that the Unionist Party had been seeking since August 1914. After December 1916 Unionists were part of a national coalition and were, theoretically, full and equal partners in that coalition. The marked decline in importance of the Unionist War Committee and the shifting of its political centre of gravity from the House of Commons under Carson's leadership to the House of Lords under Lord Salisbury's direction, was a telling Unionist indication of wide support for the Lloyd George coalition. In January 1918 when the War Committee wished to protest over what they believed to be the impending inclusion of Churchill in the war cabinet, Lord Salisbury dealt directly with Lloyd George rather than with Bonar Law.[64] The contrast was important.

Lloyd George's decision in February 1918 to appoint Lord

Beaverbrook as Minister of Propaganda and Information and Lord Northcliffe as Director of Propaganda in Enemy Countries, in addition to his decision to replace General Sir William Robertson by General Sir Henry Wilson as Chief of the Imperial General Staff, drove the Unionist backbenchers into a rage. To have politics sullied by the appointment to the government of powerful press lords and to have the politicians interfering with the soldiers was deemed unacceptable by Unionists with too much time on their hands. Strong resolutions condemning the appointments were passed by the Unionist War Committee; a crisis seemed imminent. Backbench spirits and Salisbury's aspirations were bolstered by the advent to their ranks of Austen Chamberlain who was then temporarily out of office. In the end, nothing happened. Lloyd George stalled for time and when he (not Bonar Law) finally met the Unionist War Committee in early March to discuss the press appointments he left them 'convulsed with laughter' by 'telling them pretty plainly that the type of man he wanted for propaganda was not to be found in the Committee, but was to be found in Northcliffe, Beaverbrook and company'.[65]

The Maurice debate of May 1918 also raised the possibility of serious Conservative disunity. On 7 May a letter from General Maurice, the former Director of Military Operations, who disputed parliamentary statements by both Bonar Law and Lloyd George about the extension of the British front in France and the actual strength of the British Army in France, was published in four major London papers. These allegations came as little surprise to Lord Salisbury. As chairman of the Unionist War Committee, he had discussed them in detail with General Maurice and then had attempted to verify the assertions with General Sir William Robertson in late April. Maurice told Salisbury that he had come to see him at the request of senior Army commanders who were 'most anxious that some one of influence should be told that the troops at the Front are losing confidence in the Government' because of their awareness that some of Lloyd George's statements about Army strengths were untrue.[66] Asquith challenged the government in the House of Commons about Maurice's claims and Lloyd George determined to treat his demand for a Select Committee as a Vote of Censure. Thus, when 230 members of the Unionist War Committee, with Carson again active in their midst, met to consider what action it should take, it was forced to ignore the validity of Maurice's assertions and sustain the government the following day. To have done otherwise would have

meant the defeat of the Lloyd George coalition and the return of
Asquith to power. This was anathema' to virtually all Conservatives.[67] Lloyd George was tightening his grip on the Conservatives.

The emergence of organised backbench opinion in the Conservative Party was an important development of the wartime
period. A new pattern of relationships between the party leadership and the parliamentary rank-and-file was firmly established.
This pattern was carried over to the 1922 Committee. The war
years also saw important changes in the Unionist Party that did
not relate so much to the dynamics of the structure of the party but
rather to the meaning of modern Conservativism. The war
knocked away the foundations of some cherished Conservative
principles, hastened the advent of some articles of Conservative
faith and raised a host of new problems that were to challenge
interwar Conservativism.

Unrelenting opposition to Home Rule had been one of the articles of faith of pre-war Unionists. Yet six weeks after the war
began Home Rule was on the statute book balanced only by the
vague assurances of an Amending Bill during the suspensory
period. In the spring of 1916, following the Easter Rising in
Dublin, the monolithic Unionist view of how to deal with the Irish
question was shattered by the spectacle of Bonar Law and Carson
joining forces to suggest a wartime Home Rule settlement. Law
supported Lloyd George's proposals for Ireland because they provided as fully for Ulster as had those which the Unionists had put
forward at the time of the Buckingham Palace Conference in July
1914. Carson had naturally put Ulster's interests ahead of those of
the wider cause of Unionism in the rest of Ireland and England.
The Southern (Irish) Unionists, led by Lord Midleton and openly
supported by Walter Long and Lord Lansdowne, were ve-
hemently opposed to any Home Rule settlement. That opposition
was skillfully fostered in the ranks of the party in England and
Scotland.[68] So uncertain was the situation that one Unionist whip
predicted after a five-hour meeting of M.P.s that 'if there had been
a vote I think B. Law would have had 60 percent in his favour,
though reluctantly so.'[69] Yet Law was apparently far more in
touch with Conservative opinion than were Conservative M.P.s. A
survey of the Unionist provincial press undertaken by the Conservative Central Office concluded that the balance of opinion favoured a settlement in Ireland as against the continuance of
martial law.[70] Though they were probably in a minority in their

party, the men of 'principle' like Lansdowne and Long eventually succeeded in wrecking the Home Rule settlement by making its terms impossible for Redmond. Less than two years later the same Walter Long was the leading proponent of a federal solution to the Irish question. In 1921 the Unionists were to accept a Home Rule Ireland with the exclusion of Ulster. As the *Morning Post* had observed as early as 12 July 1916: 'The Unionist Party is, in fact, dead; the cause for which it existed has been surrendered.'

The war also moulded Conservative thinking on a number of important constitutional questions. One of the central issues which was resolved during the war was the matter of the franchise. Military and industrial service in the common cause by millions of citizens of the United Kingdom made it increasingly difficult for the Conservatives to continue supporting a franchise limited by property or rental qualifications. Indeed, it was the Conservative Party itself that was instrumental in making the franchise a political question during the war. This development occurred in the summer of 1916 because of the refusal of the Unionist and Liberal War Committees, aided by the Conservative-dominated 'Beach' Committee[71] in the House of Lords, to grant the government a further extension of the life of Parliament unless a guarantee for the enfranchisement of the nation's servicemen was forthcoming. Ultimately the House of Commons refused to accept any registration legislation from the government.[72] The impasse was resolved by the establishment of a Speaker's Conference on electoral reform and registration in October 1916. However, for the Conservatives to turn to the active consideration of universal manhood suffrage brought with it the reality of a massive unpropertied working class infusion into the electorate with the attendant fears of socialism. To counter this threat the Conservatives, with varying degrees of enthusiasm, resorted to three expedients in the 1916–18 period. A small number of Milnerite M.P.s tried, with some success, to promote a new patriotic and imperialistic Labour Party to present a working class alternative to the pacifism and socialism of the existing Labour Party.[73] Further, the Unionist Party moved hesitantly but slowly towards accepting limited female suffrage as a 'conservative' counter-weight to the threat from labour. Lord Selborne, who considered that 'the existing franchise gives organized labour a larger share of power than it is entitled to considering its proportion to the whole population', put the Conservative case clearly: 'I think that an enlargement of the franchise, and especially the introduction of women voters, will tend to correct that error.'[74] Finally, the party (especially the peers) actively debated the idea of Proportional Representation. Some Unionists argued that such a scheme would help compensate for the large number of seats that would be lost as a result of redistribution in traditionally Conservative agricultural constituencies, while others contended that Proportional Representation would ensure at least some Conservative representation from the heavily industrialised areas. In February 1918 the Representation of the People Bill was finally passed into law after nearly a year of contentious debate. Universal manhood suffrage and a limited female franchise meant that the size of the electorate had been more than doubled. The traditional Conservative principle of property being equated with political responsibility was swept away by the politics of war. This new mass electorate established the need for a more broadly based Conservative Party.

While some articles of Conservative faith were cast aside during the war years, however, others were more firmly entrenched by that experience. Foremost among Conservative gains was the adoption of the concept of using tariffs both to protect essential industries and to generate revenue. The Unionist Business Committee played an important role in this economic transformation by arguing a persuasive case for tariffs as a weapon in the war against Germany. Symbolic victory was achieved in the early autumn of 1915 when the Liberal Chancellor of the Exchequer, Reginald McKenna, agreed to the introduction of duties on selected imports. Lloyd George threw a note across the cabinet table to Walter Long: 'So the old fiscal system goes, destroyed by its own advocates.'[75] Although the McKenna duties were limited to luxuries, the momentum had been established. Representatives of the Allied governments met in Paris in June 1916 to examine common economic matters and referred back to their governments a series of resolutions for economic action in both the war and postwar periods.[76] The Balfour of Burleigh Committee on Commercial and Industrial Policy was established in 1916 to consider postwar economic policy for Britain and its final report in 1917 accepted the need for the protection of key industries against unfair foreign competition.[77] 'We have', as Bonar Law told his cheering supporters at a party meeting called to endorse the continuation of the coalition beyond the end of the war, 'all that we have ever asked in regard to [Imperial] preference', an assurance of protection against dumping and the 'freedom of action, unfettered by any pledges, . . . to take the course which is best to preserve the production of this country.'[78]

The major unresolved question of principle for the Conservatives raised by the war was that of defining the role of the state in the economic and social life of the nation. In an enormous number of areas the state assumed an influence – both direct and indirect – that had been inconceivable before 1914. Conservatives were enthusiasts for the increased activity of the state to meet the demands of war; the campaigns for conscription and tariffs were two of the more obvious examples of this Conservative pressure for state intervention. The difficulty for Conservatives was that of trying to determine how much of the *ad hoc* wartime experiment would or should be permanently carried over to the postwar years. When Bonar Law, for example, at the end of 1917 gave public indications of his favourable disposition towards a levy on capital after the war, Sir George Younger, chairman of the party organisation, reported to Balfour: 'The feeling [in the party] is so strong against the slightest support of any such suicidal policy that it is impossible to say whether anything short of entire repudiation would satisfy our people.'[79]

Far more fundamental to the meaning of modern Conservatism than the question of capital taxation was that of determining whether it was Bonar Law or Lloyd George who was leading the party at the end of the war. The anticipated challenges to postwar Britain were considered to be at least as demanding as those of the war. Foremost among those challenges was 'Bolshevism' at home; failure to deal with it would leave the British 'with empty purses and days of bloodshed and misery'.[80] At the same time there was a deeply held conviction that there could be no return to the partisan politics of the pre-war years. Lloyd George seemed to be the only man adequately equipped to lead the nation in peace as he had led it in war. Indeed, Bonar Law himself considered Lloyd George's leadership to be completely logical and of benefit to both the party and the nation. Law discussed this in an October 1918 letter to Balfour on the possibility of a wartime election:

> if an election were fought in this way, Lloyd George as the leader of the fight would secure a greater hold on the rank and file of our Party and he would also be so dependent on that Party after an election that he would permanently be driven into the same attitude towards our Party which (Joseph) Chamberlain was placed in before, with this difference – that he

would be the leader of it. That would, however, I am inclined to think, be not a bad thing for our Party, and a good thing for the nation.[81]

Although there was no wartime election, the Coupon election produced results similar to those forecast by Bonar Law. Until 1922 there was a steady and growing undercurrent of debate in the Conservative Party about what to do with Lloyd George; in the end, only Bonar Law had the necessary prestige to destroy the very coalition that he had so carefully fashioned.

The experience of war was fundamental in the evolution of the modern Conservative Party. War brought the party squarely into the twentieth century by both destroying many of the fundamental landmarks of pre-war Conservativism and by creating a host of new challenges that could not be dealt with successfully by pre-war solutions. Ireland, the Welsh Church and the power of the House of Lords were essentially issues of the past; by 1918 the principles had been conceded if not *de jure* then at least *de facto*. The war raised the issue of the role of the state in society and the economy in such a way that Conservatives could no longer afford to ignore it. The other fundamental change in the Conservative Party brought on by the war was the permanent emergence of backbench politics. A pre-war unity based almost exclusively on opposition to Home Rule was destroyed by the strains of patriotic opposition and party coalition. Backbenchers discovered that they had power and that they were more than mere voting fodder. That power was exercised with brutal clarity in 1922 when the Conservative Party appeared to its adherents to have been taken away from the Conservatives.

Notes

1. F. S. Oliver, *The Endless Adventure*, 3 vols (London, 1930–5) vol. I, p. 31.

2. Henry Bentinck, *Tory Democracy* (London, 1918) pp. 78–85; F. E. Smith, *The Unionist Party and Other Essays* (London, 1913) *passim*.

3. Robert Blake, *The Unknown Prime Minister: The Life and Times of Andrew Bonar Law, 1858–1923* (London, 1955) p. 140.

4. 65 *H. C. Deb.*, 5s, cols 1601–02.

5. *The Times*, 31 Jul 1914.

6. Long to Law, 9 Aug 1914, Bonar Law MSS, Beaverbrook Library, London, 34/3/28.

7. Lord Robert Cecil to Selborne, 18 Aug 1914; copy in ibid., 34/4/54.

8. Younger to Law, 5 Sep 1914, ibid., 34/5/16.

9. Hills to Law, 6 Sep 1914, ibid., 34/5/20.

10. [Asquith's Proposals] 7 Sep 1914, ibid., 49/d/3; Sir Charles Petrie, *The*

Life and Letters of the Right Hon. Sir Austen Chamberlain, 2 vols (London, 1939–40) vol. II, pp. 5–6.

11. 66 *H. C. Deb.*, 5s, cols 882–93, 15 Sep 1914. In the case of the Welsh Bill only the date of disestablishment was postponed; preparations for disestablishment and disendowment were undertaken. Kenneth O. Morgan, *Wales in British Politics, 1868–1922* 2nd ed. (Cardiff, 1970) p. 271. There was no Home Rule Amending Bill passed though one was promised for the next session.

12. *The Times*, 15 Sep 1914; *Gleanings and Memoranda* (Oct 1914) pp. 352–61.

13. Memo in Austen Chamberlain MSS, Birmingham University Library, AC 12/29; partially used by Petrie, op. cit., pp. 14–15; Selborne to Lord Salisbury, 18 Sep 1914, Salisbury MSS, Hatfield House, S(4) 75/186 and memo by Lord Hugh Cecil, Quickswood MSS, Hatfield House, QUI.18/191–4.

14. Lord Beaverbrook, *Politicians and the War* (London, 1960 ed.) pp. 44–5.

15. Blake, op. cit., p. 229.

16. Lord Hugh Cecil to Law, 11 Sep 1914, Bonar Law MSS, 34/6/36.

17. Executive Committee, National Union, 6 Aug 1914, 1911–17 Minute Book, pp. 156–8. Conservative Central Office, London.

18. Neal Blewett, *The Peers, the Parties and the People: The General Elections of 1910* (London, 1972) pp. 266–76; R. B. Jones, 'Balfour's Reform of Party Organisation', *Bulletin of the Institute of Historical Research*, 37 (1965).

19. MS Asquith 26, Bodleian Library, ff. 13–35. The truce did not embrace Independents who were successful in a number of electoral challenges, often in constituencies where party machinery had fallen into a state of disrepair.

20. [Steel-Maitland], 'Retirements and Bye-Elections', n.d. [14 Dec 1914] Bonar Law MSS, 35/4/36.

21. Executive Committee, National Union, 6 Aug 1914, 1911–17 Minute Book, pp. 156–8.

22. William H. Oakley, *Guildford in the Great War* (Guildford, 1934) p. 22.

23. Arthur Fawcett, *Conservative Agent: A Study of the National Society of Conservative and Unionist Agents and Its Members* (Driffield, Yorks, 1967) p. 20; Roy Douglas, 'Voluntary Enlistment in the First World War and the Work of the Parliamentary Recruiting Committee', *The Journal of Modern History*, vol. 42 (1970) *passim*.

24. Younger memoranda, Sep 1918, Bonar Law MSS, 95/2.

25. Alan Beattie, 'British Coalition Government Revisited', *Government and Opposition* (Oct 1966–Jan 1967) p. 8.

26. Crewe to Hardinge, 8 Jan 1915, Crewe MSS, Cambridge University Library, C/24. The House of Lords was meeting at the time.

27. Blake, op. cit., pp. 238–9.

28. Law to Balfour, 3 Feb 1915, Balfour MSS, British Museum, Add. MS. 49693, f. 205.

29. F. S. Oliver to Chamberlain, 30 Jan 1915, A. Chamberlain MSS, AC.14/6/3.

30. The main known sources for the Unionist Business Committee are W. A. S. Hewins, *The Apologia of an Imperialist: Forty Years of Empire Policy*, 2 vols (London, 1929) vol. II, *passim*; Minute Books of the U[nionist] B[usiness] C[ommittee] and its subcommittees and the Hewins diary in the Hewins MSS, Sheffield University Library; and the scrapbooks of press clippings, etc., made by Sir William Bull, the parliamentary secretary of the U.B.C., deposited at the Hammersmith Public Library, London.

31. Alfred Bigland, *The Call of Empire* (London, 1926) pp. 41–2; Viscount Long, *Memories* (London, 1923) p. 219.

32. U.B.C. Minute Book, 22 Feb 1915, Hewins MSS.

33. Average attendance figures were developed from the U.B.C. Minute Books; Hewins claimed that membership included 'most of the Conservative members who were not at the front'. Hewins, op. cit., p. 11.

34. J. P. Cornford, 'The Parliamentary Foundations of the Hotel Cecil', in Robert Robson (ed.), *Ideas and Institutions of Victorian Britain: Essays in Honour of George Kitson Clark* (London, 1967) *passim*; Ivor Bulmer-Thomas, *The Growth of the British Party System*, 2 vols (London, 1965), vol. I, pp. 240–1.

35. Long, op. cit., p. 219.

36. U.B.C. Minute Book, 1 Feb 1915, Hewins MSS.

37. Hewins, op. cit., 10 Feb 1915, p. 13.

38. Copy of a circular letter from Bull, 13 Feb 1915, Bull MSS, H920 BUL, 1914–15, ff. 70–1.

39. David Lloyd George, *War Memoirs*, 2 vols (London, n.d. [1938]) vol. I, pp. 193–4. Lloyd George opened this campaign with the full support of Kitchener, ibid., pp. 257–9.

40. Rev. Henry Carter, *The Control of the Drink Trade: A Contribution to National Efficiency, 1915–1917* (London, 1918) p. 48. Carter, a leading figure in the Wesleyan Temperance Society, wrote extensively on the question of drink but with a certain academic detachment. A close reading of *The Times* and the *Observer* supports Carter's claim of the dominance of the drink question in public debate in the spring of 1915.

41. Memoranda by Sir William Plender, 30 and 31 Mar 1915, MS Asquith 94, ff. 12–24.

42. Blake, op. cit., p. 239.

43. Law to Lloyd George, 7 Apr 1915, Bonar Law MSS, 37/5/5; reported in *The Times* the following day.

44. Chamberlain to Mrs Chamberlain, 28 Apr 1915, A. Chamberlain MSS, AC.6/1/166.

45. 71 *H. C. Deb.*, 5s, cols 284–311.

46. 71 *H. C. Deb.*, 5s, cols 1295–1310, 6 May 1915.

47. *The Times*, 7 May 1915; Beaverbrook, op. cit., p. 69; A. J. P. Taylor, *Politics in Wartime and Other Essays* (London, 1964) p. 19.

48. Hewins, op. cit., 7 May 1915, recording events of 6 May, p. 30.

49. Beaverbrook, op. cit., p. 68.

50. Roy Jenkins, *Asquith* (London, pb. ed. 1967) p. 411.

51. From the Cross Benches, *Observer*, 2 Apr 1916.

52. See, for example, his widely praised defence of the government in response to Unionist critics in the House of Commons, 71 *H. C. Deb.*, 5s, cols 1968–76, 14 Dec 1915.

53. *The Times*, 7 Jan 1916.

54. Ibid., 29 Mar 1916.

55. Ibid., 14 Jan 1916.

56. *Morning Post*, 21 Jan 1916, cited with approval in the *National Review*, Feb 1916, pp. 833–6; the *Outlook*, 15 Jan 1916.

57. Law to Asquith, 17 Apr 1916, MS Asquith 16, ff. 147–53.

58. *Morning Post*, 5 May 1916.

59. Beaverbrook, op. cit., p. 288; Blake, op. cit., p. 298.

60. West Africa, Committee on Edible and Oil Producing Nuts and Seeds Report . . . Cd 8247 (1916); Evidence Taken before the Committee, Cd 8248 (1916).

61. Steel-Maitland to Milner, 7 Nov 1916, Steel-Maitland MSS, Scottish Record Office, Edinburgh, GD.193/71; see also 87 *H. C. Deb.*, 5s, 8 Nov 1916, *passim*. Steel-Maitland was Bonar Law's under-secretary at the Colonial Office.

62. 'Nigerian Division-Summary', Carson MSS, Northern Ireland Public Record Office, Belfast, D.1507/5/69; *Morning Post*, 10 Nov 1916.

63. 86 *H. C. Deb.*, 5s, cols 1479–82.

64. Memo by Lord Salisbury, n.d. [25 Jan 1918], Salisbury MSS, S(4) 80/293–4.

65. Lt Col. C à Court Repington, *The First World War*, 2 vols (London, 1920) vol. II, p. 241.

66. Note of Lord Salisbury's interview with General Maurice, n.d. [Apr 1918], Salisbury MSS, S(4) 82/88–88a; note of Lord Salisbury's interview with General Robertson, n.d., [25 Apr 1918], ibid., S(4) 82/87–87a; Margot Asquith, *The Autobiography of Margot Asquith*, 2 vols (London, 1920–2) vol. II, pp. 273–4.

67. L. S. Amery, *My Political Life, vol.* II; *War and Peace, 1914–1929* (London, 1953) p. 154; John Gooch, 'The Maurice Debate 1918', *Journal of Contemporary History*, vol. 3, no. 4 (1968) pp. 222–3.

68. Patrick Buckland, *Irish Unionism.* I: *The Anglo-Irish and the New Ireland, 1885–1922* (Dublin, 1972) ch. 3.

69. Bridgeman diary, 7 Jul 1916, Bridgeman MSS.

70. 'Ireland, Mr. Lloyd George's Proposals. Summary of views of Provincial Papers', n.d. [mid-Jun 1916], Bonar Law MSS, 63/c/65; D. G. Boyce, *Englishmen and Irish Troubles: British Public Opinion and the Making of Irish Policy, 1918–1922* (London, 1972) p. 33.

71. A 'Ginger Group' of activist peers and elder statesmen – Cromer, Milner, Sydenham, Loreburn, Peel, Donoughmore, Morley of Blackburn, and Balfour of Burleigh – formed in 1915 and led by Lord Midleton after the death of St Aldwyn (Sir Michael Hicks Beach).

72. 85 *H. C. Deb.*, 5s, cols 1891–1961, 16 Aug 1916.

73. J. O. Stubbs, 'Lord Milner and Patriotic Labour, 1914–1918', *English Historical Review*, vol. 87 (Oct 1972).

74. Lord Selborne to Lord Salisbury, 12 Sep 1916, Salisbury MSS, S(4) 78/83–9.

75. Hewins, op. cit., pp. 47–56.

76. Cd 8271 (1916).

77. Cd 9035 (1918).

78. Proceedings of a Meeting of the Unionist Party, 12 Nov 1918, Bonar Law MSS, 95/3.

79. Younger to Balfour, 14 Jan 1918, Balfour MSS, Add. MS. 49865.

80. *Observer*, 29 Jun 1919.

81. Law to Balfour, 5 Oct 1918, Blake, op. cit., p. 385.

2 England's Irish Question

DAVID HARKNESS

The two supreme services which Ireland has rendered Britain are her accession to the Allied cause on the outbreak of the Great War, and her withdrawal from the House of Commons at its close.[1]

When Winston Churchill, looking back in the late 1920s upon the war and its immediate aftermath, made this relieved comment, he assumed that the Irish question which had so troubled British political life during the nineteenth and early twentieth centuries had in large measure been answered. The withdrawal of Dillon's remnant of the Irish Nationalist Party from Westminster and the more strident refusal of Sinn Fein, triumphant in the 1918 elections, to attend there at all, had been followed by the 'Articles of agreement for a Treaty between Great Britain and Ireland' in December 1921. This Agreement formally separated the bulk of Ireland's political representatives from the British Parliament, leaving that overburdened legislature mercifully freer to proceed with what it considered more significant affairs, both national and international.

But if it can be agreed that England's Irish question derived from a persistent and increasingly forceful Irish demand for an end to union and for the establishment of full sovereign independence for an Ireland, the territorial integrity of which embraced the whole island, then we can understand why Churchill's relief was as shortlived as it was ill-founded. For although the great majority of the Irish withdrew from the British domestic scene, they withdrew only as far as the imperial arena, where, with their new found Dominion status, they initiated a deal of provocative activity not always to the liking of London. Furthermore, not all Ireland's representatives left Westminster since thirteen M.P.s remained on behalf of the six northeastern counties of Ulster, for which the British government still retained ultimate responsibility although day-to-day management was surrendered to a local parliament in Belfast. Also the fact that Ireland's English question remained very much alive in the form of a continuing intervention, control and restraint brought to bear by London upon Irish affairs (the island was partitioned, and political and economic pressures upon the Free State remained formidable) meant that for Westminster, even in the domestic sphere, the Irish question could not entirely depart. Churchill himself was to be less grateful for Ireland's role during the Second World War and even in the inter-war years there were many matters of moment to disturb Anglo-Irish relations and to revive at times that triangle of tension between London, Dublin and Belfast that had been so vibrant in the decade after 1910.

Churchill's over-sanguine relief did, of course, strike a widely responsive note in Britain, a point easily understood in the 1970s when Irish events have once again created an intractable and divisive embarrassment for the British people. What is of concern here, however, is to describe the form in which the denouement came in the 1920s and 1930s, before war cast its peculiar influence once more upon a relationship between neighbours so often strained because always unequal. And how, too, it must be asked, did British governments, and British political parties, respond to the range of challenges and problems posed by Irishmen, northern as well as southern, in this phase of the Irish question?

For more than half the period from 1922 to 1939 Anglo-Irish relations were formally conducted on the Irish side by the supporters of the Treaty of 1921, led throughout by W. T. Cosgrave. Upon the defeat of his Cumman na Geadheal Party in February 1932, a change of tone but no real change of direction in these relations became apparent. Under de Valera, the Fianna Fail government, which then assumed office and retained it beyond the Second World War, displayed a more strident nationalism and indulged in more unilateral actions in its dealings with the government of His Britannic Majesty. Yet the three main areas of Anglo-Irish contact during these years had emerged quickly enough before the divide of 1932: numerous matters of constitutional practice and definition, both international and imperial; closely related bilateral arrangements dealing with finance, trade, and defence; and Northern Ireland, a by no means exclusively British concern. In combination these problems compose the 'Irish question' between 1922 and 1939. They are examined in turn below, but it must be remembered that although at different times one or another was in the forefront they were each, throughout the period, interdependent, continuous and concurrent.

The Irish were preoccupied initially by a civil war over the terms of the Treaty with Britain, which established a twenty-six-county Dominion but left Britain a six-county Northern Ireland. The pro-Treaty party of Cosgrave, affirming its authority by the middle of 1923, had then to face up to the daunting task of state-building. Irish presence at the 1923 Imperial Conference was, in consequence, more in the nature of interested observation than constructive participation. But Cosgrave's men did perceive new opportunities. Hardly enthusiastic imperialists, they found themselves committed to membership of an empire, part of which was in the process of adjusting itself into a freer association to be called a Commonwealth of Nations. Determined to establish beyond question their national sovereignty, the Irish soon learned to exploit the movement for autonomy and equality already under way within the British Dominions. They also took steps, however, to assure their international standing in relation to the world outside the British empire and they perceived that at Geneva, among the ranks of the League of Nations, lay an opportunity for securing recognition and support beyond the immediate influence of Britain.

The post-war world of the early twenties was far from secure or settled, and the withdrawal of the United States and the continued uncertainty concerning Soviet Russia threw a heavy responsibility upon the British empire and particularly upon the leading British statesmen who were willing to assume the task of engineering a stabler and a more just international order. For Lloyd George, for Baldwin, for Curzon, for Austen Chamberlain and for Ramsay MacDonald, there were advantages in speaking to foreign powers with the weight of the empire in attendance. They had little desire to precipitate Dominion autonomy or to make looser the ties that bound the colonies of white settlement to the mother country. But in Canada and South Africa a reluctance to be committed by purely British decisions on international affairs was already manifest, and the new Irish Free State in the years ahead was to embrace and at times accelerate this trend towards national awareness and independence.

This then is the context of the first aspect of the Irish question in the inter-war years; the field of international, and more precisely, inter-imperial relations. Action at Geneva preceded activity in the Commonwealth, though it is worth noting that the Treaty of 1921 itself pioneered the use of the term 'Commonwealth' in an inter-national document and that the Irish Free State Constitution of 1922 contained further extensions of the principle of Dominion autonomy.[2]

In 1922 the Irish government began its groundwork in Geneva, and it submitted formal application for membership in April 1923 and was admitted on 10 September the same year. Its next move was to underpin this recognition of international status by complying with a League injunction that any treaties between member states must be registered with the League for all nations to see. On 11 July 1924 the Irish Free State had its treaty with Britain – the treaty which gave it its being – formally registered at Geneva. This action brought the Irish into direct conflict with the British, whose notion of empire precluded the registration of in-ter-imperial agreements, which (being family matters *inter se*) were deemed to be not international and therefore to require no public display. Thus, confronting each other early on, were two incompatible views of the imperial association: the one viewing it as something apart and radiating from London as the spokes of a wheel; the other striving for the sake of national dignity to have the equality and autonomy of the member states clearly recognised by the world community. The Irish government therefore used the League to complement the Commonwealth and sought by estab-lishing direct relations with foreign powers to make apparent its emergence from the tutelage of its former master.

In pursuit of this ideal, and before the year 1924 had ended, the Irish Free State succeeded in establishing the first Dominion embassy: at Washington that October, after much to-ing and fro-ing by the British ambassador, Sir Esmé Howard, Professor T. A. Smiddy was accredited to the United States government as Irish Free State minister plenipotentiary, thus breaking the diplomatic unity of the empire. Other statements of independence were made under the Cosgrave government in the following years. In 1926 the Free State stood as a last-minute replacement for Spain as a can-didate for the League Council, the non-permanent membership of which was then being raised from six to nine. This bid, frowned upon by Britain, was unsuccessful; but the principle of Dominion eligibility had been secured and, after Canada was successful in 1927, the Free State replaced that Dominion in 1930. In 1929 after considerable delay in deference to British desires to preserve a single Commonwealth approach (designed to protect the special British view of Commonwealth relations *inter se*), the Irish lost patience and finally signed the 'optional clause' of the Permanent Court of International Justice at Geneva. By so doing the Free State agreed to submit to that court any dispute that might arise between it and any other contracting member. Britain wished to exclude intra-Commonwealth disputes and in the end qualified its own signature in this manner.

Because of their history and peculiar geographical and intra-Commonwealth relationship, nearly every gesture by the young Irish Free State appeared to be directed against Britain; and this was bound to be so since it was from under Britain's wing that the Irish were escaping. It is not surprising, therefore, that the Irish record inside the Commonwealth association during these years proved even more persistent and assertive. At successive Imperial Conferences and gatherings Irish delegates strove, with much success, to make obvious to the world (and to the sometimes reluctant Dominions themselves) the absolute nature of their independence and the responsibilities and obligations that full sovereignty imposed. By 1921 the British Dominions, wisely if gently instructed by Smuts of South Africa and soon more tetchily by Mackenzie King of Canada, had begun to emphasise their individual international identities at the expense of their corporate association. The Irish Free State, claiming ancient nationhood, had joined what it saw as a British association largely under threat and only on being convinced that Dominion status could become synonymous with sovereignty. It thus naturally favoured the centrifugal trend, and in 1926, in 1929, and in 1930, successive Free State delegations at the central councils of the Commonwealth did much to make real their early hopes and in consequence operated throughout in opposition to traditional British interests.

The 1926 Imperial Conference, which publicly declared the autonomy of the Dominions and pronounced them, together with Britain, to be 'equal in status, in no way subordinate one to another', was the occasion of much close constitutional debate. It was one thing to make a dignified declaration; it was quite another to translate that declaration into practice. Thus, while

General Hertzog, who was now leading South Africa and who was determined to have his country's sovereign status endorsed, might be satisfied with words, Kevin O'Higgins, heading the Irish delegation, demanded much more: the complete sweeping away of the 'anomalies' and 'anachronisms' of the old imperial structure which from his point of view both restricted the Dominions to a position of subordination to Britain and confused foreigners as to the real advances towards sovereignty which they had already made. He listed a number of practices relating to the position of the Crown and the Parliament of Westminster – survivals from the days of undisputed British domination – and requested both the excision of such dead, obscuring wood and the creation of proper machinery by which the Commonwealth nations, voluntarily continuing in association and choosing thereby to give allegiance to a common king, could co-operate from positions of visible equality. Let the theoretical powers of Westminster over Dominion legislation be removed, he asked; let the Dominion governments be seen to advise their King freely; let the position of the Governor-General in the Dominions be unambiguously that of representative of the King and not also of the British government; let foreign governments deal directly with the Dominions on Dominion business; let those Dominions desirous of legal autonomy be no longer bound in the last resort to submit to the decisions of a British court of appeal, the Judicial Committee of the Privy Council. If these changes could be made the Commonwealth would gain new strength. As O'Higgins put it in conclusion:

> The co-operation resulting from the bond of a common King will be effective only because it is free co-operation and to the extent to which it is free. Antiquated forms dating from a period when common action resulted from the over-riding control of one central government are liable to make co-operation less efficacious, because they make it seem less free.[3]

To put all this into effect was a task beyond an already busy Imperial Conference, though the position of the Governor-General was satisfactorily dealt with and the Irish did agree to postpone their assault on the Judicial Committee of the Privy Council. Also a committee of experts was called into being to examine the other offending items and to report back. This body of experts – the Committee on the Operation of Dominion Legislation – did not meet until 1929. In the intervening time it was the Irish who assembled the most formidable array of papers and it was the Irish who, when the committee actually met, sent the strongest and ablest team to its deliberations (though Patrick McGilligan, a tough, astute and versatile academic and politician, replaced O'Higgins who had been assassinated in 1927). Throughout October and November 1929 this committee, which had to deal also with the complex field of Dominion merchant shipping legislation, carried out its brief to make recommendations concerning the whole range of legal relationships between the Dominion parliaments and the Mother of Parliaments in London. The results of these labours are embodied in the Statute of Westminster which was enacted in 1931 after considerable debate at the Imperial Conference of 1930. That conference, with its twin tasks of tidying constitutional relationships and resolving the economic problems which stemmed from the world-wide depression, provides ample illustration of the degree to which the inter-war Irish question was an imperial one. As usual the British and Irish were strongly at odds.

Ramsay MacDonald still headed a minority Labour administration when the Imperial Conference met on 1 October 1930. He was beset by economic difficulties, and the national press had encouraged quite unrealistic expectations of relief through Commonwealth economic measures. Philip Snowden's free trade orthodoxy combined with differing individual Dominion interests to frustrate joint progress on the economic front, while in the constitutional sphere the Irish pegged doggedly away to secure the provisions recommended by the 1929 Committee. To MacDonald these provisions now seemed on the one hand irrelevant and on the other dangerous; for he did not want the lack of success in the sphere of trade and finance to be compounded in the eyes of the British public by legal and constitutional concessions which seemed to threaten the very existence of the empire. To a disappointed electorate would be added a furious 'die-hard' opposition in Parliament. So the strong Irish contingent, which was unable itself to contribute to the economic debate, since Ireland already conducted most of its import and export trade with Britain, roused much resentment by sticking so closely to its constitutional agenda.

Looked at from the Irish point of view, there should have been no problem. Once the constitutional changes had been agreed the Conference could have devoted all its energies to economic matters. But the British prevaricated even over what they had apparently conceded in 1929, as they did also over renewed attempts to remove the appeal to the Judicial Committee of the Privy Council (which it was suggested could be replaced by a Commonwealth Tribunal). And attempts to establish direct Dominion access to the King in relation to his duties on their behalf, to replace the portmanteau term, 'British subject' with separate Dominion nationalities and to clarify *inter se* relations with reference in particular to the application of international treaties – all of these were resisted and, apart from some progress on the question of nationality, in effect thwarted in the 'Inter-Imperial Relations Committee' chaired by Lord Sankey.

Though thankful that the 1929 Committee's report was at last accepted and was to be embodied in a bill for approval by all the Dominions and for enactment at Westminster in December 1931, the Irish remained angry and disillusioned over the number of issues left unresolved by this conference. Thus, while the eventual Statute of Westminster was following its course through the several Dominion parliaments, the Irish took the initiative in establishing their own direct access to the King and at the same time ended their dependence on the Royal and National Seals of England, necessary for the authentication of state documents, by creating a new Great Seal of Irish Free State. But they could get no agreement from Britain to dispense with the provision for appeals to the Judicial Committee of the Privy Council, a matter bound up with the 1921 Treaty but already effectively circumvented in practice by *ad hoc* Dublin legislation which made disputed Irish court decisions law in the face of contrary Privy Council decisions. Nor could they abolish by agreement the controversial Oath of Allegiance which the Treaty had imposed upon Members of Dail Eireann, the Irish parliament. Dissatisfaction on both these issues was to spill over to the next Irish administration and to result in unilateral abolition, the promise of which, indeed, featured prominently in Mr de Valera's 1932 election campaign.

The supersession of Cosgrave by de Valera in February 1932 had repercussions in the more immediately domestic arena, but also intensified the imperial aspect of Britain's Irish problem. The fact that he disagreed with his predecessor about the inviolability of the Treaty, and the fact that he could take advantage of the terms of the Statute of Westminster, meant that Mr de Valera was well placed to take a more intransigent stand upon the inalienable and fundamental rights of nationhood. Not only did he abolish oath and appeal in 1933; he also 'minimised' the role of the Governor-General in that year, defined Irish nationality in 1935 (in the process purporting to deprive Irish citizens of their British subjecthood), rearranged the duties of the Sovereign in 1936 so that the King's function remained solely in the realm of external relations, and in 1937 implemented a new Irish Constitution which loosened further the royal connection and created what was, in effect, a thinly disguised Irish Republic.

That all this could happen despite a barrage of continuous British protest is illustrative not only of the reality of the new Dominion autonomy but also of the different perspectives of the Anglo-Irish relationship. At this difficult time of economic crisis, followed by deepening gloom in Central Europe, the British were preoccupied by a host of major global issues at the same time as they were endeavouring to rebuild the strength of the pound and the buoyancy of the British economy and to preserve a measure of Commonwealth unity in a world of deteriorating international conduct. The Irish, while not unconcerned about the general world scene, were as usual devoting themselves almost exclusively to their relations with their nearest neighbour. Single-mindedly they set about the final removal of British constitutional connections and forms, keeping just within the possible limits of Commonwealth membership in the interests of ultimate Irish national unity. As measure succeeded measure British legal and imperial officials, in anxious consultation with their other Dominion counterparts, strove to define the boundaries of that membership and to draw up contingency plans in the event of the Free State overstepping them.

In all this the British were unlucky. Angered by the unilateral legislation of 1933 and alarmed by hints in that year of Irish secession, they had to proceed cautiously lest they damage Cosgrave's chances of return to office. As time went by and the less tactful J. H. Thomas was replaced by Malcolm MacDonald as Dominions secretary, some advantage was seen in coming to terms with the man who was clearly the outstanding Irish leader. But it seemed necessary to the British government to insist upon the Irish Free State's continued membership of the Commonwealth and appropriate also to lay down the requirement that all Dominions must retain the Crown as 'a vital part of the Legislature . . . and the Head of its Executive Government'.[4]

In mid-1936 de Valera gave 'courtesy' intimation that he proposed to eliminate the Crown from Irish domestic affairs, a proposal which (to Lord Hailsham for one) would definitely put the Free State outside the Commonwealth. The cabinet tried to tighten yet further the fundamental tenets of the association, 'the necessary and essential elements which must remain if the status of a Dominion within the Empire is to be retained'.[5]

In general terms three criteria were agreed:

(1) That the King should be head of the executive government
(2) that the King should be part of the legislature, and
(3) that the nationals should owe to the King allegiance.[6]

With particular reference to the Irish Free State, the decision also consisted of three points:

(1) The whole position turns on allegiance – not on the acceptance of a Governor-General or on the Crown's assent to legislation.
(2) Mr de Valera should be asked if he were willing to make an unambiguous declaration, in some prominent position in the new Free State Constitution, containing the substance of the doctrine of allegiance.
(3) Otherwise we shall be unable to regard the Free State as satisfying the requisites for Membership of the Commonwealth.[7]

Unfortunately, having reached these decisions and laid careful plans to work slowly towards their implementation, the British were overtaken by the sudden abdication crisis and the need to coordinate Dominion concurrence in unprecedented constitutional adjustments. Mr de Valera took the opportunity to implement, by emergency legislation in advance of his new Constitution, his plan to remove the King from Irish internal affairs. Clearly this legislation undercut the agreed minimum conditions of Commonwealth membership, but the cabinet, now aware that Canada and South Africa were unlikely to favour Irish expulsion on these grounds, had to be satisfied that Article 1 of the existing Irish Constitution did declare that 'the Irish Free State is a co-equal member of the Community of Nations forming the British Commonwealth of Nations.' Early in 1937 it learned with horror that this article would not be contained in the new Constitution, to be made law later in the year. The Marquess of Zetland, Secretary of State for India, regretted the impact on that aspiring Dominion; Prime Minister Baldwin accused his Irish counterpart of wanting 'the finest possible line with which successfully to wangle Unemployment Insurance and Old Age Pensions for persons of Irish Free State origin resident in the United Kingdom'.[8] But Malcolm

MacDonald felt it would be a pity to throw out the Irish now that Mr de Valera had chosen to utilise the King in his most important (because personally handled) functions in regard to Irish external relations. He advised consultation with the other Dominions in advance of some formula to be agreed at the forthcoming Imperial Conference. The other Dominions willingly accepted the Irish legislation. In the event the Irish did not attend the Imperial Conference held in May and June 1937 and no further formula was produced, though Dominion leaders were once more consulted on the actual terms of the new Irish Constitution, which had by then been published and was clearly less satisfactory than had been hoped.

The imperial aspect of the Irish question in this period was rounded off by the fact of Irish non-involvement in the Second World War. Though Malcolm MacDonald had warned Mr de Valera in the autumn of 1937 that he 'could not admit that one member of the Commonwealth had a right to remain neutral if the others were at war'[9] the Irish premier had made little secret of his desire for neutrality in any future conflict between the great powers; and the fact that his decision was not held to be incompatible with continued Commonwealth membership showed not only how complete was now the autonomy of the Dominions, but also how much more flexible the Commonwealth association had become since 1921.

In 1921 the British authorities had refused to contemplate the creation of an Irish republic and had insisted upon answering the Irish question in terms of partition and Dominion status. Then the compromise seemed to satisfy cleverly the principal British interests: the preservation of the unity of the empire and of the allegiance of the King's subjects, and the creation of safeguards for the defence of the United Kingdom and for the position of the protestant people of Northern Ireland. But almost two decades later the Irish thorn in the domestic side of Britain (and here we come to the second area of the Irish question in the interwar years), was still proving more than a minor irritant there. And in addition part of the question remained unanswered at home.

Above all, the appendix of partition grumbled on in Ireland. The Irish signatories to the Treaty thought that the terms of that agreement would undermine the position of the Northern statelet so recently established by the Government of Ireland Act, 1920. Article 12 of the Treaty, they thought, would lead to such an alteration of the boundary between the two parts of Ireland as to make the smaller unit unviable, and would thus lead inevitably to the restoration of unity. Owing to the civil war and to other preoccupations this matter was unfortunately left in the air. So were a number of details concerning the financial relations between Britain and the Free State – details which were to lead to considerable friction in the 1930s and which were themselves to be closely connected with the boundary settlement. This settlement itself constituted the most obvious domestic intrusion of the Irish question into British affairs in the twenties. Boundary revision was to be undertaken, according to the terms of the Treaty, by a commission consisting of representatives of both parts of Ireland, under an independent, British-appointed chairman.

Details of the operation of this commission and of the report which it submitted (only to be suppressed for political reasons) have emerged slowly in recent years.[10] But the outline events have been clear enough since the commission, delayed by the civil war in the Free State and by obstructive non-co-operation in Northern Ireland, made its survey and submitted its report in 1925. Under the chairmanship of Mr Justice Feetham of the South African Supreme Court (and with Eoin MacNeill, Minister for Education in Mr Cosgrave's Cabinet, representing the Free State and J. R. Fisher, a prominent Ulster Protestant appointed by the British, representing the Belfast government) the commission examined the existing border to 'determine in accordance with the wishes of the inhabitants, so far as may be compatible with economic and geographic conditions, the boundaries between Northern Ireland and the rest of Ireland'.[11] But it is clear now that the commission set about its task with an interpretation of the old Article 12 so qualified as to deny the possibility of fulfilling the aspirations of the Irish signatories. Chairman Feetham was clear in his own mind that 'no wholesale reconstruction of the map' was authorised and that the commission's job was 'not to reconstitute the two territories, but to settle the boundaries between them'. Economics, geography and popular will would have to be subordinated to one paramount consideration:

Northern Ireland must, when the boundaries have been determined, still be recognisable as the same provincial entity; the changes made must not be so drastic as to destroy its identity or make it impossible for it to continue as a separate province of the United Kingdom with its own parliament and government for provincial affairs under the Government of Ireland Act.[12]

Had such an interpretation been put to the Irish representatives in 1921 it is inconceivable that the Treaty would have been signed. Yet MacNeill in 1925 had little hope of a successful outcome from the commission. He seems to have accepted or misunderstood his chairman's interpretation and he certainly set about his business with an integrity that denied his government any inkling of how things were proceeding. Only a leakage in the *Morning Post* on 7 November, when the report was substantially complete, alerted the Dublin authorities to the disastrous turn of events. On 20 November MacNeill resigned and the politicians set about diminishing the damage already done by the *Morning Post*'s reported details.

Before these details had become known there had already been correspondence between Dublin and London on the practical problems and actual arrangements for the transfer of territory from north to south. But to Dublin the transfer of even small amounts of its own territory to the Northern regime, which the *Morning Post* asserted was contemplated by the commission, was unacceptable; and the meagre, if greater transfers in the opposite direction were in no way calculated to make unviable the northern state. Public outcry from Irish nationalists was immediate. Publication of the actual report had to be prevented and alternative arrangements concluded.

Between 28 November and 3 December a compromise was hammered out. Bitterly disappointed, the Irish Free State accepted the existing boundary without alteration, rather than fix in cast iron a new boundary which would only perpetuate partition. Putting as good a face upon the matter as possible Cosgrave publicly expressed his faith in a voluntary growth of mutual respect and understanding which would finally lead to the union of Irish hearts. In this respect he felt that the tripartite agreement, which he now signed with Prime Minister Craig of Northern Ireland and the British government, would provide a hopeful start.

This boundary agreement made an important concession to Northern Ireland by transferring to the Belfast government powers over it reserved in the Treaty for the abortive Council of Ireland. The agreement also conceded *de facto* the freehold of the six counties so that no longer would Craig's Unionists have to fear erosion of their territory. But this is not the end of the story. The boundary agreement was accompanied by a compensatory financial settlement designed to compensate the Irish Free State for the disappointment of its hopes. This financial settlement – an important milestone in relations between Dublin and London – is best seen in the context of what had preceded it and as an essential preliminary to the series of economic disputes which arose once Mr de Valera assumed office in Dublin. These in turn contributed the shrillest domestic notes to the Irish question in the inter-war period.

Article 5 of the 1921 Treaty had stated that the Irish Free State would assume liability for the service of the United Kingdom Public Debt and towards the payment of war pensions 'in such proportion as may be fair and equitable, having regard to any just claims on the part of Ireland by way of set off or counter claim . . .' In 1923 a 'provisional' financial agreement was arrived at between British and Irish representatives, though it was not made public at that time. In brief the Irish Free State government then agreed to collect and pay over Land Purchase Annuities (i.e. moneys due from Irish tenant purchasers to the British Debt Commissioners who were the servicers of loans originally advanced under various Land Acts dating from 1891–1909); and it agreed to pay a contribution towards interest due on other land stock and to pay a certain proportion of Royal Irish Constabulary, and some other, pensions. In return the British government agreed to guarantee further land purchase bonds raised in the Irish Free State.

Details of this agreement were clarified further during 1924, but by the agreement accompanying the boundary commission fiasco, the British government in December 1925 waived any claim to a Free State contribution to the United Kingdom Public Debt. In return the Free State agreed to a specific payment of £250,000 per annum for sixty years (from 1927) in discharge of obligations relating to damage to property in Ireland during the years 1919–25. To this arrangement was added one other – the Heads of Ultimate Financial Settlement – agreed in March 1926 by Winston Churchill as Chancellor of the Exchequer and Ernest Blythe, the Free State Minister for Finance. While tidying away all remaining points of detail this agreement also reaffirmed the Free State liability regarding Land Annuities.

This was the situation when Mr de Valera came into office in the spring of 1932. His political campaign, directed at aspects of the 1921 Treaty, included a repudiation of Irish liability in respect of these same Land Annuities. Believing that Ireland had been exploited for many centuries he felt, indeed, that liabilities for compensation and payment should be admitted by Britain. Thus, when battle was joined over the Land Annuity issue, he was disinclined to accept British protestations of injured innocence. From March to April 1932 an acrimonious correspondence was conducted between de Valera and J. H. Thomas, the Dominions Secretary, prior to the meetings which took place in Dublin and London on 7 and 10 June respectively. During this period de Valera widened the quarrel, linking financial disagreement to Irish resentment at the continuation of partition and at the British naval utilisation of certain Irish ports, as well as at the constitutional issues referred to above. In the middle of June de Valera proposed arbitration, but not by an empire tribunal as Britain insisted (the boundary commission had convinced the Irish leader that there the 'dice would always be loaded against the Free State'),[13] and not just upon the Land Annuity issue, but on the whole range of financial relations between the two countries.

It was the Land Annuities question that came to a head first, however, for de Valera refused to sanction the half-yearly payment of interest which fell due at the end of June, leaving the British government to find the money (approximately £1,250,000) due to the holders of the Irish Land Stock. Aggrieved, and reluctant to saddle the British taxpayer with this additional burden, the British government passed the Irish Free State (Special Duties) Act and proceeded under its provisions to levy special duties (designed to raise an amount equivalent to that withheld) on certain articles imported from the Free State.

In response to this action de Valera quickly conferred with his British counterpart, Ramsay MacDonald, but their failure to agree was aggravated by misleading newspaper accounts of their respective attitudes. Economic 'war' was joined when the Irish in turn imposed duties upon goods imported from England, and the British followed up by refusing to enter into any Anglo-Irish trade agreements at the important Imperial Economic Conference at Ottawa later in the year.

The 'economic war' heralded return of the Irish question to the British domestic scene with a vengeance. While the rights and wrongs of the actual Land Annuity dispute are of relatively minor relevance here, the fact of disagreement over a wide range of issues 'constitutional, financial, defence and economic'[14] imposed new strains on both sides of the Irish Sea and renewed the tensions already present in the six counties of Northern Ireland.

A major attempt to negotiate a settlement in London on 14 and 15 October 1932 revealed the extent of the gap between the two parties. It became clear, too, that the Irish were not only convinced their case was morally correct but also that they felt they had insufficient resources to meet the outstanding bills. While de Valera pleaded the case along lines of natural justice, instancing over-taxation of Ireland since the Union and furthermore demanding a fair share of the assets of the imperial partnership dissolved in 1922; his Minister for Finance, Sean McEntee not only sought a clean slate to enable a friendly renewal of relations but also admitted frankly that the 'plain fact was that the Irish Free State could not afford to make the payments'.[15] The British negotiators were profoundly unimpressed. They asserted that everything had been settled in the previous agreements and produced statistics to prove that there was no net burden on the Free State Treasury: the Land Annuities were, after all, raised from the tenant purchasers and did not constitute part of the Irish government's revenue; and, as far as pensions were concerned, these were a normal government charge, many of the payments went to Free State citizens, and monies departing to Britain were more than balanced by war pensions paid by Britain to citizens of the Free State. Besides, the Free State had been freed, most generously, from its obligation to bear a share of the Public Debt of the United Kingdom, which, it was agreed had been incurred for the benefit of all the peoples of the United Kingdom, including those now belonging to the Free State. For the war years alone that debt amounted to £6,785,000,000.

There was thus no meeting of minds here and even on the matter of arbitration Neville Chamberlain argued sourly that he thought the Irish so constituted that they would never accept a decision unless it accorded with their own views. J. H. Thomas concluded that nothing could have been more unconvincing than the various Irish claims, while de Valera lamented that while the Irish and British peoples ought to be moving closer, their failure to reach agreement here would only postpone such an event.

The negotiations failed and for six years a mutually damaging economic war disrupted arrangements between the two countries, despite several attempts to initiate further talks. By March 1933, having remained silent while de Valera sprang a surprise election in Ireland and slightly improved his position, the British cabinet's Irish Situation Committee reviewed the state of the tariff war. Against some £4,660,000 deemed to have been withheld by the Free State, only £2,123,000 had been raised in duties (though £1,750,000 had been withheld before the duties had been imposed). A tax on Irish stout was considered but rejected in view of the resentment which would most probably be felt by the British electorate! The problem that remained was how the United Kingdom could hit the Free State without hurting itself more.

It was not until the close of 1934 that a minor breakthrough occurred. Finding that Irish delegates were studying Polish coalfields, the British responded to a suggestion from the Irish High Commissioner, J. W. Dulanty, that an amelioration of the tarriff war might be effected by reciprocal import reductions – by the Irish on the duty upon British coal and by the British on that levied upon Irish cattle. Fearing the imminent conversion of Irish furnaces to take the very different type of coal from Poland, which would lose this market to British coal forever, the British agreed and in January 1935 a coal-cattle pact was concluded to the benefit of both Irish farmers and consumers and of British miners and carriers.

Anglo-Irish relations nevertheless remained at a frigid level until Malcolm MacDonald, who took over from J. H. Thomas late in 1935, brought his conciliatory spirit, already evidenced in the field of Commonwealth constitutional affairs, to bear upon matters economic. Indeed his approach was from the beginning a comprehensive one, which sought a general settlement between neighbours that might strengthen their bilateral bonds as well as remove from the Commonwealth a canker that could only do damage to the association as a whole. In his own words, 'such a settlement would greatly strengthen our position in world affairs, would increase our security from the point of view of defence, and would materially assist British trade and industry.'[16] By 1936 the Irish question was both international and domestic, and its resolution had become urgent.

As a result of a number of private conversations with de Valera which established their mutual trust, Malcolm MacDonald was able to persuade his colleagues that a better political relationship with the Irish might be worth some financial sacrifice. In a comprehensive settlement, he argued, it might be possible to return to Irish custody the naval installations retained under the terms of the Treaty, if by so doing co-operation was secured at a political level. In the field of finance a face-to-face settlement would, he thought, be preferable to arbitration, and a carefully worked out, once-for-all, lump-sum payment would provide the best basis for a solution. Regarding trade, a successful financial settlement would lead to the abolition of tariff duties and to the conclusion of

a general trade agreement, possibly along the lines of those concluded at Ottawa. Neville Chamberlain thought the financial
price for this might be too high, for on his estimate the capital
value of the sum upon which the Irish were defaulting stood in the
area of £100 millions while it was rumoured that the Irish would
be unable to raise more than £10 millions. Lord Hailsham
refused to believe that de Valera had changed his spots and
expected only another damaging failure to reach any agreement.
But against a background of rather alarming constitutional developments, the cabinet authorised MacDonald to continue his ex-
plorations throughout 1936 and 1937.

On 24 November 1937 a letter from Mr de Valera suggesting a
meeting at governmental level provided the excuse needed for
positive action. A favourable reply was communicated to the High
Commissioner, Dulanty, on 1 December, and what was to prove
the final round of negotiations was set in motion. Meetings and
letters followed one another from the middle of January 1938 until
agreements were signed on 25 April. Negotiations were by no
means straightforward and towards the end were threatened with
complete breakdown. But pertinacity and mutual interest pre-
vailed.

Before the first major encounter took place, from 17–19 January, the British negotiators – Neville Chamberlain (Prime
Minister since mid-1937), Sir John Simon, Sir Samuel Hoare, and
Malcolm MacDonald, backed by Inskip, Stanley and Morrison –
admitted that 'Mr. de Valera and his colleagues were extremely
hard bargainers.' Indeed, Chamberlain went so far as to add that
'Mr. de Valera's mentality was in some ways like Herr Hitler's. It
was no use employing with them the arguments which appealed
to the ordinary sensible man.'[17] As it turned out, Mr de Valera's
strategy was to link a defence treaty to an end to the partition of
Ireland; he also linked defence to finance for, clearly, Eire (which
the Free State had become by its Constitution enacted in 1937)
would need more money to shoulder its new responsibilities in
connection with the naval ports should they be returned (They
had been run down under the British and now stood in need of
heavy expenditure, a principal British reason for handing them
back!). The Irish, therefore, could not afford to pay out much
money to the British exchequer and this was particularly so if it
was realised that Eire would be defending Britain's flank and purchasing British equipment with which to do so. But, de Valera
added, it would be difficult to enter into a defence pact with

Britain while partition lasted. And there could be no going back on the Land Annuities. There could be a lump sum financial payment to settle other outstanding money matters, but it should be small for the above reasons and also in order to allow Ireland to build up its agricultural resources, which were so vital an asset in any time of war.

The British were already finding it difficult to preserve an overview of all the matters under negotiation. But they remained convinced that any generosity towards Eire must be reciprocated in respect of Eire concessions towards Northern Irish trade. Haggling over lump-sum compensation ranged from an Irish offer of £6 millions against a British claim reduced to £50 millions, to an Irish £8 millions and a British £37 millions. After further British concessions reducing the sum to £25 millions over three years, de Valera said £10 millions was his limit; but when asked whether or not this was exclusive of putting the ports on a war footing he replied 'Yes', and agreement was then deemed possible. Trade, however, provided a much more complicated picture, and after a defence treaty draft was presented by Britain, it was agreed to adjourn so that departmental officials could hammer out trade details during the ensuing weeks. On his departure de Valera stressed privately to MacDonald that some movement on partition would be the surest guarantee of acceptance of an agreement by public opinion in Eire. His own parliamentary position, he pointed out, was far from being a strong one.

On 23 February the negotiators were ready to resume their talks. But there had been no movement by Britain on partition. There could, therefore, be no defence treaty. But, remonstrated Chamberlain, Britain could not compel the North to join Eire! Nor could Britain evade responsibility for the blatant discrimination against Catholics there, replied de Valera. Tempers warmed and Chamberlain accused the Irish of presenting a three-leafed shamrock, none of the leaves having any advantage for Britain: on finance, the British were being asked to surrender their claims for only token payment; on trade, they were asked to surrender revenues with only an Irish Commission to look into the possibility of relief for British goods; and on defence, surrender of the ports, with no hard guarantees of future co-operation, was demanded. Could not Eire at least give preferential customs duties to Northern Irish goods as a *quid pro quo*?

The Dublin cabinet considered this request until 3 March, when further discussions revealed a complete Irish rejection of concessions to Northern Ireland for as long as discrimination and gerrymandering continued there. And on this issue deadlock threatened to bring to nought the whole range of agreements. High unemployment in Northern Ireland and hostile reaction there to the possibility of British naval withdrawal from the Southern ports left Chamberlain little room to manoeuvre without some genuine gesture from Dublin. But in the end it was Britain once more who had to yield. The other Dominions and public opinion at home were keyed up to expect a settlement; and real advantage was expected for British trade if one could be concluded. Attempts were made to press Belfast into accepting the agreement but when the Northern Ireland Premier, Craigavon, and his finance minister, J. M. Andrews, continued to insist that free entry for a long list of Northern Irish goods must be granted by Dublin, they had to be bought off with a series of rearmament contracts instead. This face-saving solution was not reached until the second week in April and it meant that the long sought general settlement could at last be concluded.

On 25 April 1938 three principal agreements were signed. The financial dispute was resolved by British acceptance of a lump sum of £10 millions, though the £250,000 p.a. agreed in 1925 was to continue and by the abolition of the special tariff duties levied by both sides. With the end of the economic war, an agreement was made providing for full freedom of trade, subject only to certain quotas and preferential duties and an Irish review of British import prices. Finally, although no defence treaty was concluded, Britain abandoned the Treaty ports, which were anyway deemed by her own experts to be untenable in the face of a hostile population, to be unusable for purposes of war and to require a prohibitive degree of expenditure to remedy their deficiencies. The complete settlement, in the words of Malcolm MacDonald, was 'not a good agreement on paper but . . . it would open a new chapter in Anglo-Irish relations . . . and our generosity would have its effects in Ireland.'[18] It is only fair to recall that in the unhappy history of postwar international debt settlements, the surrender of a claim of some £90 millions by Britain was neither unusual nor significant, and in relation to the Treaty ports, an agreement concluded in the same spirit of appeasement that was being applied concurrently to Mussolini's Italy was felt to be appropriate, more especially because Eire was a member of the Commonwealth. The particular hope here was that de Valera would modernise the port installations and make them available to Britain in any future conflict, though de Valera would give no assurances other than that the ports would never be offered to the enemies of Britain. Chamberlain, who had grown to respect and like the Irish Prime Minister, looked forward to a new era of friendly co-operation.

It must be remembered, however, that one item had been omitted from these agreements – the item closest to the heart of de Valera and his colleagues – partition. Eire with its autochthonous constitution, its ports no longer available to the forces of a foreign power, and its international identity established, had surely now succeeded in satisfying all the demands of independent sovereignty so long sought by an Ireland struggling to escape British control. For Eire, defined as the twenty-six county bulk of Ireland's thirty-two county island, the answer might be yes; but Eire, in its own estimation, applied to that whole island and the one aspiration yet unfulfilled, the integrity of the national territory, was the most crucial of all and the one destined to perpetuate for Britain that Irish question which it was by now supremely anxious to resolve, but which was to return with renewed violence and embarrassment in the post-World War Two period. De Valera had, as early as 1934, assured Britain that if an all-Ireland Republic were achieved within the British Commonwealth of Nations, then he would be prepared himself to take up arms against the enemies of Britain. But truncated Ireland remained and Eire remained neutral during World War Two, refusing to countenance alliance with a Britain that had, in the Irish government's view, both created partition and continued to uphold it at the same time as it had failed in its duty as trustee for the Roman Catholic minority within Northern Ireland.

Partition, the continuing existence of the six Northern Irish counties as part of the United Kingdom, albeit administered in domestic affairs by their own parliament at Stormont, remained the heart and core of the Irish question. For both Ireland and Britain the settlement of 1921 had not solved this problem. For both countries the inter-war years marked here, as elsewhere, Years Between': between two periods of sustained and widespread violence, though the 'twenties and 'thirties themselves were not free from trouble and rancour so far as Northern Ireland was concerned. The partition of Ireland, legally performed by the Government of Ireland Act, 1920, had seen little rejoicing in either part of the island and was enacted at the height of a guerrilla war between nationalist Sinn Fein and the British forces. Until the boundary commission had been disposed of in 1925, the Northern regime had rested on shaky foundations, though its uncompromising intention from the start had been summed up in the phrase, 'What we have we hold.' As the Roman Catholic minority there was assumed to be hostile, nationalistic and Republican, it was treated with suspicion. And this minority, in its turn, was determined to win through to an all-Ireland state and could not but regard the Belfast regime as temporary. Nor were its members in any way inclined to lend to that state support or comfort. Community relations got off to a poor start in Northern Ireland. Even after 1925 continuing pressures ensured that they remained at a low level. Though the boundary commission had removed an immediate threat, the Unionist authorities never really threw off their characteristic seige mentality – outnumbered as they still were in Ireland as a whole, and subject to pressure from a substantial minority within whose aspirations can only have seemed akin to treason.

In the uncertain first two years of its existence there was much open conflict and some loss of life in Northern Ireland; but the civil war in the Free State and the uncertainty surrounding the boundary commission produced something of a lull both in rural conflict and city pogrom. After 1925 the Unionist government concentrated upon the consolidation of its power, and was aided for a time in this by the continuing non-co-operation of the minority during the overhauling of both education and local government. Gradually the elected representatives of the nationalists faced up to reality, however, and by 1927 Joseph Devlin (who was until his death in 1934 the outstanding representative of Northern Irish nationalist opinion) headed a group of ten members in the Stormont Parliament. This Parliament, it is perhaps worth noting, was composed of a Senate of twenty-six (two ex-officio, twenty-four elected by the Commons on a basis of proportional representation) and a House of Commons of fifty-two Members. The latter, where authority lay, was distinguished by the steady predominance of the Unionist majority throughout the period – the Unionist representation stood continuously at the forty mark, or slightly below – and in the continuity of its personnel and hence of its social composition. When inside the first decade the Unionist vote began to show signs of splintering in favour of tenant and temperance candidates outside the official party, Craigavon, the prime minister,* ended the prevailing system of proportional

* James Craig, knighted in 1918, became Viscount Craigavon in 1926. He was prime minister of Northern Ireland from 1921 until his death in 1940.

representation in 1929. This act successfully ensured that the main electoral issue was again the choice between unclouded support for and opposition to the Union with Britain.

The 1929 election preceded the worst depredations of the world-wide economic depression, which brought to the province in the early 1930s a heavy increase in unemployment. In these circumstances sectarian strife surged up once more and minor riots in 1931 and 1934 were followed by violence and death in 1935, reminiscent of the worst days of 1922. In the wake of these outrages the Council for Civil Liberties conducted a far reaching investigation and published a report in 1936 which strongly condemned the Stormont government's use of its emergency powers (embodied at the height of the early troubles in the Special Powers Act, 1922). These powers, the report declared, had been used to intimidate the minority community. In circumstances so far removed from the British system, where parliamentary opposition has always a reasonable expectation of holding office some day, this intimidation had inevitably driven the Catholic community to extreme measures, thus worsening the tensions. The report was damning; but it merely reflected the distrust still persisting between two communities holding diametrically opposed views of the state in which they lived.

When at the height of sectarian violence attempts were made in the British House of Commons to seek information and intervention, the great weakness of the Westminster-Stormont relationship as it operated in the inter-war years became apparent. A responsible devolution of power was scrupulously observed by successive British ministers. Thus, when, for example, on 19 July 1935 George Lansbury sought in the House of Commons to make the British government answerable for the actions of police and army in Belfast, the Home Secretary, Sir John Simon, blandly replied that the Northern Ireland government was responsible for law and order there; and a year later, in May 1936, Under-Secretary Geoffrey Lloyd made a similar response to a demand by Sir Percy Harris. To opponents of the Union, however, such an attitude could only seem a totally irresponsible abdication of an overriding duty towards a body of citizens of the United Kingdom permanently subject to the will of their sworn opponents. The truth is, it seems, that the Westminster Parliament was glad to be relieved of an area remote from the centres both of population and of economic expansion. References in *Hansard* throughout the twenties and thirties make depressing reading. They are few enough, and most often they grumble about the expenditure of moneys, or relate to such matters as cattle and horse purchases, or pig production, or general commodity prices, admiralty contracts or, as a more regular item, statements of liquor revenues and post office accounts. Indeed, it took until 1928 for the *Hansard* index to dignify Northern Ireland with a separate heading, previous references appearing under 'Ireland, Northern'. From the start the British Parliament expressed little interest in the affairs of the six Northern Irish counties across the water. And lack of interest produced in time almost total ignorance.

It is true that during the detailed trade surveys that preceded the Anglo-Irish agreements of 1938 a close look was given to the economic situation in Northern Ireland and strenuous efforts were made to persuade the Eire authorities to grant concessions Craigavon disliked what he saw of these negotiations, but though he distrusted the British ministers he was anxious not to see Eire driven from the Commonwealth. On the British side, although there was anxiety about Northern Irish unemployment and mounting political disquiet, harsh words were spoken in cabinet about Belfast intransigence, which seemed destined at a late stage to jeopardise all hope of a settlement. The Ulster Protestants, if they wished to remain British, would have to toe the line and accept this settlement and see it in the context of broader British policy.

Little knowledge, little sympathy: these characterised the Westminster view of the most intransigent element in the Irish question in the inter-war years – the continued existence of that 'Protestant state' for those 'Protestant people' in northeast Ulster. The Irish question, then, survived the years of reappraisal, survived the Second World War, and persists today. Circumstances did change after the war, with the creation of a welfare state in Britain and all the repercussions that this had for the citizens, majority and minority, of Northern Ireland. But, sadly, the lack of knowledge at Westminster, and the lack of sympathy, did not change. Thus, in the so very different climate of the late sixties, when the Irish question once more burst upon the British parliamentary scene, it was the ignorance and the abdication of responsibility established bv successive British governments in the inter-war years that was to make so very much more difficult the final answering of that intractable riddle.

Notes

1. W. S. Churchill, *The Aftermath* (Thornton, Butterworth, 1929) p. 283.
2. These points are discussed in D. W. Harkness, *The Restless Dominion: the Irish Free State and the British Commonwealth of Nations 1921–31* (Macmillan, 1969).
3. P.R.O., CAB.32/56, E(IR/26)3.
4. P.R.O., CAB.24/262, C.P.124(36) See also D. W. Harkness, 'Mr. de Valera's Dominion: Irish Relations with Britain and the Commonwealth, 1932–8', *Journal of Commonwealth Political Studies*, vol. viii, no. 3 (1970) for this, and notes 5–9.
5. P.R.O., CAB.27/527, 1SC(32), 108.
6. P.R.O., CAB.27/524, subcommittee meeting, 20 Jul 1936.
7. Ibid., 21 Jul 1936.
8. P.R.O., CAB.27/524, 15 Dec 1936.
9. P.R.O., CAB.27/271, C.P. 228.
10. See e.g. Geoffrey J. Hand, 'Introduction', *Report of the Irish Boundary Commission* (Irish University Press, 1969) and 'MacNeill and the Boundary Commission', F. X. Martin and F. J. Byrne (eds), *The Scholar Revolutionary: Eoin MacNeill 1867–1945, and the Making of the New Ireland* (Irish University Press, 1973).
11. *Articles of Agreement for a Treaty between Great Britain and Ireland*, Article 12.
12. P.R.O., CAB.24/176, C.P. 533, Letter Feetham to P.M., 17 Dec 1925 (See also D. W. Harkness, 'The Boundary Commission,' *Irish Times*, 23 Jan 1968).
13. P.R.O., CAB.27/530, p. 23. See also CAB.27/522, C.P. 350 (32), 'Record of Conference held October 14 and 15 1932 between representatives of the United Kingdom and the Irish Free State', p. 20.
14. P.R.O., CAB.27/522. 'Irish Situation Committee: explanatory note'. It was to deal with these matters that this cabinet committee was set up. Its first meeting was held on 7 April 1932.
15. P.R.O., CAB.27/522, C.P. 350 (32) op. cit., p. 29.
16. P.R.O., CAB.27/523, Minutes of 23rd meeting of Irish Situation Committee, 12 May 1936.
17. P.R.O., CAB.27/642, I.N.C. (38) (Cabinet preparations for Irish negotiations 17/1/38) p. 17.
18. CAB.23/93, p. 159; see also D. W. Harkness 'Economic war ends; ports returned', *Irish Times*, 2 Jan 1969.

3 The Defeat of the General Strike

GEOFFREY MCDONALD

On 4 May 1926, in response to a policy decision of the T.U.C. General Council, workers in the railways, road transport, the docks, iron and steel, printing, heavy chemicals, building, gas and electricity supply, withdrew their labour in support of the coal miners, who were already out on strike. It was a massive demonstration of solidarity. By it, the T.U.C. hoped to force Baldwin's Conservative government to alter its policy on the coal industry. The T.U.C. wanted the government to accept the union contention that, before the miners were asked to accept reasonable wage reductions, the government should guarantee that speedy and effective reorganisation of the capital side of the coal industry would be implemented. In effect, the T.U.C. were demanding equality of sacrifice in coal, and were serving notice that they would not let the miners bear the brunt of the adjustment necessary to restore the prosperity of the economically depressed British coal trade.

On 4 May T.U.C. leaders were confident of victory. The committee structure at T.U.C. headquarters was reorganised so as to control and co-ordinate the overall union effort. Union leaders talked of calling out additional workers in order to intensify the pressure upon the government to achieve a rapid victory. However, on 12 May, only nine days later, the T.U.C. ended their General Strike unconditionally, without securing terms either for the miners, or for the strikers in other industries. The government had achieved an outright victory.

This essay analyses the policies adopted, and measures taken, by the Baldwin government to deal with the General Strike of

1926. It concludes that the government's policies and actions – its supply and transport organisation, its unconditional surrender policy and Baldwin's conciliatory tone – both compelled and persuaded the T.U.C. to end their strike unconditionally so that in effect the government defeated the General Strike.

Before examining the reasons for the defeat of the General Strike it is necessary to look at the events which led up to it, in order to understand why both the government and the T.U.C. believed they were justified in resorting to the politics of confrontation. An analysis of these events shows that, ironically, the conflict of 1926 arose out of an attempt by the government and the T.U.C. to seek co-operatively a peaceful solution to the problem of the coal industry.

The dispute in the coal industry, which underlay the General Strike, had presented the government with a difficult problem in 1925. The insensitive and heavy-handed approach of the coal owners towards the miners' living standards had offended moderate public opinion. Baldwin realised that in a fight between the owners, and the miners supported by the T.U.C., the government could not afford to appear as the ally of the owners. Therefore Baldwin sought a neutral position which would be acceptable to moderate public opinion. He appointed a Royal Commission to investigate the coal mining industry and subsidised the miners' living standards for nine months. He offered to accept the Commission's report if the owners and miners did, and throughout April he acted as conciliator between the miners and owners. Finally he strove with the T.U.C. to reach a last-minute coal settlement. Although in reality, Baldwin's actions from March to May 1926 were less than expert, and perhaps were even unhelpful, they gave the appearance of being, and probably were, the work of a sincere; well-intentioned man striving to preserve industrial peace. In effect Baldwin defused the government's coal policy as a political issue.

After the publication of the Report of the Royal Commission on the Coal Industry on 11 March 1926, both the government and the T.U.C. had worked for a compromise coal settlement along the lines of the Report. Neither the government nor the T.U.C. welcomed all aspects of the Report, but both tacitly rejected the hard-line official policies of the Miners' Federation and the coal owners' Mining Association and agreed that some combination of reorganisation of the capital side of the industry and some reduction of labour costs offered the best hope of a compromise coal

settlement. However, although neither the government nor the
T.U.C. wanted a confrontation, a series of miscalculations on
both sides placed them on a collision course, from which they
proved unable to escape.

In late April 1926, when collective bargaining in coal was
clearly failing, owing to a hardening of both the owners' and the
miners' negotiating positions, the T.U.C. decided to intervene.
Baldwin was receptive and Arthur Pugh, the then T.U.C. Chairman, advised Baldwin on how to handle the miners. Pugh told
Baldwin that to gain the miners' confidence he would have to discuss reorganisation of the coal industry before proceeding to discuss wage reductions.

Baldwin, however, also received advice from Lord Weir,
Honorary President of the National Confederation of Employers'
Organisations, who insisted that there should be a return to an
eight-hour working day in the coal industry. Baldwin was
attracted by this suggestion, believing that the miners might
accept longer hours, if by doing so they might minimise their wage
reductions. Accordingly he decided to ease the deadlocked coal
talks on 30 April by injecting into them a government package
solution involving longer hours.

The miners, however, rejected this initiative absolutely. They
regarded the seven-hour day as a vital non-negotiable position.
The miners were none the less not entirely negative because they
did imply that they might consider wage reductions if these were
considered alongside speedy and comprehensive coal reorganisation. Hence Baldwin's package solution had precipitated
some relaxation in the miners' position – though not, of course, in
the direction of longer hours but rather along the lines which Pugh
had already suggested Baldwin might pursue. But time was
already running out. The coal stoppage was timed to begin after
the last shift on Friday, 30 April.

At the last minute, therefore, on 30 April, the government and
the T.U.C. met to explore the possibility of a coal settlement
based on reorganisation and wage reductions. Such a solution, it
was thought, might be found if the government and the T.U.C.
entered into direct consultations. The failure of collective bargaining in the coal industry meant that the government and the
T.U.C. had in effect to arrive at a *political* solution to the coal problem. Before the government would consent to participate in a new
round of talks, however, Baldwin indicated to Pugh that the
T.U.C. would have to obtain assurances that the miners would

accept wage reductions.

That evening, on 30 April, other trade union leaders complicated matters by deciding at a conference of their executives to
proceed with a plan for simultaneous strikes in key industries in
support of the miners. As a result of this development, the T.U.C.
hoped that the miners' leaders would transfer the handling of the
coal negotiations to the General Council. On Saturday morning, 1
May, T.U.C. leaders conferred with Herbert Smith, the Miners'
Federation President, who was deliberately vague about any ces-
sion of responsibility in the dispute. Nevertheless the T.U.C.
assumed that they had obtained Smith's consent to two things:
T.U.C. control over coal negotiations and the miners' consent to
wage reductions. Smith had, however, been careful not to commit
himself to guarantee either concession.

Later on 1 May, the T.U.C., backed up by their preparations to
call a General Strike if necessary, met the government. The
T.U.C. leaders wanted to arrange a new round of talks. Through
such talks the T.U.C. hoped to obtain definite government
guarantees on reorganisation before the miners were asked to take
reasonable wage reductions. In meeting the union leaders the
cabinet had one aim only: to see if the T.U.C. could get the miners
to accept wage reductions. On Saturday evening Baldwin, on the
cabinet's behalf, put this question to Pugh, who led the T.U.C.'s
negotiating team. Somewhat to the surprise of the cabinet representatives, the T.U.C. representatives replied that Smith had
agreed to wage reductions.

The government and T.U.C. negotiators drew up a formula
which, if the miners had endorsed it, would have committed the
miners to an acceptance of wage reductions. The T.U.C. representatives, expecting no real difficulty, undertook to show this formula to the miners' leaders and Pugh promised to inform the
government of the miners' response before noon on Sunday, 2
May.

When the T.U.C. sought the miners' view of the formula on
Sunday, they found that the miners' leaders had returned to
their districts. Cook, the miners' Secretary, and the only member
of the Federation executive who had remained in London,
angrily rejected the formula and refused to commit the miners to
wage reductions. Cook would not do more than summon members of his executive to return to London that evening. Meanwhile the T.U.C. negotiating team decided to play for time until
the miners returned, by engaging the cabinet representatives in

new talks early on Sunday evening. These talks were, of course, unproductive and, when the miners' executive arrived at Downing Street late on Sunday evening the T.U.C.'s negotiating team left Baldwin and his ministerial colleagues to present the formula arrived at on Saturday evening to the miners. While Pugh was trying to tie Smith down to a definite time period during which a settlement involving wage reductions could be found, the T.U.C. negotiating team was suddenly summoned to see Baldwin.

The cabinet had decided to terminate the talks. Ministers not involved in the negotiations with the T.U.C. had been unhappy at the formula arrived at on Saturday evening. They believed that acceptance of this formula would give the impression that the government had yielded to T.U.C. pressure. Furthermore, when the T.U.C. failed to communicate the miners' decision to the cabinet before noon on Sunday and then neglected to inform the cabinet of the reason for the delay until late on Sunday afternoon, ministers became disappointed at the lack of progress in the talks. When precautionary strike orders, which union leaders had issued on Saturday evening, were intercepted at the G.P.O. and conveyed to Baldwin on Sunday afternoon, the ministers were further disquieted. In response to this increasingly depressing situation the cabinet decided to activate the government's supply and transport organisation. The cabinet also drafted and held in reserve, pending a final breakdown in talks, a letter terminating negotiations with the T.U.C.

These divisions of opinion within the cabinet about the value of continuing the talks had appeared after the T.U.C. representatives had left the government negotiators late on Sunday evening to discuss the formula with the miners. Baldwin and the negotiating team wished to continue but other ministers did not. Then, the *Daily Mail* incident (in which the local NATSOPA chapel halted production of the paper in protest against a 'For King and Country' editorial by Thomas Marlowe, the paper's editor), which ministers took to be a result of the strike orders issued on Saturday evening, was reported to the cabinet.

Churchill among others insisted that negotiations could not continue until the T.U.C. accounted for this incident and cancelled strike orders unconditionally, and to this the cabinet agreed. The letter, held in reserve, was stiffened and Baldwin summoned the T.U.C. representatives to him to receive it.

The T.U.C. were stunned at this hardening of the cabinet's attitude. When Pugh and Walter Citrine, the acting T.U.C. General Secretary, returned to Number 10 to disclaim responsibility for the *Daily Mail* incident, the Office Keeper, who met them, apparently said Baldwin was in bed and everyone had gone home. Pugh and Citrine left, probably unaware of the attendance of four private secretaries in the building. Thus, before the T.U.C. had a chance to decide whether to follow the miners' policy or to threaten dissociation from it, the government had in effect ended the weekend talks. Attempts by Ernest Bevin on Monday, 3 May – one day before the General Strike was timed to begin – to negotiate a coal settlement foundered upon the miners' intransigence and the government's refusal to reopen talks until the General Strike orders had been cancelled. Angered by the sudden end to the weekend talks, and feeling that it was the government's attitude which had brought matters to this impasse, the T.U.C. decided to prosecute their fall-back policy of a General Strike with vigour.

Thus, in a sense, the General Strike was the accidental by-product of an unsuccessful attempt at high level co-operation between the government and the T.U.C. to avert a coal stoppage. Neither the government nor the T.U.C. had consciously planned to have a massive confrontation. Ironically, the efforts to avoid a large scale national stoppage in the mines resulted in the T.U.C. calling a series of large scale national stoppages in other trades in support of the miners. Yet once the decision to strike had been taken, the episode entered a new phase marked by a radical shift in the mind of the T.U.C. For, despite the fact that the T.U.C. had striven to preserve industrial peace, once outright industrial war had been declared the T.U.C. was determined to win the struggle and to force the government to accept its policy on coal. The government for its part was faced not only with a major industrial crisis but also with a major threat to its authority when the T.U.C.'s General Strike took effect on 4 May. Believing that the General Strike represented an attack upon constitutional government, the government was as determined as the T.U.C. to emerge the victor at the end of the battle.[1] As a result of a catalogue of mistakes and misunderstandings the politics of confrontation replaced the politics of consultation.

II

To defeat the General Strike the government needed to rely heavily upon its supply and transport organisation. This organisation had been developed within the scope of the Emergency Powers Act of 1920 which allowed the government, during a state of emergency, to take possession of materials, to control food distribution and essential services, to regulate road transport and, generally, to do all it considered necessary to defend the community. In 1923 Baldwin's first ministry had begun the initial work upon the organisation and at the start of his second ministry Baldwin had appointed his Home Secretary, Joynson-Hicks, to chair a cabinet supply and transport committee to press ahead with the scheme.

The cabinet committee had to shape a supply and transport organisation within guidelines laid down by the Treasury, which wanted the government to act essentially as a co-ordinator and not to incur financial responsibilities by resorting to compulsion and requisition except as a last resort. In the event of an emergency, the cabinet committee had decided that Joynson-Hicks would chair a headquarters organisation which would be responsible for the national oversight of ten divisional supply and transport organisations, each chaired by a Conservative junior minister. These divisional organisations would be responsible for co-ordinating local supply and transport committees within their areas. At both national and divisional level, Conservative ministers, civil servants, the armed services, local authorities, the police, representatives of business organisations and volunteers would co-operate to protect the community and to provide rudimentary services while the crisis lasted.

The cabinet supply and transport committee had also asked government departments to draw up plans, as required, for the maintenance of essential services. While coal distribution could be left under the control of local authorities and the Mines Department (which had considerable experience in this area) the distribution of foodstuffs and road transport required additional detailed planning. The Board of Trade recruited extra staff to its food department and formed a Food Advisory Council which represented the chief foodstuffs trades; it also obtained information on stocks. The Board appointed divisional and local food officers who were to chair district and local committees responsible for foodstuffs distribution. Again, detailed plans were prepared which included plans to convey yeast by destroyers to selected ports for distribution to bakeries, to convey milk to London, to maintain cold storage centres to conserve meat supplies and to hold prices in event of shortages. The Ministry of

Transport appointed divisional road officers and formed leading road hauliers into local transport committees. These local committees were to pool vehicles and concentrate their use on essential tasks such as foodstuffs distribution. The R.A.C. and A.A. supplied lists of drivers. The Home Office was made responsible for the physical protection of vehicles, while an interdepartmental group drew up a scheme to indemnify vehicle owners and drivers against damage and injury. Detailed plans to maintain petrol distribution were prepared. The Ministry of Transport also made discreet preparations to maintain metropolitan and provincial electricity supplies. The Air Ministry and the G.P.O. devised an overall communication system to keep local and divisional committees in contact with the national supply and transport headquarters in London.[2]

By late 1925, preparations for the supply and transport organisation were almost complete. The traditional view, that the government appointed a Royal Commission into the coal industry in July 1925 because its supply and transport organisation was not ready does not appear to be borne out by the evidence. On the contrary, the organisation *was* ready: all that was lacking was the will within the cabinet to use it. As Cunliffe-Lister, President of the Board of Trade, later remarked: 'It is not true, as has been suggested, that . . . our strike organisation was not ready. It probably functioned better in the spring of 1926 but it would have worked all right in the autumn or winter of 1925.' For reasons other than preparedness the government decided not to risk a confrontation in July 1925.[3]

The government, in July 1925, had, however, identified one problem in connection with its emergency plans. It would take the first two days of a crisis to make the supply and transport organisation fully operational. Committees would have to adjust to unfamiliar work and volunteers would need to be recruited and allocated. In response to the latter problems some 'concerned patriots' in the House of Lords decided to establish an Organization for the Maintenance of Supplies (O.M.S.) to compile lists of volunteers in advance, and to provide some of these potential volunteers with instruction, so as to ensure speedy and effective replacement of strikers. Throughout March and April 1926, as the date of possible conflict drew nearer, the government had continued its preparations. Finally, on the Sunday afternoon of 2 May, while negotiations with the T.U.C. were still proceeding, the cabinet authorised Joynson-Hicks to despatch telegrams activating key supply and transport organisation groups. Fortunately for the cabinet, the T.U.C. had, as has already been seen, ordered the unions to strike from Tuesday, 4 May. This allowed the government to minimise uncertainty by using Monday's postal deliveries to provide local groups with final written instructions.[4]

On 4 May, when the General Strike began, the government's supply and transport organisation came into effective operation. National and divisional headquarters took charge; local committees functioned; volunteers came forward to man the organisation. At London headquarters Joynson-Hicks, aided by Sir John Anderson, his permanent secretary, acted swiftly to deal with problems of policy as they arose. For example, they ordered local committees to ignore union rulings such as the distinction between 'allowable' domestic lighting and 'blacked' industrial power. The general smoothness of the first few days was, however, marred by friction between O.M.S. and government officials. O.M.S. leaders tried to take charge locally, to the annoyance of government officials, while the O.M.S. apparently contributed little by way of volunteers.[5]

Joynson-Hicks, and his staff in London, who received a stream of information from divisional headquarters, were able to monitor the overall situation as it developed. They could thus locate problems as they arose and theoretically devise solutions, and order and co-ordinate local responses.

And from the viewpoint of national headquarters, three important general problems presented themselves during the course of the strike. First, aggressive picket lines and sporadic rioting in some urban areas soon placed a considerable strain upon the ordinary police forces, and the 'special' or 'volunteer' constables who were assisting them. By 5 May headquarters believed the most important need was for more 'special' constables to avoid a breakdown in law and order and to protect vehicles transporting key materials. The government called upon leading City business houses and institutions, Army and Air Force reservists, Colonial and Indian civil servants on leave, and Oxford and Cambridge colleges for assistance. On 6 May, Joynson-Hicks issued a general appeal for volunteers. So great was the response that by the next day the authorities had as many 'special' constables as they felt they needed.

On 7 May, however, the problem of bolstering the ordinary forces of law and order had assumed a different form. The 'special' constables were not proving 'reliable' – they tended to create incidents through over-aggressive behaviour – while the need for supplementary police forces continued to increase. Alarmingly, in the view of military authorities, local supply and transport officials were turning, in the absence of other more suitable forces, to the army to provide armed troops in small detachments to guard key points and vehicles. There existed the danger of a 'military' incident which could have inflamed the situation. National headquarters considered that the most urgent need was for a new force, beyond the control of the police, which would be available to deal with difficult situations before resort was had to the armed forces.

On 7 May, therefore, the cabinet authorised Joynson-Hicks, Sir Laming Worthington-Evans, Secretary of State for War, and Churchill to plan a force of hand-picked men available for instant despatch to centres of trouble. The result was the Civil Constabulary Reserve: a paid, full-time, sworn-in body of trusted men, disciplined and in good health. These were, in effect, Territorial Army units, dressed in civilian clothes, and supplied with steel helmets and truncheons. On 9 May the government began to establish this new force and by 11 May 4600 reservists had been recruited in London alone. They were never used; for serious outbreaks of violence did not in fact occur. However, the creation of the reserve did not mean that the original problem of the 'incorrect' use of soldiery had been solved. Indeed the problem grew daily more serious. By 12 May, in London alone, there were seven battalions, one squadron of cavalry, and two armoured car companies in use with armed troops posted at various points. According to a War Office Report a 'military' incident was avoided more because of the population's good sense than because of the correct use of soldiers by supply and transport authorities.

Foodstuffs distribution was, of course, another important area. Existing retail and wholesale foodstuffs were sufficient to tide the community over the first couple of days of the strike. The supply and transport organisation concentrated upon replenishing local wholesale stocks, leaving the distribution to local retailers up to ordinary business channels. By 7 May, however, the narrow margin of local wholesale food supplies had been depleted in some areas, and shortages developed, especially in the South Midlands. The government decided it had to open the strike-bound and picketed London docks to release the foodstuffs within them. An Admiralty and Port of London Authority contingency plan existed, and J. T. C. Moore-Brabazon, Parliamentary Secretary at the Ministry of Transport, was appointed Special Commissioner for

London's dockland. Supply and transport officials gathered 500 volunteers, prepared billeting, and concentrated naval vessels, troops, armoured cars, and over 100 lorries nearby. On Saturday morning 8 May, a large convoy of vehicles with full military escort, designed to deter and dissuade picket intervention was sent to open the docks. Headquarters waited anxiously because they feared violence might occur.[6] Fortunately, dockland offered no resistance. Thus by Monday, 10 May, the foodstuffs position had improved.

By 12 May, the last day of the strike, the supply and transport organisation was operating with increasing confidence and efficiency. Food, petrol, coal and electricity supplies were being maintained. Law and order was being preserved. However, it is easy to over-estimate the inherent effectiveness of the organisation because, fortunately, it never had to respond to an aggressive T.U.C. challenge to its authority and control. While the T.U.C. devised a system of permits to try to control the distribution of essential supplies, they did not resort to aggression when road hauliers, with government support, ignored them.

However, whether or not the supply and transport organisation would have been overwhelmed if tested more severely, its importance lay in the opportunity it gave for 'loyalist' elements to participate in official resistance to the union movement and in the appearance it gave of coping adequately with the disruption caused by the General Strike.[7]

III

Although the cabinet had the physical security of the supply and transport organisation to allow it to withstand the shock of the General Strike, it had to obtain sufficient parliamentary and community support to allow it to persist with its demand for the unconditional surrender of the T.U.C. Baldwin's tactical moves since July 1925 had been designed, at least partly, to ensure such support in the event of a crisis.

At the same time, however, Baldwin heightened public awareness of the constitutional dangers inherent in T.U.C. sympathetic action in support of the miners. Thus the constitutionality of a General Strike became the dominant political issue in May 1926 and overshadowed and eclipsed the entire coal problem. By portraying himself as the defender of

the constitution and parliamentary democracy and as the pro-
tector of the community against misguided T.U.C. blackmail
tactics, Baldwin was fighting from a position of some strength
upon ground of his own choosing. Because the cabinet had cast
the dispute in such terms, it assumed that it would be able to
count upon widespread and unquestioning parliamentary and
public support.

But it soon became apparent that it had miscalculated. The
cabinet itself remained firm throughout in insisting upon unconditional surrender. It had to because to negotiate with the T.U.C.
before it had surrendered would have been in breach of the constitutional principles the cabinet claimed it was defending. Ministers were extremely nervous lest the government might in some
way give the appearance of victory to the T.U.C. Cave, the Lord
Chancellor, on behalf of himself and four other ministers, advised
Baldwin to get the T.U.C. to withdraw its General Strike 'absolutely' in writing, before Baldwin consented to meet the T.U.C.
Otherwise, Cave feared that the T.U.C. might claim to have
obtained conditions, thus setting a 'fatal precedent'.[8] However, on
the back benches, some Conservative M.P.s were uneasy.

The right-wing 'diehard' Conservative M.P.s led by Colonel
John Gretton, of course, saw nothing but the constitutional issue
in the affair and insisted upon unconditional surrender. However,
other Conservative M.P.s, while supporting the government on
the constitution, were also concerned about the 'industrial'
aspects of the situation. They had become rather disquieted about
the government's handling of the negotiations with the T.U.C. –
especially when in the House of Commons on 5 May J. H.
Thomas accused the cabinet of ending T.U.C. – miner talks which
were near to success. Thomas had intimated that the strike could
be called off if the government offered to resume negotiations.
Thomas's speech shook many Conservative M.P.s who believed it
had damaged the government's position.

Baldwin had to act firmly to restore party morale. He did this
by providing an 'unvarnished' account, from the government's
viewpoint, of the weekend negotiations of 1 and 2 May. Baldwin
said that these talks had been held to discover if the miners would
accept a compromise coal settlement, if negotiations were ex-
tended over another fortnight. However, said Baldwin, the
miners had not shown any willingness to compromise, nor had
the T.U.C. demonstrated any capacity to bind them. Furthermore, emphasised Baldwin, the government had not ended the

talks absolutely on Sunday, 2 May. These could have been resumed had the T.U.C. repudiated the *Daily Mail* incident and cancelled its General Strike orders. Baldwin's rebuttal undercut Thomas who was unable to restore his credibility among Conservative M.P.s.[9] This would have required raising the possibility that the T.U.C. might have left the miners to strike alone, if only the government had not ended the talks so suddenly on Sunday – an impossible admission for Thomas to make now that the T.U.C. was conducting a General Strike.

After this, Conservative M.P.s on the whole supported the government's unconditional surrender policy and there was also strong support for the government in the constituencies. Business opinion was likewise generally solid behind the cabinet. The Federation of British Industries assisted the government's supply and transport organisation by providing information on the state of coal stocks, lorries and employment. In individual industries where workmen had gone out in sympathy with the miners, employers' organisations reinforced the government's call for unconditional surrender by demanding that their men return to work or face possible retaliation. Newspaper proprietors and managements had resented the attempts at censorship, followed by strike action, on the part of their printers, and the surviving press generally supported the government. Churchill supplemented this with his *British Gazette* and, since the B.B.C. was subject to government censorship, the cabinet had the support of most of the existing means of communications.

This was fortunate for the government because, as the strike continued, an increasing number of influential 'independent' groups began to question the government's policy. While the government emphasised the constitutional issues and the T.U.C. (supported publicly by the Labour Party) asked for a resumption of talks, a 'middle' opinion grew up, which, while not necessarily pro-union, did not support the government's unconditional surrender policy. It became obvious that the government might not be able to count upon a widespread and unquestioning public, or even parliamentary support if this 'middle' opinion gained wide dissemination.

Influential Protestants tended to be critical of the government. The Presbyterian Central Assembly, meeting in Liverpool, was more critical of the government than of the T.U.C. and supported the workers' right to a decent standard of living. Fearing civil disorder, it urged Baldwin to start talks with the T.U.C.

Many Anglican leaders also wanted a negotiated peace. On 7 May the Archbishops of Canterbury and York, three Bishops and some nonconformist leaders met at Lambeth to consider means of focusing Christian opinion on evolving a solution to the strike. A three-point appeal – apparently the mildest version the Archbishop of Canterbury could obtain after several hours effort – was framed as the basis of a possible concordat. In the view of the Lambeth meeting the T.U.C. should end its strike; the government should give a subsidy; the owners should reopen their mines on pre-strike terms; and all these steps should be taken simultaneously to facilitate new talks. The basic premise of these churchmen was that securing industrial peace was of more importance than the constitutional issue. However, when the Archbishop asked Baldwin for permission to broadcast his appeal over the B.B.C. the government refused to allow him to do so.

Some business leaders were not altogether happy with the government's policy. Sir Allan Smith, Director of the Engineering and Allied Employers' National Federation, saw Baldwin on 7 May. He said that the strike was not revolutionary but could help the Communists. He advised Baldwin to contact Pugh, to discuss industrial aspects of the situation. This would, he said, help Pugh and the moderates to end the General Strike. In Birmingham the Cadbury family, and in Manchester a group of businessmen led by C. P. Scott, editor of the *Manchester Guardian*, called for negotiations. The printers' union had, however, closed the *Manchester Guardian*, despite Scott's request that the T.U.C. intercede to allow the newspaper to continue publishing an 'independent' view.[10]

Although, in effect, the support given to the government by most of the existing means of communication shielded it from the growth of 'middle' opinion within the community, it had to contend with a steadily growing stream of criticism within Parliament.

Front-bench and back-bench Labour M.P.s, of course, supported the T.U.C. in its call for the government to reopen talks. The Liberals, who represented a middle force within Parliament, gradually moved towards the Labour position. From the start, Lloyd George, apparently hoping to 'co-ordinate and consolidate all the progressive forces', had blamed the cabinet for the crisis and had called for a negotiated peace. Initially, however, Asquith, Simon, Grey and Runciman supported the cabinet's stand. But on 9 May, these Liberal leaders tabled a Commons resolution based upon the Archbishop of Canterbury's appeal, while on 11 May Simon, in a powerful speech, said the country could not allow a fight to the finish. Simon suggested that both the T.U.C. and the government should act to end the conflict.[11]

Despite such pleas the Conservative majority in the House stood firm; the government was able to ignore the calls for a negotiated peace and to persist with its demand for the unconditional surrender of the T.U.C.

IV

While the government insisted upon absolute surrender, Baldwin tried to make it as easy as possible for the T.U.C. to withdraw unconditionally. In this he was helped by leading Liberal politicians who tried, privately, to encourage the T.U.C. to devise reasonable coal settlement proposals which might satisfy the government. Contact with these mediators provided the cabinet with indirect access to T.U.C. thinking, and enabled Baldwin to compose a key speech so as to draw out the sentiment for peace which he knew existed within the General Council.

Lord Wimborne, a Liberal coal owner, tried with some success to develop a peace formula with Thomas and reported his initiative to the cabinet; but it was Samuel, the Chairman of the Royal Commission which had investigated the coal industry, who, independently of Wimborne, became the chief negotiator with the T.U.C. When Samuel first approached the cabinet it advised him that it would feel bound to consider most carefully and sympathetically any peace terms he arranged. However, ministers impressed upon Samuel that he could commit the government to nothing, because any cancellation of the T.U.C. strike orders had to be absolutely unconditional.

Samuel accepted the government's position. Accordingly, when he made contact with Thomas and the T.U.C. negotiating team, Samuel advised them that, while he could not bind the government, the latter would view with sympathy any terms he arranged. Samuel further interested the T.U.C. when he expressed unhappiness with the government's overall handling of the coal problem. He blamed the government for the current crisis and also talked of it probably having to coerce the coal owners. Samuel gained the confidence of the T.U.C. negotiators and together they proceeded to frame detailed proposals for a settlement of the coal industry dispute. Samuel kept the cabinet informed on the progress of these negotiations.[12]

From Samuel, Wimborne and others, Baldwin obtained insights into the situation within the T.U.C. General Council. Upon being informed that T.U.C. moderates (which probably meant Pugh and Thomas) would be helped by some gesture to induce their colleagues to end the strike, Baldwin prepared his 'Man of Peace' speech which was broadcast on Saturday, 8 May. Wimborne, on Baldwin's instruction, advised Thomas to take particular note of this broadcast.

In the speech Baldwin remained firm on the constitutional issue. There would be no negotiations until the T.U.C. ended the General Strike. However, on the industrial aspects of the situation, Baldwin was conciliatory. He repeated the pledge he had given in March: the government would accept the recommendations of the Royal Commission into the coal industry, if the miners and owners did. In any event, once the General Strike was ended, Baldwin promised to consult both the owners and miners, and to work for a coal settlement involving reorganisation of the capital side of the coal industry. He insisted that the government was resisting the General Strike to defend the constitution and not in order to cut the miners' living standards. Finally, Baldwin asked the unions to trust him to offer a 'square deal' to both sides in the coal dispute.[13] This broadcast received a good reception with the T.U.C.

However, in contrast to Baldwin's conciliatory tone, a cabinet committee headed by Viscount Cave had prepared a tough trades disputes and trades union bill for introduction to the House after the weekend of 8–9 May. This bill was certain to provoke considerable Labour and union opposition; it allowed the courts to freeze union funds and employers to bring actions for damages against the unions, and it placed sympathetic strike action outside the protection of the 1906 Act. In effect, this bill would have undercut Baldwin's conciliatory initiative.

Baldwin, naturally, was hesitant about proceeding with such a bill, and there were many others who shared his apprehension. Cabinet officials did not want Baldwin's conciliatory approach impaired. Leading civil servants, Warren Fisher and Otto Niemeyer at the Treasury, Brooke at Transport and Edward Gowers at Mines, feared upsetting what was essentially a peaceful situation by a bill that would be regarded as an attack upon trade unionism. Eyres-Monsell, the Conservative Chief Whip, reported that some M.P.s doubted its wisdom while the majority opposed provocation. Granet, President of the Railway Companies Association, also expressed doubts about it. While various moves were being initiated to try to prevent the bill from reaching the House, news that the T.U.C. was considering an end to the strike reached the cabinet, which then resolved to shelve the bill. Baldwin's moderate tone was preserved, but it had been a narrow victory.[14]

V

Although events might quite easily have turned out badly for the government in May 1926, in the end they did not. Although the supply and transport organisation might, in fact, have proved fragile if put to a severe test by the T.U.C., although the cabinet did not receive the widespread and unquestioning parliamentary and public support upon which it had counted, and although Baldwin's conciliatory initiative was very nearly undercut, none of this proved of comfort to the T.U.C. From the T.U.C. viewpoint the strikers were confronted by a supply and transport organisation which gave the appearance of coping adequately with the disruption, and with a firm and unwavering government demand for unconditional surrender. Together with Baldwin's conciliatory call for an end to the conflict, these government policies and actions had a progressive impact upon the T.U.C. They both compelled and induced the T.U.C. to consider ending its General Strike without obtaining definite terms from the government.

After the first forty-eight hours the T.U.C. realised that a massive demonstration of solidarity in support of the miners' cause, no matter how impressive, was itself insufficient to force the government to accept the T.U.C.'s coal policy. As union leaders were unwilling to intensify the industrial struggle by an aggressive assault upon the government's supply and transport arrangements, they had to accept the fact that the government's organisation had largely neutralised their strike policy. They had to accept that the quick victory, upon which they had counted implicitly, was not going to materialise.[15]

Given this situation the T.U.C. resolved to rely upon 'middle' opinion, which was welling up, to influence and pressure the government to reopen negotiations with the T.U.C. The T.U.C. tried to encourage town councils and church and business groups to call for a resumption of negotiations. They hoped to foster an atmosphere which would force the cabinet to contact the T.U.C., even if striking could not achieve this aim. At the same time Thomas, who had become the T.U.C.'s chief negotiator, began to make preparations for the time when the cabinet would re-establish contact with the T.U.C.

On Thursday, 6 May, when Samuel had contacted the T.U.C. offering private discussions on coal, Thomas had accepted. He believed Samuel would serve as a useful mediator in the event of new talks between the government and the T.U.C. Thomas also believed that Samuel, because of his apparent sympathy for the miners' cause and his disquiet over the government's policy, might be prepared to use his authority as ex-Chairman of the coal Royal Commission, and his influence as a leading Liberal politician, to assist the T.U.C. in presenting its case to the cabinet in any new talks.[16]

However, the events of the weekend of 8 and 9 May dealt a blow to T.U.C. hopes of forcing the cabinet to reopen talks. The T.U.C. was impressed by a number of factors. The government appeared to be tightening its control over the industrial situation. The supply and transport organisation was proving increasingly effective in food distribution and road transport. The police were arresting unionists for irregular picketing as well as for breaches of the peace, and magistrates were delivering sharp sentences. The government also appeared to be gaining in confidence. Despite the growth in 'middle' opinion, Baldwin showed in his broadcast on Saturday, 8 May, no relaxation of the demand for unconditional surrender. Instead, as has been noted, Baldwin advised the T.U.C. to end their General Strike and then to trust him to seek fair treatment for the miners. By the end of the weekend the T.U.C. realised that it was unlikely that the government would now reopen talks with them.[17] From this point onwards the T.U.C. concerned itself with the manner and timing of the General Strike's ending.

By Monday, 10 May, Thomas and the T.U.C. negotiating team had decided upon a shift in tactics. Over the weekend, Thomas had negotiated a settlement with Samuel, which gave the T.U.C. essentially what they had been pressing the cabinet for during the negotiations on the weekend of 1 and 2 May directly prior to the General Strike. The Samuel terms provided for definite government guarantees on speedy and thorough reorganisation before the miners were asked to take wage reductions (which would be decided by a National Wages Board). Thomas decided to force the miners to accept Samuel's proposals by threatening to leave them to strike alone if the Federation remained rigid. Thomas calculated that if the T.U.C. and

Miners' Federation ended the General Strike and coal strike simultaneously, on the basis of the Samuel proposals, this would have a dramatic effect upon public and parliamentary opinion. The government would in Thomas' view come under immense pressure to accept the Samuel scheme, to avoid a resumption of strike action.[18]

However, despite the efforts of Thomas, Pugh and Bevin on Monday and Tuesday, 10 and 11 May, the Miners' Federation refused to accept Samuel's settlement. Smith was angry that the T.U.C. and Samuel had framed the proposals without consulting the miners. He pointed out that there was no guarantee that the government would, in fact, accept Samuel's plan and that anyway the scheme was unacceptable because it foreshadowed wage reductions. Smith challenged the T.U.C. to end the General Strike if it so desired, as the miners were prepared to continue their strike alone.

Pugh, Thomas and other union leaders were aware that the very best they could now achieve was to force the government to reopen talks, and this was increasingly unlikely. The continued rigidity of the miners' leaders, however, had demonstrated to the T.U.C. that even if they did secure a new round of talks they would probably be embarrassed by being unable to get the miners to accept any reasonable compromise that resulted.

Pugh, Thomas and other union leaders were unwilling to continue under such conditions and resolved to begin considering an early end to the General Strike. A number of factors strengthened them in this resolve. From the beginning of the General Strike union leaders realised that their action might provoke harsh government and employer reaction, mob violence and disorder, but they were prepared to take such risks in support of the miners' cause. Now, however, as continuation of the General Strike seemed to offer little prospect of success, the T.U.C. began to examine the risks more seriously.

It has been suggested that the real reason for surrender was fear that control of the strike might pass from responsible union officials and T.U.C. headquarters into the hands of irresponsible extremists, and '. . . bring a highly hypothetical civil war into the realm of actuality'. One historian has written that it was not fear of a breakdown in solidarity but '. . . fear that the strike might get out of their hands that primarily moved the most influential members of the General Council.' However, while control was often passing to local Councils of Action, for example, in South Wales and Camden Town, T.U.C. sources indicate that this was not the major immediate reason for termination.[19]

Contrary to this argument, fear of a breakdown in solidarity had become a major concern within the General Council by Tuesday, and this fear coming on top of the realisation that continuation of the General Strike offered little prospect of success induced the T.U.C. to terminate the strike on the following day, Wednesday, 12 May.

When T.U.C. leaders discovered that a quick victory was not possible, they wondered how long rank and file solidarity could be maintained. Union leaders after all did not want the General Strike to impair the fighting strength of their own unions. They feared that if some of their rank and file returned to work it could injure morale and weaken union attempts to arrange a resumption of work without victimisation by employers.

On 10 and 11 May, therefore, union leaders were becoming worried as they received increasing reports of small returns to work among, for example, printers and railway clerks. Indeed, there appeared to be a crumbling of solidarity among some groups. By the morning of 12 May the T.U.C. Intelligence Committee believed it could detect a discernible drift back which it considered '. . . sufficient to cause serious perturbation'. The T.U.C. believed that the overall strike movement had reached its peak and that the General Strike had to be ended as a matter of urgency.[20]

Thomas helped the waverers on the General Council to vote an end to the strike by raising the possibility that there was some sort of tacit understanding between Samuel and Baldwin. Once the General Strike was over, suggested Thomas, Baldwin would feel bound to accept the Samuel proposals.[21] Bevin and other union leaders, perhaps remembering Baldwin's Man of Peace broadcast on 8 May, apparently hoped that this would be so.

However, the majority of union leaders decided to end the strike, late on Tuesday evening, 11 May, because they believed that serious breakaways were imminent. In their haste T.U.C. leaders did not attempt to secure definite guarantees for their own rank and file, let alone for the miners. Accordingly, on Wednesday, 12 May, a deputation of T.U.C. leaders called upon Baldwin in Downing Street to inform him that their strike was over.

Thus, the government's policies and actions had, in effect, defeated the General Strike. The government's supply and transport organisation largely neutralised the T.U.C.'s strike policy and destroyed their hopes of a quick victory. The government's adherence to a policy of unconditional surrender dealt a blow to the T.U.C. hopes of forcing the cabinet to resume negotiations. By the end of the weekend of 8 and 9 May the T.U.C. realised it was unlikely that they could force the government to reopen talks. From this point onwards the T.U.C. concerned itself with the manner and the timing of the General Strike's ending. They had lost confidence in victory. The miners' intransigence and the erosion of solidarity from 10 May onwards only hastened the T.U.C. upon a course of action which they had already tacitly agreed.

VI

When the T.U.C. deputation arrived at No. 10 on Wednesday, 12 May, Horace Wilson, permanent secretary at the Ministry of Labour, met them to verify that they had come to end the strike and not to bargain. When the T.U.C. representatives met the Prime Minister and some of his ministers and announced the end of the General Strike, Baldwin made no mention of Samuel's terms and remained completely non-committal. Pugh and Thomas did not discuss the problem of reinstatement of their men, nor did they raise the problem of the continuing coal stoppage. Bevin became concerned and tried to question Baldwin on these matters, but was rebuffed. Baldwin was determined to ensure that the T.U.C. surrender was completely without conditions. The meeting then terminated, leaving the T.U.C. representatives in no doubt that there had been no tacit understanding between Baldwin and Samuel over coal. The T.U.C. was confronted with the reality of their unconditional surrender: the government retained its freedom of manoeuvre over coal. The General Strike had achieved nothing.[22]

Afterwards there were recriminations on the General Council. Union branch leaders sought information on terms achieved only to find there were none. Areas such as South Wales felt a severe letdown. The T.U.C. urged unionists to refrain from controversy over the decision to end the strike, but Cook, the miners' secretary, attacked the T.U.C. and a bitter row developed. Union leaders were faced, immediately, with difficulties over securing for their members a resumption of work on old terms. Over the long term they were confronted with a prolonged industrial stoppage in coal, which reduced economic activity in coal consuming and coal carrying trades. The rest of 1926 proved to be bleak for the trade union movement as union membership declined, funds were drained, and the unions were weakened in industrial negotiations.

By contrast, for the government and for Baldwin personally May 1926 was regarded as a victory. Baldwin was congratulated by the cabinet. When he entered the House to announce the termination of the General Strike, he was hailed by Conservative M.P.s and by some Liberals. There was also an air of self-congratulation within Conservative and business circles.[23] With its large Commons majority and over half its term to run, the government was in a position of strength for any future dealing with the union movement.

Baldwin and the government did not, however, use the commanding position which they held in the aftermath of their victory to mount a concerted attack upon union standards or privileges. Instead, immediately after the General Strike Baldwin intervened to assist unions to hold to their old agreements. Throughout 1926 he tried to arrange a coal settlement that was fair to the miners, but he was defeated by the intransigence of both the miners and the owners. In the 1927 Trade Disputes and Trades Union Act the government did not attempt any radical reconstruction of the system of collective bargaining; nor did it remove from the unions the immunity from actions in tort which they enjoyed under the 1906 Act. Finally, late in 1927 Baldwin actively encouraged a reconciliation between industrialists and labour, which was attempted in the Mond–Turner Talks of 1928 and 1929.

VII

The General Strike was thus an unintended consequence of an unsuccessful attempt to avert a coal stoppage, by the government and the T.U.C. But once direct confrontation occurred both sides were determined to win the struggle. In the end, of course, it was the government which was victorious.

But the battle might quite easily have gone the other way: the supply and transport organisation might in fact have proved quite fragile if put to a severe test by the T.U.C.; the cabinet might not have continued to receive the widespread and unquestioning parliamentary and public support on which it was counting and Baldwin's conciliatory initiative could easily have been undercut. From T.U.C. viewpoint the unions were confronted by a supply and transport organisation which gave the appearance of coping adequately with the disruption caused by the General Strike, a firm and unwavering government demand for unconditional surrender and Baldwin's conciliatory call for an end to the conflict.

Together these government policies and actions made a progressive impact upon the T.U.C. and within nine days had defeated the General Strike.

Notes

The following abbreviations for paper collections are used in the notes:
CAB – Cabinet
W.O. – War Office
LAB – Ministry of Labour
F.B.I. – Federation of British Industries
T.U.C./G.S. – T.U.C. General Strike collection
B.P. – Baldwin Papers

1. For details of the negotiations before the General Strike, see: G. W. McDonald, 'Aspects of Industrial Politics 1924 to 1929' (unpublished thesis, Cambridge, 1973) pp. 164–223.

2 For details see CAB.27/260, S.T.(24) conclusions; and CAB.27/261, S.T. (24) memoranda; H. A. Taylor, *Jix, Viscount Brentford* (London, 1933) pp. 192–4; Viscount Swinton, *I Remember* (London, 1948) pp. 42–3; Robert Rhodes James, *Memoirs of a Conservative: J. C. C. Davidson's Memoirs and Papers 1910–1937* (London, 1969) p. 230.

3. For details see CAB.23/50, 42(25)1; the traditional view was held by a succession of writers: G. Glasgow, *General Strikes and Road Transport*, p. 101; W. H. Crook, *The General Strike: A Study of Labour's Tragic Weapon in Theory and Practice* (Chapel Hill, 1931) pp. 297, 308–9; Julian Symons, *The General Strike* (London, 1957) p. 20; for Cunliffe–Lister's view see Viscount Swinton in collaboration with J. Margach, *Sixty Years of Power: Some Memories of the Men Who Wielded It* (London, 1966) p. 83.

4. B.P., vol. 22, Mitchell-Thomson to Baldwin, 29 Apr. 1926, pp. 5–6; CAB.23/52, 22(26)2.

5. The O.M.S., given its minor role, has attracted unjustified historiographical attention. For a critical assessment of the O.M.S. see CAB.27/260, S.T. (24) 31st Conclusions.

6. Crook believes that the opening of the London docks was evidence of a more forceful side to government policy and, more implausibly, that the government extremists wished to provoke disorder, which they could suppress violently as a lesson to intimidate union militants (Crook op. cit. p. 419.)

7. For details of the operation of the organization during the General Strike see CAB. 27/260, S.T. (24) conclusions; CAB. 27/261, S.T. (24) memoranda; CAB. 27/331, S.T. Information bulletins; W.O. 32/3456, Memo and Notes, from Jan 1927; T.U.C./G.S. Report of Intelligence Committee; B.P. vol. 22, Lieut. Col. B. F. Strange to Baldwin, 15 Jun 1926, pp. 92–106.

8. B.P., vol. 18, Cave to Baldwin, 11 May 1926, p. 34; see also: Joynson-Hicks to Baldwin, 12 May 1926, p. 132.

9. CAB.21/296, L.O./H/19, Thomas' speech in Commons, and Draft by Wilson for P.M.'s statement in House of Commons in reply to Thomas; B.P., vol. 61, King's letter, 6 May 1926, pp. 106–9; vol. 20, Lord H. C. Bentinck to

Baldwin, 5 May 1926, pp. 43–4; Duff-Cooper (Viscount Norwich) *Old Men Forget* (London, 1953) p. 150; and Earl of Avon, *The Eden Memoirs: Facing the Dictators* (London, 1962) p. 6.

10. CAB.21/296, L.O./H/19, Memo., 7 May 1926; B.P., vol. 16, Note of a conversation between the Prime Minister and Sir Allan Smith, 7 May 1926, pp. 115–17; vol. 20, Jones to Baldwin, 7 May 1926, p. 10; vol. 23, Baldwin, letter to Conservatives, 17 May 1926, pp. 36–7; F.B.I./W.P., General Meeting, 30 Mar 1927, Muspratt, p. 1; T.U.C./G.S., Rev. J. Fraser to T.U.C., 7 May 1926; and Note, 8 May 1926; Citrine op. cit., p. 184; and A. Bullock, *The Life and Times of Ernest Bevin, vol.* I: Trade Union Leader, 1881–1940 (London, 1960) p. 324.

11. B.P., vol. 61, King's letter, 12 May 1926, pp. 130–3; Trevor Wilson, *The Downfall of the Liberal Party 1914–1935* (London, 1966) p. 329; A. J. P. Taylor (ed.), *Lloyd George: A Diary by Frances Stevenson* (London, 1971) pp. 244–6; Symons, op. cit. p. 119.

12. CAB.21/296, L.O./H/19, Note by Lord Wimborne, 10 May 1926, 10.45 a.m; and G. Blaxland, *J. H. Thomas: A Life for Unity* (London, 1964) p. 199; CAB.23/52, 27(26), Appendix, Steel-Maitland to Samuel; LAB.27/4, Samuel to Pugh, 8 May 1926; and Symons, op. cit., p. 187.

13. CAB.23/32, 27(26) 4; B.P., vol. 22, P.M.'s Message to Nation, 8 May 1926, pp. 65–6; G. Blaxland, op. cit., p. 200; R. K. Middlemas (ed.), *Thomas Jones Whitehall Diary*, vol. II: *1926–1930* (London, 1969) p. 36.

14. CAB.21/296, E. L. (26) 1st conclusions; CAB.23/52, 27(26)1 and Appendix, Draft Illegal Strikes Bill, 1926; 28(26)1; 29(26)6; Middlemas, op. cit., vol. II, pp. 43–52.

15. T.U.C./G.S. Intelligence Committee notes; Lord Citrine, *Men and Work: An Autobiography* (London, 1964) p. 182.

16. T.U.C./G.S. Intelligence Department to Speakers, 6 May 1926; Notes for Speakers drafted by Publicity Committee; Bevin to Publicity Committee, 5 May 1926.

17. Citrine, op. cit., pp. 188–91.

18. Ibid., pp. 195–200; Bullock, op. cit., vol. I, pp. 325–7; B.P., Samuel to Baldwin, 11 May 1926, p. 34; LAB.27/9, MacMullan, pp. 41–2.

19. Symons, op. cit., pp. 210–11; Crook, op. cit., p. 398; T.U.C./G.S. Intelligence Committee reports; and Report of Intelligence Committee.

20. Citrine, op. cit., pp. 195–6; T.U.C./G.S. Report of Intelligence Committee; Intelligence Committee report for 12 May 1926; LAB.27/9, MacMullan, pp. 77–8.

21. Christopher Farman, *The General Strike: May 1926* (London, 1972) pp. 225–6; Symons op. cit., p. 231; Citrine, op. cit., pp. 195–9; Bullock, op. cit., vol. I, p. 328.

22. CAB.24/179, C.P.195 (26), Termination of the General Strike.

23. CAB.23/53, 31(26)1 & 2; B.P., vol. 61, King's letter, 13 May 1926, p. 142.

4 The Renewal of Liberalism: Liberalism without Liberals

JOHN CAMPBELL

The history of the Liberal Party between the wars is in most respects a melancholy record. The party declined from strength to insignificance in twenty years: a governing party of 260 M.P.s when the armistice was signed in 1918, it had dwindled by the declaration of war in 1939 to a mere parliamentary pressure group of eighteen members. It may be that the social upheaval of 1914–18 and the extension of the suffrage to the mass electorate spelled inevitably the doom of the Gladstonian Liberal Party and the rise of Labour in its place. Nevertheless, its own internal divisions gratuitously hastened the party's fall: the Asquith–Lloyd George split kept the party divided in the crucial years 1918–24 when Labour, to its own surprise, advanced to government; while the further three-way split – Samuel–Simon–Lloyd George – in 1931 shattered it finally at the very moment when Labour's debâcle might have offered it fresh hope. The story is one of discord, bitter recrimination, and, at first sight, total failure. Yet the Liberals possessed two tremendous assets: first, the restless genius of Lloyd George, still in the 1920s, for all his faults, the dominating and most potent personality in politics; and second, the intellectual services of a group of radical economists of whom the most notable was Maynard Keynes. When, for a brief period from 1926 to 1929, the ideas of Keynes were harnessed under the leadership of Lloyd George, the party produced a policy document which in retrospect stands out as a far-sighted contribution to the reappraisal of economic philosophy in this period. The Liberal 'Yellow Book', *Britain's Industrial Future*, had already offered in 1928 a blueprint for managed capitalism, a synthesis of social-ism and *laissez-faire*, which although not implemented until 1945 then became the accepted wisdom of all parties for the next two decades. The purpose of this essay is to trace the development of this policy by the smallest and most divided of the parties between the wars.

Lloyd George and Keynes were not the only authors of the 'Yellow Book'. Far from it, though the influence of both men was crucial in the end. Advanced elements in the Liberal Party had started feeling their way towards 'new' Liberalism before 1914. Seebohm Rowntree's famous study of poverty in York (1901) demonstrated the inhumanity of unfettered free enterprise, and numerous books by the outcast economist J. A. Hobson – *The Physiology of Industry* (1889), *The Problem of the Unemployed* (1896), *The Social Problem* (1901) – argued the possibility of some mitigat-ion of the trade cycle by the state. Several rising Liberal politicians drew the moral from these writings. Herbert Samuel in *Liberalism* (1902), Leo Chiozza Money in *Riches and Poverty* (1909), and C. F. G. Masterman in *The Condition of England* (1909) all helped to move Liberal thinking towards interventionism. Twenty years later Rowntree, Samuel and Masterman were on the committee that produced the 'Yellow Book'. Lloyd George, on becoming Chancellor of the Exchequer in 1908, was quick to put himself at the head of the new movement – both symbolically with his attacks on the old order as epitomised by the House of Lords, and practically by his introduction of national insurance for ill health and unemployment. Masterman was his first lieutenant. This legislation is usually taken as marking the foundation of the 'wel-fare state'. But though they continued to look back to their pre-war achievement for inspiration, the Liberals after the war tended to leave to Labour the ambition of extending it. The war turned their thinking to other applications of the principle of inter-vention.

The new emphasis was partly dictated by finance. The pro-jected reforms of the Liberal ministers in the postwar coalition – notably Christopher Addison's Housing Act and H. A. L. Fisher's Education Act – were mutilated by the Geddes Economy Com-mittee in 1922. The cry of 'retrenchment' remained – even in 1929 – a powerful one in Liberal ears, and the depressed climate of the 1920s was not propitious for heavy calls on national expenditure. Regulation of industry was cheaper than provision for the indi-vidual and could be represented as striking at the root of poverty, not just at its branches. Perhaps more important, government control of industry during the war, unpopular though it was with all classes, had provided practical experience of the administration of intervention. The Ministry of Reconstruction, set up under Addison in 1917 to build the land fit for heroes, was an important testing ground for new ideas. A passage from Addison's diary offers an early statement of the doctrine that grew into the 'Yellow Book':

> The War has thrown all preconceived ideas as to trade organization into the melting pot, and every thinking man . . . agrees that if we are to regain and hold our position in the markets of the world there must be a new outlook on the part of both employers and employed; the old jealousies between firms must be abandoned once and for all, and what is equally important, the 'Ca'canny' methods . . . must be discontinued. The war . . . has proved that in the face of national necessity we can rise to heights of industrial organization and cohesion such as would have been deemed impossible.[1]

The Ministry of Reconstruction was generally reckoned a failure. Many key industries were returned to free enterprise, with no strings retained. But the Ministry had implanted in the minds of many of those involved in it (of whom at least two, Rowntree and Francis Acland, were later involved in the 'Yellow Book') and of a wide section of non-socialist progressive opinion the idea that some government control of industry was both desirable and compatible with Liberalism. One of its minor successes was the establishment in several industries of 'Whitley Councils' – joint committees of management and workers to negotiate wages, hours and conditions, named after the chairman of the committee that recommended them. They were far from fulfilling all the high hopes placed in them, but they were a significant step in the direction of better industrial relations. The extension and development of 'Whitleyism' to foster a sense of partnership in industry was one of the major purposes of the Liberals of 1928. Indeed, it has remained a distinctive aspiration of Liberalism ever since, though the name is largely forgotten.

These were antecedents. The process that directly resulted in the 'Yellow Book' can be dated from a meeting of Manchester Liberals at a farm in Herefordshire in the summer of 1920. Their host was Ernest Simon, a successful businessman and dedicated social reformer, then Chairman of the Manchester City Council

Housing Committee, and the following year Lord Mayor. His guests were Ramsay Muir, Professor of Modern History at Manchester University; Ted Scott, son of the editor of the *Manchester Guardian* and later editor himself; and the writer Philip Guedalla. Their purpose was to formulate for the Liberal Party a modern industrial policy on which it could meet the Labour challenge. 'The party leaders', wrote Simon, 'still lived in the old ideas of laissez-faire; their only industrial policy was free trade.'[2] Ramsay Muir presented a draft policy far more ambitious:

> The nationalization of mines and railways, with a representative government by all the factors concerned, a drastic control of trusts and cartels by regulation, taxation and, if necessary, national ownership, the taxation of land values and increments with large power of public purchase, large public provisions for housing, health and education, public guarantees for minimum wages, leisure, and unemployed pay, coupled with a taxation policy in which indirect taxation (except of luxuries) disappears, and income taxes and death duties on an advancing scale from the sources of normal revenue, with a capital levy as an emergency measure for reducing the war debt to manageable dimensions . . . . . . In all well-established businesses, a limitation should be put upon the amount of profits distributed to shareholders, the excess profits being divided between the State, the workers in the concern, and the shareholders in proportions prescribed by law.[3]

This seminal document, published as *Liberalism and Industry,*[4] was not, however, the most important outcome of the Herefordshire meeting. In order to provide for the continuous discussion and development of their proposals, Muir and Simon determined to establish an annual Liberal Summer School. The first met at Grasmere in 1921: ninety-five enthusiasts – mainly 'North of England business men'[5] who found the new doctrine at that time too much to swallow – were addressed, not only by the founders, but by the economists Walter Layton, J. A. Hobson and William Beveridge. The second, at Oxford, drew 600 Liberals; the third, at Cambridge, over a thousand; thereafter they alternated between the university towns till 1939. In 1926 it was the Summer School which set up the Inquiry which produced the 'Yellow Book'.

It was through the Summer School that the intellectuals were recruited to the aid of the Liberal Party. Its attraction was that it was not overtly political. The 1922 School

> was not arranged by any of the official organizations of the Liberal Party, nor was any part of its expenses paid out of party funds. It was the outcome of a spontaneous discussion among a number of men and women who, believing that Liberalism is above all other political creeds dependent upon the free discussion of ideas, came to the conclusion that it was desirable to create a platform upon which such discussion could be carried on, in a manner quite different from what is usual, or indeed practicable, at ordinary official party gatherings.[6]

For one week every year the worlds of politics, business and economics were enabled to meet in an academic atmosphere where ideas could be floated and explored in the hope that they might emerge as policies, but without the pressure to draft manifestoes. For a week the politicians and political workers came back to university to be lectured by dons, professors and civil servants. The party leaders, Asquith, Grey, and after 1923 Lloyd George, came to deliver opening and closing speeches. In between, the superiority of Liberalism – the belief that free discussion almost by definition led to Liberalism – was taken for granted, never stressed. The school stood aloof from personalities: 'The thing I care about', wrote Muir in 1923,

> is to set on foot an active process of criticism and discussion – an intellectual activity independent of formal associations. We have already managed to bring together a rather striking collection of men, who confer at intervals; a sort of revival of Benthamite methods, though not of Benthamite ideas. I believe we have thought too much about leaders and organization, and enquired too little: this has been the malady of the Liberal party for a long time – I put it down to the tremendous personal ascendancy of Gladstone, which was mischievous in the long run.[7]

Muir was the 'guru' of the Summer School. Although he gave up his chair in 1921 to devote himself to the Liberal Party, sat briefly in the Parliament of 1924, and in 1931 became Chairman of the National Federation, he always remained more of a publicist and teacher than a politician or expert. His eccentricities evoked enormous personal affection, and he, more than anyone else, inspired the school with his idealism, solemn eloquence and faith in the possibility of rational progress, speaking sometimes on industrial reform but more often on such general topics as 'The Liberal Ideal'.[8] By contrast, most of the other regulars who made up the core of the Summer School were specialists: Layton (who joined Muir and Simon as a director) was editor of *The Economist*; Keynes and Hubert Henderson were also economists with civil service experience, and Simon was a recognised authority on housing. Guest speakers were equally distinguished: Sir Josiah Stamp, taxation expert and British representative on the Dawes Commission on German reparations; Professor (of Political Economy at Manchester) Henry Clay; Professor (of Sociology at London) L. T. Hobhouse; Seebohm Rowntree; A. D. MacNair, Secretary to the Sankey Commission on the Coal Industry; the banker R. H. Brand. There was one important absentee, however: Beveridge. Although he had attended the first gathering at Grasmere in 1921, he felt that his position as Director of the London School of Economics precluded political activity even of so mild a kind as speaking at the Liberal Summer School. He maintained his connection with it: he published *Insurance For All And Everything* under its auspices in 1924[9] and in 1926 even appears to have served on the committee. Nevertheless, he had little sympathy with the policies the school was developing, and in so far as he counted himself a Liberal at all between the wars, his allegiance was primarily to the old principle of free trade.[10]

In this he differed diametrically from his co-architect of the postwar welfare state, Keynes. Keynes abandoned free trade in 1930, but his Liberalism had never been based on that shibboleth anyway. A talk to the Summer School in 1925 entitled, 'Am I A Liberal?' gives the clearest indication that what kept him Liberal was the Summer School itself. He was not alone. This was the central importance of the school. With the rise of the Labour Party, threatening socialism, politics was polarising class against class. Some middle-class intellectuals – the Webbs, R. H. Tawney, G. D. H. Cole – did join Labour: so did some distinctly upper-class politicians – Arthur Ponsonby, Charles Trevelyan, Oswald Mosley – though these tended to be motivated in the twenties more by internationalist desire for peace than by conversion to socialism. For most liberal intellectuals, however, Labour was essentially a class party, the party of the trade unions; and as Keynes most bluntly put it, 'I can be influenced by what seems to me Justice and good sense; but the *Class* war will find me on the side of the educated bourgeoisie.' Despising the stupidity of the Conservatives ('They offer me neither food

nor drink – neither intellectual nor spiritual consolation'),
Keynes found himself a Liberal on the negative ground that they
alone offered a chance to the clear-sighted middle-class reformer.
'I do not believe that the intellectual elements in the Labour Party
will ever exercise adequate control; too much will always be decided by those who do not know *at all* what they are talking
about.'[11] The spirit of the Summer School – Muir's Benthamism –
kept Keynes' services at the disposal of the party. For the Industrial Inquiry in 1926 the school could call upon not only Keynes
but also Layton, Henderson, Rowntree, Hobhouse, Stamp and
more. The liberal intelligentsia was still predominantly Liberal;
the Summer School was both a contributing cause and a reflection
of that fact. Ernest Simon was another – strongly influenced by
the Webbs – who might have joined Labour at any time from
1918, but actually remained a Liberal till 1945. 'What a party!',
he lamented after a dispiriting ten months in the Parliament of
1923–4. 'No leaders, no organization, no policy! Only a summer
school! But it is still worth an effort.'[12]

A distinction must be drawn, however, between the original
founders of the Summer School and the economists who were its
brightest stars. Manchester called in Cambridge to help redress
the balance of society; but Keynes, Layton and Henderson had
different aims and different methods from Muir and Simon; and it
was Cambridge which eventually gave to the 'Yellow Book' both
its intellectual coherence and its most practical proposals. The
Manchester approach was essentially political. The programme
of *Liberalism and Industry*, as of Masterman's *The New Liberalism*, published the same year,[13] consisted of fiscal and institutional
reforms which could be carried in the traditional way through
Parliament by legislation – redistributive taxation on the one
hand, nationalisation and a framework of industrial relations on
the other. The clear purpose was to outbid the Labour Party.
Keynes and Henderson, by contrast, though they engaged readily
in political polemics, were first and foremost theoretical economists. Keynes had some private interest in social reform, particularly in what he called 'Sex Questions' – birth control, divorce,
sexual law, the position of women;[14] but his professional commitment was to understanding the economic forces of the modern
world, and to spreading that understanding. 'We have to invent',
he told the Summer School of 1925, 'new wisdom for a new age.'
Nineteenth-century economic theory – 'the assumption that economic adjustments can and ought to be brought about by the free

play of the forces of supply and demand' – had been rendered obsolete by the restrictive activities of governments, trade unions and big corporations. 'We have changed, by insensible degrees, our philosophy of economic life, our notions of what ìs reasonable and what is tolerable; and we have done this without changing our technique or our copybook maxims.'[15] His task was to rewrite the copybook, to coach the politicians in new techniques. Keynes had no interest in superficial tinkering with industrial relations; it was not from the partnership of Capital and Labour, but only from the enlightened use of Capital that he hoped to see efficiency, prosperity, and social justice flow. When he wrote of 'the end of *laissez-faire*' he meant, not the nationalisation of the railways (than which, he said in 1926, there was no 'so-called important political question' more irrelevant) but the assumption by the state of responsibility for the balance of the economy. He too looked to Bentham, and adopted his 'forgotten but useful nomenclature' to 'distinguish afresh the Agenda of Government from the Non-Agenda . . . The important thing for Government is not to do things which individuals are doing already. . . but to do things which at present are not done at all.'[16] Keynes saw the high level of unemployment since the war – still over a million in 1923 and showing no sign of dropping – not simply as a regrettable social problem which would ultimately pass with the upswing of the trade cycle, but as evidence of the inability of the Invisible Hand in modern conditions to keep the economy in balance; not as inevitable, but as an 'absurdity . . . which should be remediable if we can think and act clearly.' By 1923 he had come to the conclusion that the fundamental economic decisions affecting the value of the currency and the flow of investment could no longer be left to the interaction of individuals' self-interest, but must become the 'Agenda of Government'. 'We must free ourselves', he told the Summer School that year, 'from the deep distrust which exists against allowing the value of the currency to be the subject of *voluntary decision*. Only by wisely regulating the creation of currency and credit along new lines can we protect society.'[17] Here Keynes, as an economist, was striking much closer to the root of Britain's real problem than were the industrial reformers Muir and Simon. Yet the next stage of his attack on unemployment derived from a surprising quarter, from a rejected politician – Lloyd George.

Lloyd George fell from power in October 1922, when the Conservative Party tired of coalition under his leadership. For a year he drifted in a political limbo, trying to create a new centre co-alition and posing unconvincingly as the moderate middleman between Reaction and Revolution. In November 1923 Baldwin's plunge into protectionism forced the Asquithians to accept Lloyd George back into a united Liberal Party, and he began to recover both his energy and his natural radicalism. He began to look about for a distinctively Liberal, progressive social policy. It was his former secretary, Philip Kerr, the future Marquis of Lothian, who called his attention to the industrial problem. Kerr was an idealist – 'an ultra-refined aristocratic dreamer with senti-mentally revolutionary views', was Beatrice Webb's cutting de-scription;[18] Frances Stevenson thought him personally 'the most Christ-like man' she had ever known.[19] Like Muir he identified as the central problem of politics the conflict of capital and labour. In the spring of 1924 he showered Lloyd George with letters urging him to tackle it as only he could. With universal suffrage, Kerr argued, Liberalism had achieved political democracy; its next task must be industrial democracy. Industrial power was the modern equivalent of monarchical power in the seventeenth cen-tury. 'Labour today will no more give its labour zealously to Capi-tal than Pym and Hampden would give taxes to Charles I.' The Labour Party offered one alternative; Lloyd George must contrive another, a new Glorious Revolution to forestall the Socialist Revolution. He must talk to the socialists and understand their arguments, Kerr boldly told his master, in order to transcend them. 'You won't get the answer out of your inner consciousness, for you have never really thought about the socialist prob-lem . . . . . I don't care what conclusion you come to as long as you probe the question to the bottom.'[20] Challenged by Lloyd George to give his own ideas, he produced a plan for the self-government of industry by a permanent council of the F.B.I. and the T.U.C., representing management and workers, with a hierarchy of simi-lar bodies at all levels. He eventually hoped to see labour so involved in industry that it hired capital, rather than vice-versa. The flaw of socialism was that politicians were unfitted to run in-dustry; the economic sphere, Kerr proposed, should be as inde-pendent of the political as was the legal.[21] He despaired of Lloyd George's failure to grasp the nettle:

> Why on earth do you never come near the problem? The whole country is waiting for a lead on the subject. It's the key and only key to your future career. It's the most important problem of

our time. But you go on repeating the old shibboleths of a dead past. You really are doing what Wully Robertson and the Western Fronters did in the war. You will not ask yourself whether the war can be won on any other lines than that of 'killing Germans'.[22]

This thrust stirred Lloyd George to action, though not quite in the direction Kerr intended. Kerr's contribution to the policy, or at least the philosophy, of the 'Yellow Book' was important; but he belonged in spirit with the Manchester school of industrial reformers. Lloyd George, like Keynes, thought that the real problem of industry was unemployment. *There* was the key to his future career. The difference between them in 1923 was that, whereas Keynes wanted to attack the imbalance that created unemployment, Lloyd George wanted to attack the thing itself. High unemployment had originated during his premiership, but he had then been too preoccupied with Ireland and the settlement of Europe to give it much attention (though the Trade Facilities Act passed by his government was in fact almost the only measure taken in the whole decade directly to stimulate employment). He had already, however, the germ in his mind of a more drastic solution. 'When trade is slack', he remarked to Bonar Law and Lord Riddell in October 1921, 'you paint your factory and get it ready for new business. That is what we ought to be doing.'[23] After losing office he remained pessimistic of the prospects of an early trade revival, confidently forecast on every side, predicting in July 1923 'depression such as we have not seen in our lifetime'.[24] He was accused of fostering a sense of crisis for his own ends. He must have read Keynes's almost weekly articles on currency control in the *Nation* – the Liberal weekly which Keynes and the Summer School group had acquired as their mouthpiece in 1923 – for it was to the *Nation* on 12 April 1924, a month after Kerr's impassioned urgings that he take up the industrial problem, that he wrote a highly important letter on unemployment. He reviewed the deep-seated reasons for Britain's loss of trade since the war, repeated his lonely prediction that recovery would be slow, and urged that immediate action should be taken on 'the problems of the meanwhile', reviving his old metaphor:

A far-seeing manufacturer utilizes periods of slackness to repair his machinery, to re-equip his workshop, and generally to put his factory in order; so that when prosperity comes he will be in as good a position as his keenest competitor to take advantage of the boom. I suggest that the nation ought to follow that wise example, and that this is the time to do so. Let us overhaul our national equipment in all directions – men and material – so as to be ready, when the moment arrives, to meet any rival on equal or better terms in the markets of the world. No man who has examined the use now being made of our national resources can believe that we are making the best of them. In power – in our transport arrangements – in the use we make of our soil and of the minerals underneath it – in the organization of our industries – in the use of our capital – in the possibilities of development at home or in the Empire across the seas, and, above all, in the use we make of our fine manhood, we are not taking full advantage of the assets at our command. Capital and labour are alike strangled by vested prejudices and traditions. Both are capable of producing infinitely more wealth for the benefit of the community than they are now creating. It is of no avail to spend time on distribution if production lags behind the common need. The best means of achieving production seems to be the most urgent task of our industrial and political leaders at this hour.[25]

Public works, in the spirit of outdoor relief, had always been the standard official 'cure' for unemployment. No one until Lloyd George, however, had envisaged them on such a scale that the work itself would actually bring prosperity to the country. Lloyd George's trumpet call provoked several weeks of debate in the columns of the *Nation*. Beveridge[26] and others wrote in support; Layton thought Lloyd George too pessimistic.[27] Finally Keynes summed up in favour of the drastic remedy, calling for a large extension of the Trade Facilities Act to redirect investment, private and public, into home development: road-building, electrification, and, he suggested, prefabricated housing. 'That part of our recent unemployment', he concluded,

> which is not attributable to an ill-controlled credit cycle, has been largely due to the slump in our constructional industries. By conducting the national wealth into capital developments at home, we may restore the balance of our economy. Let us experiment with boldness on such lines – even though some of the schemes may turn out to be failures, which is very likely.[28]

The stage now seemed to be set for fruitful co-operation between Keynes and Lloyd George. Keynes went on to pursue the argument for directing savings into domestic, rather than foreign, investment and somewhat shocked the free-trade faithful at the Summer School in August by questioning the system of concessions whereby loans could be raised in Britain for New South Wales or Rhodesia more cheaply than for the Port of London.[29] Meanwhile Lloyd George was urging the House of Commons to ask itself whether Britain could still afford to maintain the free money market, declaring himself 'very much struck by a very able article by Mr. Keynes'.[30] However, for two years the alliance was not joined. *The Economic Consequences of the Peace* had made Keynes famous as a critic of Lloyd George; he was also a personal friend of Asquith. Liberal reunion in 1923 had done nothing to lessen the distaste with which the Asquithians regarded Lloyd George; his manoeuvring over party finance in 1924 increased their distrust. The Summer School tried to steer clear of the power struggle between the leaders, but it had been founded at the period when Liberal abomination of Lloyd George's government was at its height – as if to underline the fact, Sir Frederick Maurice was among its earliest 'expert' speakers – and the prejudice lingered on. Only gradually, and perhaps reluctantly, did Muir and Simon come to realise that while Asquith and his principal colleagues remained perfectly content to reiterate their traditional vague principles, Lloyd George was actively seeking a modern and practical programme for the Liberal Party, and might be of use to them. Masterman was the first to be converted back to appreciation of his old chief. In 1923 he was described as 'the most extreme opponent of Lloyd George and of any sort of reunion that would bring him back into the party'.[31] In 1924 he confessed to his wife, 'When Lloyd George came back to the party, ideas came back to the party.'[32] But Lloyd George still felt that the *Nation* was hostile to him; in so far as the political notes were written until 1925 by A. G. Gardiner, he was undoubtedly right. Late in 1925, however, Henderson (whom Keynes had made editor after a disagreement with Muir) wrote to him denying any bias:

> I may say that I am personally disposed to 'take off my hat' to the man who within so brief a period of opposition has shown that progressive social policy can mean something definite and practical and challenging – not merely the incoherent welter of phrases or absurdities which had seemed the substance of Liberal or Socialist propaganda in recent times.[33]

Nevertheless, it was one of Lloyd George's policies which served to keep him divided from Keynes until 1926. For in 1924, after his letter advocating public works and after producing an unexceptionable report on the coal mines which anticipated the Samuel Commission by two years in proposing the nationalisation of the mineral royalties and the enforced reorganisation of industry by the government,[34] he suddenly abandoned the problems of industry and took up instead the revival of agriculture – 'the use we make of our soil'. Since the near-success of the German U-Boat campaign in 1917 he had felt that Britain was dangerously dependent on imported food; and he believed deeply in the superiority of rural to town life, and in the iniquity and inefficiency of private landlords. He was now seized by the vision of combining the cure of unemployment with the restoration of the countryside, and devoted the whole of 1925 to a great campaign to settle the unemployed on the land as small farmers under the landlordship of the state. 'The best exchange for the workless', he told a mass rally in Devonshire, 'is an exchange of the green doors of the Labour bureau for the green fields of Britain.'[35] National salvation lay in the soil. The plan[36] split the Liberal Party. It was eventually adopted in diluted form as official policy in 1926, but was thereafter quietly dropped from prominence. It also split the Summer School. The Manchester politicians supported it – Muir was on the committee which formulated it; the Cambridge economists, on the other hand, though they did not oppose it, were not impressed. Keynes saw no future for Britain in rural revivalism. In February 1926, Lloyd George wrote furiously to Simon (who in fact had no editorial responsibility) complaining of 'a sustained personal attack' upon him in the *Nation*. 'Is it too late', he demanded, 'to save it from the hands of the naggers?'[37]

Three months later came the General Strike. Lloyd George took an independent line: he refused to condemn the strike out of hand, blamed the government for provoking it, and urged conciliation. For this he was blackballed by the Liberal leaders. Asquith tried to dismiss him from the shadow cabinet. The *Nation*, to its own surprise, found itself backing Lloyd George. 'Who would have believed that in a controversy between these two statesmen, Mr. Lloyd George would be triumphantly and unmistakeably in the right? Yet so it is.'[38] This was a painful moment for Keynes. It cost him Asquith's friendship, and they never met again; but it signalled his reconciliation with Lloyd George. That summer Lloyd George, perhaps as a result of the strike, partly in recognition that the land campaign had failed to take fire, turned his attention back to the industrial problem. He had set up his coal and land enquiries quite independently, as a private member trying to gain the ear of his party; now that he was Liberal leader, however – Asquith retired under cover of illness in October – and had finally won the editor and proprietors of the *Nation* to his side, he felt confident enough to entrust the industrial enquiry to the auspices of the Summer School. From the fabled wealth of his personal political fund – derived originally (though since swelled by profitable investment) from the singular circumstance of having been Prime Minister at a moment when an unusual number of peers were created in recognition of wartime services, with no conventional party chest in which to amass the customary payments – he gave Simon and Muir £10,000 'to finance a thorough enquiry', with no conditions.[39] 'He had solemnly undertaken that he would use no veto, nor interfere in any way with the findings of the committee, so that the Summer School could feel that its independence was not jeopardised; but he asked to be allowed to take part in its deliberations.'[40] So the Liberal Industrial Inquiry was set up. But the directors of the Summer School may have retained some doubts about association with Lloyd George. 'The spelling of Enquiry', the secretary of the committee noted, 'was amended to Inquiry when it was pointed out that the abbreviation to LIE would provoke rude scoffing[41] – an ironic reflection, surely, on Lloyd George's reputation for veracity.

The chairman of the Inquiry was Walter Layton, the vice-chairman Ernest Simon. Five principal subcommittees were chaired by Keynes (Industrial and Financial Organization), Muir (the Functions of the State in Relation to Industry), Simon (Labour and the Trade Unions), E. H. Gilpin (Worker Remuneration and Status), and Lloyd George (Unemployment). The Executive Committee was composed of these six plus Henderson, Masterman (until his early death), Rowntree, Kerr, H. L. Nathan, Sir Herbert Samuel and, rather half-heartedly, Sir John Simon. Other notable participants in the subcommittees included, under the category of 'experts', Sir Josiah Stamp, D. H. Robertson, L. T. Hobhouse, R. H. Brand and A. D. MacNair; Philip Guedalla and Stuart Hodgson, editor of the *Daily News*, might be classed as publicists; while the political contingent included two of Lloyd George's former ministers, Charles McCurdy and T. J. Macnamara, and several figures of the future – Ernest Brown, Sir Archibald Sinclair, W. A. Jowitt, and Mrs Corbett Ashby.[42] The others, unknown to *Who's Who*, are said in the preface to the report to have included both businessmen and trade unionists. The work of research, discussion and drafting took up the whole of 1927. There appear to have been no serious disagreements: the only resignation was Sinclair's. No recriminations have been recorded. Lloyd George kept his bargain; he did not dominate the committee, but often entertained its members for working weekends at his estate at Churt, where he delighted in feeding them entirely on home-grown produce and refreshing them with cider, buttermilk and mead.[43] 'This weekend I have fourteen professors at Churt,' he told his wife in September 1926.[44] 'He was a perfect host,' wrote Simon. 'He gave us the benefit of his vast experience; he never made the least attempt to use his position to influence our report, except by contributing to the discussion on an equality with all other members.'[45]

The report, *Britain's Industrial Future*, known from the colour of its cover as the 'Yellow Book' (Lloyd George's previous reports had been 'brown' and 'green'), was published on 2 February 1928.[46] It ran to 500 pages, divided into five sections, of analysis and detailed recommendations. It was, as the *Nation* warned, 'too full of matter to be easy to summarize'.[47] Nevertheless, a summary of precisely what it said is essential.

The short introduction first stated the Liberal belief that the opposition of individualism and socialism was, in modern conditions – where large areas of national enterprise were already in public hands, and so-called private firms were increasingly large and impersonal – unreal, anachronistic and damaging: the purpose of the book was to define more clearly what, in the interests of efficiency and social welfare should be the proper role of government in a still basically capitalist economy.

Book One comprised an analysis of the existing condition of British industry. It blamed unemployment primarily on the loss of export markets since the war, warned that the old exporting industries – coal, cotton, iron and steel – might never recover, and concluded that 'industrial revival may require a migration of labour from the threatened industries and the diversion to home development of capital normally devoted to foreign investment.'[48]

Book Two – 'The Organization of Business' – which was Keynes's particular contribution, contained the means of implementing the last point. 'The stream of national investment which is at present chaotically controlled by a multiplicity of public authorities and private interests, should be canalized by a Board of National Investment,'[49] with wide powers to issue bonds for domestic development and to approve overseas loans. There were also in this section proposals for the external control and internal reform both of public enterprises, such as the Metropolitan Water Board, and of private firms. The latter would be obliged to publish full and accurate balance sheets to assist informed investment; directors would be made answerable to and dependent on a Supervisory Council of shareholders and employees. ('Directorships are . . . the "pocket boroughs" of the present day.')[50] Large companies tending to monopoly power would be subject to more stringent public scrutiny, by special registration as public corporations. Finally, the government should be advised on its enlarged economic responsibilities by an Economic General Staff (an idea first advanced by Beveridge in the *Nation* in 1923);[51] there should be a standing cabinet committee on economic policy, and a continuous census of production co-ordinating and publishing all essential economic information; and there should be developed machinery by which the government, industrialists and trade unionists could together keep under review the entire state of industry.

Book Three dealt with industrial relations and it proposed the sort of framework of co-operation at all levels which Muir, in particular, had long been advocating,[52] culminating in a representative Council of Industry working closely with a separate Ministry of Industry. (It did not follow Kerr's vision of industrial autonomy.) Compulsory arbitration was specifically not recommended. A minimum wage, with family allowances where possible, should be established in each industry; normal wages would then be negotiable; and these would be variably supplemented by a fixed percentage of the company's profit. More ambitious profit sharing schemes were proposed as the means of encouraging 'the popular ownership of industry' (as distinct from nationalisation). Employees would become shareholders in their own firms. (Several successful schemes from Britain itself, America and New Zealand were cited as examples.) Progressive taxation and the spread of the habit of banking and investment down the social scale would help to produce 'a real advance towards that goal of Liberalism in which everybody will be a capitalist, and everybody a worker, as everybody is a citizen'.[53]

Book Four – 'National Development' – was inspired by Lloyd George. It incorporated both his earlier reports, calling for the revival of agriculture by the establishment of security of tenure and other measures recommended in the 'Green Book', and for the reorganisation of the coal industry, with nationalisation of mineral royalties as recommended in 1924. It also dealt with the expansion of education. But its principal proposal was to absorb unemployment and re-equip the country for future prosperity by a great programme of public works – road building, housing, slum clearance, electrification, afforestation, drainage, and the improvement of docks, harbours, and canals – financed from idle savings by the Board of National Investment and by Site Value Taxation, and directed by an interdepartmental Committee of National Development, responsible to the Prime Minister. This was the most striking section of the whole report, and the most controversial, affirming Lloyd George's passionate belief in the power of political will in language that is surely his own:

> We cannot acquit the timid, unimaginative, unenterprising policy of the present government of a major responsibility for damming up in the stagnant pool of unemployment so much of the available forces of willing labour, which might be employed – if only the stimulus, the encouragement, the central direction, were there to give it the lead – to make the soil more fruitful, the roads more serviceable, the housing more sufficient, and the environment of life ampler and more decent.[54]

Book Five – 'National Finance' – again owed much to Keynes. It stressed the monetary causes of unemployment and urged that, within the limits imposed by the return to gold, 'the control of our credit system . . . should be exercised more deliberately and systematically than hitherto, with a view to the maintenance of steady trade conditions.'[55] For this purpose the Bank of England should be brought under much closer public regulation. It also urged reform of the obsolete system of national accounting to enable Parliament genuinely to control expenditure; recommended some economy on armaments but no cuts in social spending, which it insisted was an essential method of redistributing wealth; and finally proposed reform of the rating system to relieve industry by transferring much of the burden to the national Exchequer, and as much as possible of the remainder to the taxation of site values.

This then was the Liberal 'Yellow Book'. It was unquestionably the unanimous product of the whole Executive Committee; it was 'put into final shape' by Layton and Henderson.[56] Yet it divides clearly into three sections, reflecting the three main sources of its inspiration, and the three distinct personalities and purposes of

Muir, Lloyd George and Keynes. Of these Keynes must be judged the most decisive influence. The initial desire for more state intervention in industry had come from Muir and the original Summer School group; this was tempered by Keynes, who emphasised regulation, publicity and credit control as the most effective forms of intervention at the expense of outright nationalisation. No immediate extension of public ownership is recommended by the report, except the acquisition of the coal royalties. The drive to make a frontal assault on unemployment came from Lloyd George; but here too it was Keynes who supplied the means, the National Investment Board. The section in which Keynes's hand is least visible is that on industrial relations, though even here he may have helped to ensure that the proposals followed the relatively practical ideas of Muir rather than the utopian fantasies of Kerr. The most serious difference among the committee members was between Keynes and Kerr. 'I don't exactly disagree with your line of approach', Keynes wrote,

> My real difficulty lies in the impracticability, or uselessness, of inscribing pious ideals on a political banner of a kind which could not possibly be embodied in legislation. No doubt things would be much better if various classes of individuals suffered a change of mind and heart and became more sensible; and it is important for everyone to beseech them to be as sensible as possible. But a political programme, I think, must go rather beyond this.[57]

When it was published Kerr conceded, despite the absence of his own ideas, that the 'Yellow Book' was 'extremely good'. But he put his finger on its weakness. 'It is so good', he wrote to Lloyd George, 'that it is a poor electioneering document. It lacks the impact, from a political point of view, of a simple rallying-cry like Protection or Nationalization.'[58] This was borne out by the press reception: no two papers could agree on what the report said. Given that it must somehow be discredited, the Tory papers could not decide, as the *Nation* wrily pointed out, whether 'to denounce it as outrageous, or to pooh-pooh it as platitudinous'.[59] *The Times* pooh-poohed it, in an editorial entitled 'Common Ground': 'The Report is useful as an incorporation of recent facts and current ideas in a compendious form.' The *Evening Standard*, too, considered it 'sedative rather than exciting . . . Too much of it is in the nature of pious aspirations.' One of the *Standard's* columnists, however, dubbed it 'a pompous and ridiculous manifesto, whose impudence is only exceeded by its impossibility'. The *Daily Telegraph* merely thought it too complicated, but the *Daily Dispatch* held that it was the purest communism; while the *Yorkshire Post* declared: 'The Socialist will read the Report with glee; the true Liberal will grieve for the mutilation of his faith.' The *Glasgow Herald* took the opposite view, seeing no distinction on this evidence between Liberalism and modern Conservatism, with which opinion the Labour papers naturally agreed, deeming the book an individualist's charter.[60] The novelty of the 'Yellow Book' approach was simply not understood – unless the unanimous Tory and Labour jeers may be taken to mean that the threat to their entrenched ideologies had been understood only too well.

The 'Yellow Book' as it stood was an immensely valuable statement of a new Liberal philosophy; but it was clearly not an election manifesto. For the 1929 general election, the Liberals determined to concentrate on one single issue – 'the word written today on the hearts of the British people and graven on their minds'[61] – unemployment. Lloyd George's national development programme was lifted from the 'Yellow Book' and re-presented in more popular form as the 'Orange Book', under the challenging title, *We Can Conquer Unemployment*. The plans for road building, housing and electrification were broken down, detailed and costed; extension of the telephone system was added; in all 600,000 men were to be put to work for two years at a cost of £250 millions, to be raised by a special loan which the work itself would repay in a few years. At a Liberal candidates' luncheon on 1 March 1929, Lloyd George gave a solemn pledge:

> If the nation entrusts the Liberal Party at the next General Election with the responsibilities of government, we are ready with schemes of work which we can put immediately into operation: work of a kind which is not merely useful in itself but essential to the well-being of the nation.
>
> The work put in hand will reduce the terrible figures of the workless in the course of a single year to normal proportions, and will, when completed, enrich the nation and equip it for successfully competing with all its rivals in the business of the world. These plans will not add one penny to the national or local taxation.[62]

The pledge was greeted with derision by the Tory press: as 'A programme of imposture' by the *Daily Telegraph*, as 'Make-Believe' by the *Scotsman*, as 'Specious' by the *Glasgow Herald*. 'The money', jeered *The Times*, 'will doubtless be found at the end of the rainbow.'[63] Lloyd George's past promises were thrown back at him, by Leo Amery among others: 'Where is your ninepence for fourpence now? How modest a slogan it seems when you compare it with this hundred millions for nothing!'[64] The Labour Party, however, regarding unemployment as its special concern although utterly lacking a remedy, did not know whether to deride the Liberal scheme or claim it as its own, and finished up doing both. In one and the same speech Macdonald accused Lloyd George of 'talking through his hat' and of 'gleaning in other people's fields to palm off other people's fruits as his own'.[65] The government, too, while claiming that it was itself conquering unemployment,[66] was sufficiently worried to publish an official Treasury reply to Lloyd George, which repeated the orthodox view that investment in public works could only divert resources required elsewhere and actually increase unemployment.[67] To this Keynes made the memorable rejoinder: 'Mr. Baldwin has invented the formidable argument . . . that you must not do anything because it will mean that you will not be able to do anything else . . . There is not a single economist in the country who will come forward to support the White Paper's arguments'.[68] The government did, however, have some more telling criticisms. One, that skilled men could not be expected to work as navvies, was only partly answered by Lloyd George's demonstration that construction work would stimulate a host of other, manufacturing industries.[69] Another, that roads need surveying and careful routing and could not possibly be planned and built in two years, seems unanswerable, unless local authorities already had detailed schemes which they only wanted the money to put in hand. These objections, however, were raised solely in a spirit of obstruction. Lord Grey, on the other hand, the symbol of continuing Asquithian resistance to Lloyd George within the Liberal Party, persuaded to give his blessing to the unemployment pledge in the interest of unity, offered, though profoundly sceptical, a cautious endorsement which may stand as a sensible qualification of Lloyd George's expansive claims without destroying them:

> Even if the policy does not succeed in doing all that is hoped of it, even if the pledge turns out to be over-sanguine, even if the policy takes two or three or four years to accomplish all the results we hope for, it will not be by any means a failure; it will still remain the right policy.[70]

Lloyd George's pledge dominated the 1929 election; yet it remained a quiet campaign. The Liberals won 5 million votes, 23 per cent of the total, but only fifty-nine seats; the Tories won slightly more votes than Labour ($8\frac{1}{2}$ millions), but slightly fewer seats. Labour took office for the second time, dependent as in 1924 on the Liberals, but determined as in 1924 to ignore them. They had no policy for unemployment, but would take none from the Liberals. Unemployment rose. They rejected Mosley, the only man in the Labour Party who had read Keynes and understood him. The government collapsed in the face of crisis in 1931; Macdonald and Baldwin formed the National government which remained in office until 1940. Lloyd George, who could not otherwise have been excluded, was ill at the critical moment. The Liberal Party split three ways: the unemployment policy was lost: Lloyd George fell out with Keynes: the Summer School lost its intellectual distinction and its sense of direction: the *Nation* merged with the *New Statesman*. With the failure of its last great effort the Liberal Party went into eclipse.

Yet, as Grey reluctantly but generously admitted, the policy had been right. Not only the unemployment policy, though unemployment was reduced by similar means in Germany, in Italy, in Sweden and in the United States (it did not necessarily require a dictator, as Baldwin claimed), but the whole philosophy of the 'Yellow Book', of which it was the emergency application, has been seemingly vindicated, as it were posthumously, since the last war. Simon lived until 1960 (and joined the Labour Party), Layton until 1966; but Muir died in 1941, Lloyd George in 1945, and Keynes in 1946. In 1945 the Labour Party of Attlee, Bevin, Dalton, and a reformed Cripps ushered in a period of managed capitalism which substituted for the divisions of the interwar period that broad political consensus which was christened in the 1950s 'Butskellism': it meant some nationalisation but not much, regulation of monopolies, full employment maintained by monetary controls, close government involvement in industrial relations through a Ministry of Labour, with the government eventually brought together with industrialists and unions in a National Economic Development Council. 'Butskellism' did not add up to the perfect incarnation of the 'Yellow Book'– the profit-sharing proposals have remained, as Keynes predicted, a pious ideal – but it derived from the same philosophy and the same economies, and fulfilled, belatedly, many of its hopes.

Of course, the 'Yellow Book' was not a complete prophecy of

the postwar world. One of the central pillars of that world, the structure of social services loosely known as the 'welfare state', was never mentioned in it. Of Beveridge's 'five giants on the road of reconstruction',[71] the 'Yellow Book' was directly concerned only with Idleness, marginally with Ignorance and Squalor, indirectly with Want, and not at all with Disease. But Beveridge himself gave no hint (indeed had no idea) in the thirties of the programme he was to unfold in 1943; nor had Labour any advanced plans for a National Health Service before the war.[72]

Neither, more important, was the 'Yellow Book' by any means the only piece of enlightened forward thinking between the wars. In the decade after its appearance, as the economic crisis deepened and endured, and politics seemed to polarise more violently between left and right, numerous other groups and individuals put forward similar programmes of constructive state action short of socialism. The vogue word suddenly was 'planning'. In 1930 Sir Oswald Mosley offered his Memorandum to the Labour government and left the party when it was refused. In 1931 a group led by the banker Basil Blackett, containing several industrialists, the economist Arthur Salter and the zoologist Julian Huxley, set up P.E.P. – Political and Economic Planning – which published periodic pamphlets calling for just that. In 1935 Blackett, Salter and Huxley were involved with Harold Macmillan, Lord Allen of Hurtwood, and others in producing *The Next Five Years*, a sort of British Five-Year Plan,[73] Among the signatories of this plan – politicians of the 'soft centre' drawn from all parties, economists, and laymen ranging from Lord Rutherford to A. A. Milne – were Layton and Rowntree of the 'Yellow Book', Hobson, and Mrs Corbett Ashby. (Lloyd George was deliberately not invited to sign, for fear of his taking over; but he too organised in 1935 a rather impoverished band of 'experts', mainly Welsh, whom he named the Council of Action for Peace and Reconstruction. He revived the 1929 programme under the title, 'Organizing Prosperity',[74] talked of a 'New Deal' in imitation of Roosevelt, and actually had his proposals formally considered by the cabinet; but it was his last effort.) Finally, in 1938 Harold Macmillan published *The Middle Way*, a recipe for Tory collectivism which he, Boothby, and a number of other frustrated young Conservatives had been concocting, unheeded by their party, since 1927.[75] All these manifestations of what has been called 'middle opinion'[76] demonstrate the growing acceptability before the war – at least to a certain sort of cross-bench mind – of the sort of mixed and managed economy ideas that were to triumph after it, when the barriers of Treasury orthodoxy were overthrown by a new professionalism. But they all came after the 'Yellow Book' and owed a debt, mostly unacknowledged, to it. Above all they can all be broadly characterised by the word 'Keynesian'.

Keynes only published his *General Theory of Employment, Interest and Money* in 1936.[77] But the understanding which the *General Theory* formulated was already present behind all the financial proposals of the 'Yellow Book'. Although even he had not, in 1929, yet suggested that the government had only to put money into the economy to stimulate recovery – it did not matter economically whether any roads or houses actually got built – the concept of the 'multiplier' was clearly expounded in his pamphlet for the 1929 election, *Can Lloyd George Do It?*[78] It was failure of that appeal that drove Keynes back to Cambridge to develop the full theoretical case for the sort of action which common sense had told him – and Lloyd George – was necessary and right. The *General Theory* is now seen as a great landmark in modern economics which has only in the last few years come to seem inadequate. But it was not derived solely from the 'inner consciousness' of Maynard Keynes. It was evolved over a period of years at the Liberal Summer School, in the columns of the *Nation*, and in the Liberal Industrial Inquiry. Keynes, with Layton and Henderson, provided the economic expertise; Lloyd George, on the crucial question of unemployment, provided the political drive; Muir and Ernest Simon founded the Summer School which kept them together. It should not be forgotten that the ideas which transformed Britain after 1945, which both the major parties completely accepted for a generation, were developed at a time when neither of those parties was producing any constructive ideas at all. It is surely a paradox that the economic reappraisal which interwar Britain so desperately needed was, at least initially, provided largely by the depleted ranks of the dying Liberal Party.

Notes

1. Paul Barton Johnson, *Land Fit For Heroes: The Planning of British Reconstruction, 1916–1919* (Chicago, 1968) p. 7. Johnson's page reference to Addison's *Four and a Half Years* (London, 1934) is incorrect.

2. Sir Ernest Simon in *Ramsay Muir: An Autobiography and Some Essays*, ed. Stuart Hodgson (London, 1943) p. 181.

3. 'The New Manchesterism', *Nation*, 1 Jan 1921.

4. Ramsay Muir, *Liberalism and Industry: Towards a Better Social Order* (London, 1920).

5. *Nation*, 8 Oct 1921

6. *Essays in Liberalism* (London, 1922) p. v.

7. Muir to H. A. L. Fisher, 9 Feb 1923 (Fisher papers).

8. See particularly Miss Sydney Brown in Hodgson, op. cit. pp. 204–7.

9. *Insurance For All and Everything* (London, 1924), no. 7 in the 'New Way' series published by the Council of the Liberal Summer School.

10. For information about Beveridge I am indebted to Mrs José Harris of the London School of Economics.

11. 'Am I a Liberal?' reprinted in J. M. Keynes, *Essays in Persuasion* (London, 1931) pp. 323–4.

12. Mary Stocks, *Ernest Simon of Manchester* (Manchester, 1963) p. 69.

13. C. F. G. Masterman, *The New Liberalism* (London, 1920).

14. 'Am I a Liberal?', op. cit., pp. 331–3.

15. Ibid., pp. 336–8.

16. J. M. Keynes, 'The End of Laissez-Faire', (London, 1926) reprinted in *Essays in Persuasion*, pp. 313–7.

17. J. M. Keynes, 'Currency Policy and Unemployment', *Nation*, 11 Aug 1923.

18. Beatrice Webb diary, ed. M. Cole (London, 1952) 3 Jun 1917, p. 85.

19. Frances Stevenson diary, (A. J. P. Taylor (ed.), *Lloyd George: A Diary* (London, 1971)) 7 May 1921, p. 214.

20. Kerr to Lloyd George, 4 Feb 1924 (Lloyd George papers, G/12/5/2).

21. Kerr to Lloyd George, 7 Mar 1924 (ibid., G/12/5/4). See also P. Kerr, *The Industrial Dilemma* (London, 1926), the 'New Way' series, no. 14).

22. Kerr to Lloyd George, 1 Mar 1924 (ibid., G/12/5/3).

23. *Lord Riddell's Intimate Diary of the Peace Conference and After* (London, 1933) 8 Oct 1921, p. 328.

24. Parliamentary Debates, House of Commons, Fifth Series, vol. 166, col. 1951, 16 July 1923.

25. D. Lloyd George, 'The Statesman's Task', *Nation*, 12 Apr 1924.

26. *Nation*, 19 Apr 1924.

27. *Nation*, 3 May 1924.

28. J. M. Keynes, 'Does Unemployment Need A Drastic Remedy', *Nation*, 24 May 1924.

29. J. M. Keynes, 'Foreign Investment and National Advantage', reprinted in *Nation*, 9 Aug 1924.

30. Parliamentary Debates, House of Commons, Fifth Series, vol. 174, col. 2399, 19 June 1924.

31. *The Political Diaries of C. P. Scott, 1911–1928*, ed. Trevor Wilson (London, 1970) 9 Mar 1923, p. 438.

32. Lucy Masterman, *C. F. G. Masterman* (London, 1939) p. 346.

33. H. D. Henderson to Lloyd George, 9 Nov 1925 (Lloyd George papers, G/10/2/2).

34. *Coal and Power: the Report of an Enquiry presided over by the Rt. Hon. D. Lloyd George* (London, 1924).

35. Speech at Killerton Park, Devon (Sir Francis Acland's estate), 17 Sep 1925, to an audience of 25,000 (*The Times*, 18 Sep 1925).

36. *The Land and the Nation: the Rural Report of the Liberal Land Committee* (London, 1925).

37. Lloyd George to E. D. Simon, 23 Feb 1926 (Lloyd George papers,

G/18/3/2). The last part of this letter was in fact deleted.

38. *Nation*, 29 May 1926.

39. Sir Ernest Simon in Hodgson, op. cit., p. 183.

40. Roy Harrod, *The Life of John Maynard Keynes* (London, 1951) p. 375.

41. Note by W. M. Eagar on a file of L.I.I. papers (Eagar papers).

42. Information about the membership of the L.I.I. from the Eagar papers.

43. Copies of an elaborate menu are preserved in the Samuel and Eagar papers.

44. Lloyd George to Dame Margaret Lloyd George, 22 Sep 1926, *Lloyd George: Family Letters, 1885–1936*, ed. K. O. Morgan (Cardiff & London 1973) p. 207.

45. Simon in Hodgson, op. cit., p. 183.

46. *Britain's Industrial Future: being the Report of the Liberal Industrial Inquiry* (London, 1928). It cost 2s. 6d.

47. *Nation*, 4 Feb 1928.

48. *Britain's Industrial Future*, p. 3.

49. Ibid., p. 61.

50. Ibid., p. 90.

51. *Nation*, 29 Dec 1923, 5 Jan 1924.

52. See, as well as *Liberalism and Industry*, *Politics and Progress: a Survey of the Problems of Today* (London, 1923).

53. *Britain's Industrial Future*, p. 261.

54. Ibid., p. 281.

55. Ibid., p. 414.

56. Walter Layton, *Dorothy* (London, 1961) p. 79.

57. Keynes to Kerr, 31 Aug 1927 (Lothian papers, GD.40/17 229/320).

58. Kerr to Lloyd George, 7 Feb 1928 (Lothian papers, GD.40/17 229/348).

59. 'The Reception of the Industrial Report', *Nation*, 11 Feb 1928.

60. All these judgements and excerpts are taken from the above article in *Nation*, 11 Feb 1928.

61. *We Can Conquer Unemployment: Mr. Lloyd George's Pledge*, (London, 1929) p. 5.

62. Speech to Liberal candidates' luncheon at the Connaught Rooms, London, 1 Mar 1929 (*The Times*, 2 Mar 1929).

63. *Daily Telegraph, Scotsman, Glasgow Herald and Times*, 2 Mar 1929.

64. *The Times*, 2 Mar 1929.

65. Speech at St Pancras Baths, 1 Mar 1929. (*The Times*, 2 Mar 1929).

66. Baldwin speech at Drury Lane, 18 Apr 1929 (*The Times*, 19 Apr 1929).

67. 'Memoranda on Certain Proposals Relating to Unemployment', issued in May 1929. See R. Skidelsky, *Politicians and the Slump* (London, 1967) pp. 72–4.

68. *The Times*, 29 May 1929.

69. E.g. Speech at Plymouth, 19 Apr 1929, in which Lloyd George claimed that road-building gave work to forty-seven other trades. (*The Times*, 20 Apr 1929).

70. Lord Grey, speech to the Liberal Council at the Hotel Metropole, 10 Apr 1929 (*The Times*, 11 Apr 1929).

71. The Beveridge Report, Cmnd 6404 (Session 1942–3) p. 6.

72. See Arthur Marwick, 'The Labour Party and the Welfare State in Britain, 1900–1948', *American Historical Review* (Dec 1967).

73. *The Next Five Years: An Essay in Political Agreement* (London, 1935).

74. *Organizing Prosperity: A Scheme of National Reconstruction* (London, 1935).

75. *The Middle Way*, (London 1938). *Industry and the State* (London, 1927), by this group, actually predated the *Yellow Book*, but its influence cannot be compared.

76. Marwick, 'Middle Opinion in the Thirties: Planning, Progress, and Political "Agreement"', *English Historical Review*, (Apr 1964).

77. *The General Theory of Employment, Interest and Money* (London, 1936).

78. J. M. Keynes and H. D. Henderson, *Can Lloyd George Do It?* (London, 1929), p. 25.

5 Revolt over India

GILLIAN PEELE

Today the word 'imperialism' is a familiar part of the political vocabulary only as pejorative term used to describe the relationship between economically advanced and developing nations or, more rarely, the highest stage of capitalism according to Leninist doctrine. Yet in the interwar period the word 'imperialism' and the concept of empire were at the heart of Great Britain's political culture. There was very little need to remark on the fact that Britain possessed an empire and even less need for the average citizen to demonstrate his feelings about it; it was simply accepted as a part of the existing order of things rather like the monarchy and the weather. Reminders of the imperial system were everywhere: there was a school holiday for Empire Day, there were labels saying 'Empire made' and the banner of a popular daily newspaper proclaimed that it stood for 'King and Empire'. In the speeches of politicians appeals were frequently made to the cause of empire and no party could afford not to show enthusiasm for the organisation, although frequently also the word seems to be a rather more altruistic-sounding way of saying 'Britain'

To be sure, there were critics of empire among the intellectual circles of the period; and on the left, too, there was a certain amount of organisation and debate designed to influence the future development of the whole structure but particularly its policies for the peoples of Africa and Asia.[1] But it would, nevertheless, be a mistake to see the sentiments expressed by George Orwell or the *New Statesman* after Kingsley Martin became editor in 1931 as

114

in any way typical of the mood of the majority of the general population or reflective even of the consensus of articulate political opinion. The amount of attention devoted to the pamphlets, articles and books of the enemies of the imperial idea is disproportionate to the amount of attention which they received in their own time, however influential they may seem in retrospect and however much amusement one may gain from discovering consistency and originality in their theses.[2]

The existence of the empire as a fact of political and international life was, of course, of particular importance to the Conservative Party, which naturally identified defence of the integrity of the empire with patriotism and claimed a monopoly in both.[3] But underneath the strident rhetoric which marked the gatherings of constituency workers and such bodies as the Junior Imperial League[4] and the Primrose League[5] lay a host of uncertainties about the future of Britain's relationship with the other component parts of the empire. Indeed, to some commentators, the war which had ostensibly been the most triumphant moment in the empire's history was the precipitant of problems calculated to destroy the complete imperial edifice. One such problem was that the Dominion governments – in particular South Africa and Canada – were impatient of their lack of autonomy in foreign policy and, fearful that their own electorates would not accept mere convention in the matter, were demanding some legal formula to embody their newly recognised rights.

The year in which that legal formula was embodied in the Statute of Westminster was 1931 – a year in which the British government was more than usually aware of another great difficulty: cost. Britain had emerged from the war with her territorial extent the greatest it had ever been. But this fact meant that her commitments were also the greatest *they* had ever been – and that at a time when her economic position was ill-suited to meet them. It has been argued that one reason why Britain resorted to all sorts of expedients in her attempt to cut the cost of defence expenditure in particular was that politicians of all political parties knew that the working-class voter would be unwilling to pay for imperial projects when the money could be used more profitably on social services at home. Attractive though this view is in some respects, it fails to take account of the fact that the Treasury would have sought to cut expenditure by the Colonial Office and the service departments whatever the outlook of the British electorate because it believed that a balanced budget was a necessary prerequisite of a return to economic prosperity. The rise of *demos* did not stop a Labour government from contemplating cuts in the unemployment benefit in 1931; there is no reason to credit it with responsibility for the British determination to make the Dominions, for example, pay a greater share of the cost of their own defence.

But one of the greatest uncertainties of the interwar years surrounded the possession which in many ways was the symbolic keystone of the empire. India had cast its thrall over the British for a period far longer than the Raj itself[6], but the relative brevity of the Raj's life seemed overshadowed by the spectacle, mystery and prestige of the Indian empire. Even now it is difficult not to feel slightly nostalgic when reading of King George V's Durbar at Delhi in 1911, where it was noted that 'His Queen wore a crown with 4,149 cut diamonds, 2,000 rose diamonds, 22 emeralds, four rubies, and four sapphires. He had 20,000 of his British and Indian troops drawn up in full-dress parade before him. There were trappings of Maharajahs, Rajas and princelings galore to make that December day . . . a gorgeous memory for everyone present and there were 50,000 of them at least.'[7]

Beneath the pomp and glitter of British rule, however, the political aspirations of the Indian elite were growing and a nationalist movement – incoherent and weak at first – was gaining in strength. The participation of India in the war had given that movement an added impetus, and a measure of autonomy at the provincial level, deemed generous by the British but disappointing to Indian opinion, was accorded under the so-called Montagu–Chelmsford legislation of 1919.[8] In ten years the implications of both the indigenous Indian developments and the pragmatic British reaction to them were to burst upon the British political scene and force government and society alike to contemplate the possibility that the sun might indeed be going down over their empire in the East.

The 1919 legislation introduced the rather clumsy form of government known as dyarchy to India and provided that the experiment of applying the principles of self-rule to people of non-european origin should be reviewed after ten years. Reaction to the reforms themselves, of course, differed. In India those who were willing to work the reforms split off from the main body of the Congress Party, and within Congress itself fissures developed as disagreement about the tactics to advance Swaraj arose.[9] All sections of Indian opinion took the 1919 Act's preamble as a definite declaration of intent, however, and began to organise accordingly. In Britain, on the other hand, the emphasis was placed on the gradual nature of constitutional evolution and Westminster, for the most part, seemed convinced that it – rather than the forces on the spot – could control the timing of advance. With the formation of Baldwin's 1924 Cabinet, Lord Birkenhead, the only man in Lloyd George's government to oppose the Montagu–Chelmsford reforms,[10] became Secretary of State for India. It was Birkenhead, nevertheless, who – partly to pre-empt a future Labour government and partly as a response to the Viceroy, Lord Irwin's assessment of the situation – decided to appoint a Parliamentary Commission to investigate the working of the 1919 reforms before the time specified in the Act. The Commission was chaired by Sir John Simon but found no favour in India because it was without Indian representation and (apart from Simon himself) seemed a rather undistinguished group of men.[11] Although it was boycotted by the Congress Party (which had temporarily managed to unite a number of different sections of Indian opinion in criticism of the Commission's composition), at the beginning of 1929 Simon himself still adhered to the view that his investigations would produce a report of relevance to the Indian situation.[12]

On the British side a major change occurred when the general election of 1929 produced a minority Labour government. The commander-in-chief of the Indian army, Field Marshal Sir William Birdwood, frankly admitted to Sir Laming Worthington-Evans, the former Secretary of State for War, that it was 'a matter of great regret' that neither Worthington-Evans nor his party would be presiding over the destinies of the army at that crucial period.[13] But as far as the Viceroy, Lord Irwin, was concerned the replacement of the opinionated Birkenhead by the malleable Wedgwood Benn offered an opportunity for seizing the initiative from Westminster and the India Office; and that in turn might allow a substantial amelioration of the government of India's position and be more in Britain's long-term interests than those unfamiliar with the intricacies of Indian politics would at that stage appreciate.

The problem as Irwin saw it at the end of 1928 and as he expressed it to Malcomn Hailey was that whatever the Simon Commission proposed would be rejected by the majority of Indians; what he wanted was a device which could crack the unity of Indian factions – a unity cemented only by the activities of the Simon Commission – and rally the moderates around proposals which, even if they were limited by the need to safeguard certain areas of concern to the British, might nevertheless be sold if properly packaged:

> In a different atmosphere . . . control in essential subjects might be accepted, possibly by the majority, or at least by considerable sections of organized political thought, and it would be worth a great deal to break the present, admittedly not very happy, partnership of Liberal and Congress Parties. If we are to do this it seems vital to present the problem in a new guise.[14]

The new guise consisted of a proposal for a Round Table Conference which would involve all sections of Indian opinion and which could thrash out even those constitutional and political questions which were excluded from the Simon Commission's remit. Indeed, the proposal effectively meant that the elaborate mechanism of the Commission would be consigned to oblivion if a realistically composed assembly could be convened. But Irwin desired to add to this aspect of his plan a further proposal – that he, on behalf of the governments of India and Great Britain, should make a statement confirming that the ultimate goal of British policy was that India should achieve Dominion status.

It is not necessary to go into the lengthy and complicated discussions which preceded the Viceroy's announcement of the intention of the government in London to call together representatives of Indian political life and his declaration that Dominion status was indeed the ultimate end of British rule in the subcontinent.[15] What is of importance is the fact that this statement of Irwin's – which was made on 31 October 1929 – ushered in a period in which politicians of all parties in Britain were forced to reconsider their assumptions about the character of the empire, and in which a section of the Conservative Party found the issue of such importance that they were prepared to challenge the leadership's policy on every possible occasion for the next seven years. The opposition was not, however, completely confined to Parliament or even to the extra-parliamentary wing of the Conservative Party – although of course both bodies were very much involved in the struggle. Outside the ordinary channels of political activism, the Indian question sparked off the creation of pressure groups of various kinds which recruited to their aid a number of men and women whose feelings had hitherto rarely occasioned political organisation of any kind. Apart from the rather populist empire free trade movement – which had a rather different appeal and

which after all had the aid of some rather important daily newspapers to give an outlet for the movement's views – few issues relating to the conduct of imperial policy had aroused such interest
or indeed such organisation. It is the purpose of this essay to trace
the development of these groups and to show their relationship
with the ebb and flow of rebellion on the backbenches at Westminster.

The Irwin declaration occasioned a debate in both Houses of
Parliament. In a sense the House of Lords rather stole the thunder
of the Commons debate because it witnessed both a weighty
attack on the action of Irwin by Lord Reading – his predecessor in
Delhi – and a rather counter-productive tirade by Lord Birkenhead. What was clear in the Commons debate, however, was that
the Indian problem might prove another opportunity for
Baldwin's personal enemies to discomfort him; and it might even
allow mischievous figures outside the ranks of Conservative par-
liamentarians to take advantage of the Tory leader's difficulties.
As Davidson, the chairman of the Conservative Party, wrote to
Irwin after the debate:

> About three weeks ago those in our party who regard SB as an
> ineffective, supine Leader, and whose sympathies are clearly
> Coalition in character decided to use the Indian situation to get
> rid of him for once and for all, and the opportunity was so
> favourable that there can be no doubt that they believed they
> would be successful, aided by the *Daily Express*, the *Daily Mail*,
> and Lloyd George . . .[16]

Yet Davidson recognised that not everyone who had been
worried by the contents of the Viceroy's statement was motivated by malice and he admitted that it was not only the 'die-
hard' element in the party who were concerning themselves with
the issue: even the moderates were in what Davidson called 'a
state of suspended animation' – presumably waiting for the
Simon Commission's report before making up their minds. And
many of Baldwin's senior colleagues were unhappy. Salisbury,[17]
for example, was deeply dissatisfied with the trend of events in
India and even Churchill, whose criticism of the Irwin declaration was probably what led Davidson to associate their Indian
stance with a hankering for the old coalition with the Liberals
against the Labour Party, was acknowledged to have some
genuine interest in the problem. Unfortunately because much of
Irwin's strategy depended upon assuring Indian leaders that the

British government's initiative presaged a real advance for the country while simultaneously assuring British critics at home that the gestures he had been making were essentially of form and that no crucial British interests in India would be sacrificed; this meant that the repeated demands of prominent British politicians like Churchill for a clarification of the limits and safeguards to be placed on any constitutional experiment were embarrassing to the government of India. Indeed Irwin, although he wrote soothingly to Churchill at the end of 1929 expressing the opinion that he could not forget views like Churchill's because he shared them, wrote also to Salisbury asking him to try and restrain Churchill's eloquence because it was having a bad effect in India.[18]

The decision of the Congress Party to boycott the first session of the Round Table Conference was a blow to Irwin's policy which had in part been designed to split the moderates from the extreme wing of the organisation and get them to the conference table.[19] This failure had become clear by March 1930 but what had become equally clear by that date was that the opposition to the government's policy was going to split the Conservative Party seriously; Baldwin, motivated by friendship for Irwin, by dislike of the die-hard sections of the Conservative ranks, and by his own tolerant attitude to Indian affairs, was going to find himself increasingly out of step with the backbenchers on his own side who were demanding a more militant form of opposition on the issue.

The period was one of great personal difficulty for Baldwin since the press lords – Rothermere and Beaverbrook – had been conducting a spasmodic but highly disruptive campaign on the question of protection and imperial preference. Even if their doctrines did not convert many of the parliamentary party (with the possible exception of men like Patrick Hannon[20] and W. Grant Morden), they did attract large numbers of the Conservative rank and file and did force Tory M.P.s to focus upon the quality of Baldwin's leadership and the quality of the party's policy on the fiscal issue. And as Baldwin well knew, when the questions raised by the *Daily Mail* and the *Daily Express* were widened to these more general issues, the dissatisfaction inside the party was widespread. (The incident of the Twickenham by-election[21], where Central Office had withdrawn its support from a candidate because he stated that he subscribed to the doctrine of empire free trade but where several backbench M.P.s – notably Sir Henry Page Croft and others associated with the Empire

Industries Association – had insisted on lending support to the
heretic's campaign, was embarrassing enough; it was to be followed by even more humiliation for Baldwin in October 1930
when Central Office again withdrew support from an official candidate at South Paddington whose views were then publicly
defended by a range of backbenchers including J. R. Remer, the
M.P. for Macclesfield, Colonel John Gretton, the M.P. for
Burton, and Page Croft – all figures of seniority and distinction on
the backbenches if not men of great popularity with Baldwin.)
Only Rothermere and the *Daily Mail*, however, seemed interested
in extending the campaign against the conduct of Conservative
policy to embrace other issues apart from the fiscal one, and Beaverbrook himself decisively rejected a plea for him to join forces
with Churchill.

The evolution of Churchill's obsession with Indian affairs requires some comment because he was to become the spearhead of
the campaign against the government's policy towards India even
when, after the formation of the National government in August
1931, that government was largely dominated by the party to
whose ranks he had so recently returned.[22] Although Churchill
had been driven back to Conservatism by (among other factors)
his hatred of socialism and his disapproval of the Liberal Party for
putting the Labour Party in office in 1924, he was anything but a
docile new recruit. Too idiosyncratic in his views to be a good
party man at the best of times (and it might be added too assured
of his own brilliance to suffer the restraints of discipline easily), he
had incurred the wrath of many a backbencher during his period
at the Exchequer because of his refusal to go very far in the direction of safeguarding British industry, much less towards the comprehensive tariff policy which so many Conservatives were hailing
as a political and economic panacea. The enjoyment of office did,
however, keep Churchill in regular step with most of his cabinet
colleagues – except perhaps Amery – in a way which was not possible when the Conservatives went into opposition in 1929.

It is somewhat strange that politicians seem to fear the repetition of dangers already experienced more than the emergence
of completely new ones, just as they frequently predict for personalities which were once politically powerful a resurrection of
strength which a rational assessment of the situation would
hardly warrant. But then anyone who seeks to understand political developments must realise that political actors are not
rational and that their subjective impressions of the world in

which they move are the ones which determine their attitudes and their decisions. And it cannot be denied that, for whatever reason, Baldwin and some of his colleagues really felt and feared that Lloyd George was not the isolated figure he seems in retrospect but was in 1930 capable of regrouping around him the forces alienated from Baldwin. Large political parties are of course co-alitions of very different ideological and social groups, and although it is easy to impose upon them from a hindsight a unity and stability which they may not have possessed at the time to the extent that potential divisions are present in the calculations of those who contribute towards policy or whose actions have a public audience, they must be considered and charted by the analyst of politics.[23] It has already been shown that the result Davidson most feared from a division in the Commons over the propriety of the Irwin declaration was that Baldwin and two-thirds of the Tory party would have gone into the same lobby as the Socialists while Lloyd George, Churchill, the pro-coalitionists and the die-hard wing of the party, together with an additional number of Baldwin's personal enemies, would have gone into the other lobby. It might seem now that Churchill's position was much weaker than it appeared at the time because it was hardly likely that he would be able to unite, with any hope of perma-nence, Liberals – committed to free trade and by and large liberal in their conception of the development of the empire – with back-bench Conservatives who shared Churchill's attitude to India but who were with the exception of Lord Salisbury and his immediate family determined to press for protection. For a short period – possibly until to Baldwin's relief a clean break was made on the Indian issue in January 1931 – Churchill seemed a personal and political threat to Baldwin of scarcely less importance than the threat posed by Beaverbrook.

As far as Churchill himself was concerned there were two rather crude and inaccurate views which circulated over this period to explain his commitment to a position which divided him from the Conservative leadership and kept him out of office for almost a decade. The first view is that Churchill was indeed as he himself stated more concerned about the future of India than about any other issue in public life; his dedication to the fight against the government proposals for Indian constitutional reform when they were finally published in 1933 as a white paper[24] was thus inspired by a deep-seated feeling that Britain was making a terrible mis-take and betraying a sacred trust for the welfare of the millions of

Indians who inhabited the subcontinent. The second view of Churchill's behaviour over the years 1929–35 was summed up by *The Economist* in 1933 when it said:

> In *choosing* India as the issue *best calculated* to dissociate the Conservative Party from Mr. Baldwin and break up the National Government, Mr. Churchill and his die-hard supporters *chose* wisely and well. To surrender our Empire in India! To give way to sedition! How many true Conservatives breathe with a soul so dead as to be deaf to such an appeal as this.[25]

In this explanation Churchill was motivated rather more by considerations of personal political advantage than by any conviction about the effects which government policy would have on India. The whole of Churchill's personal involvement in the Indian issue was thus a manoeuvre to jockey himself into the Conservative leadership and to achieve this goal by ranging against Baldwin the backbench members who could see no real advantage to their party from a coalition with the remnants of the 1929–31 government and who could see real disadvantage in the National government's commitment to many of the policies which the former Labour Prime Minister had initiated or sanctioned. Certainly Churchill earned the distrust of many members of the Conservative Party during the period of the India revolt because of this deep suspicion that ambition and not principle was motivating his activities.

The reality – if one can ever properly understand what propels another human being to act in a certain way – was probably rather different. It is true that Churchill had very little detailed knowledge of the Indian political scene and that Indian affairs had not hitherto taken up a great deal of his concentration. It is also true that Churchill had not expressed any grave reservations about the implementation of the Montagu–Chelmsford proposals. However, it is equally true that Churchill was not a cynical or scheming politician in the sense that would have fitted the explanation suggested by *The Economist*, and similar ones propagated widely at the time of the rebellion. (Apart from anything else Churchill was too impetuous a character to be efficiently Machiavellian as his all too frequent lapses of political judgement reveal.)[26] What appears to have happened is that between the Irwin declaration and the beginning of 1930 Churchill developed the firm opinion that the whole British Empire was in danger from a paralysis of nerve on the part of the politicians at home. He gave a long statement of his position to Irwin himself in January 1930 in which he explained his belief that it was the duty of the Conservative Party to act as the core of national and imperial opposition to Socialist policies and that the Liberal Party would to a certain extent feel obliged to join in criticising policies damaging to the safety of the empire. Churchill felt that he could not disclaim responsibility for the direction in which events were moving; but he claimed that, given the succession of blows which had been dealt to the Empire in Ireland, in Egypt and of course in India, he did not wonder that some people in the far-flung corners of the imperial system doubted the determination of British public opinion to defend the empire against internal subversion and felt that conciliation and compromise were the only courses open to them in any conflict. However, Churchill also thought that the emergence of the Indian issue had in fact helped those who wanted to preserve the empire because it posed alternatives in stark simplicty – and in this respect he also welcomed the enunciation of the extreme nationalists' demands. The real danger was that in attempting to meet the needs and desires of so-called moderate opinion in India Britain would be pushed down a slippery slope towards abdication without realising it. And abdication would, in Churchill's view, automatically entail the horrors of anarchy, civil war and famine; such evils had beset China, even though the Chinese were in Churchill's opinion a stronger and more capable people than the Indian races.

The initial reaction of Churchill to the Indian question was thus one of outrage that the supine leaders of British opinion could not see that a threat to British power (which it never occurred to Churchill to think could be anything but a power for stability, order and hence for good in the world) was inherent in a threat to the fabric of empire. In opposition, of course, Churchill himself was not called upon to respond practically to the demands of Indian or indeed any other events, so that he was free to castigate the men whose portfolios chained them to short-term solutions to problems and blinded them to the long-term dangers of weak and appeasing policies. But parallel with this increasingly pessimistic assessment of the turn events were taking in the world as a whole there appeared between 1929 and the middle of 1930 an increasing sense of personal frustration in Churchill's *weltanschaaung*. The leaders of the Conservative Party, and particularly Baldwin, seemed to Churchill to lack vision. They were small and mediocre figures whose indifference to Britain's decline also made them contemptible. It thus became important to change these men and to replace them with leaders who could alert the nation to the danger it was facing and could rally it to meet the crisis. Baldwin, whether as Leader of the Opposition from 1929 to 1931 or as Lord President of the Council and then Prime Minister from 1931 to 1937, lacked the ability and the will to master the situation. Churchill's analysis of the predicament naturally led him to believe that he would make a better leader than Baldwin, but his determination to expose Baldwin's weaknesses stemmed from a much broader emotion than personal rivalry. Not that Churchill's own evaluation of the political situation produced entirely consistent tactics or emotions; in September 1930 he could write one letter to Beaverbrook begging him to broaden his campaign into a wider crusade on imperial themes[27] and on the following day write warmly to Baldwin (who had returned the proofs of *My Early Life* with flattering comments).[28] And in October when Baldwin was again experiencing acute difficulties over the fiscal issue and when it was assumed that an accomodation with the protectionist wing of the party would involve Churchill's resignation from the Opposition Business Committee at the very least, the Conservative leader received from Churchill a conciliatory letter saying that although Churchill wanted to reserve his position on the question of taxing staple foods he would continue to work hard for the success of the Conservative Party and for Baldwin's leadership of it:

> As I am putting things on record let me add that in my opinion if you had not been subjected to so much ill treatment and intrigue this year, you would have been able in 1931 to lead our party into as great a victory as 1924.[29]

Churchill's was not the only opposition to the policy which the MacDonald government with Baldwin's acquiescence was adopting towards India, to be consolidated and heightened during 1930. Lord Lloyd, the former Governor of Egypt, had been enunciating his critical opinions on the issue and when he met Lord Lee of Fareham in Venice in April 1930 he was quick to give his opinion of Irwin. Irwin, he thought, was 'so stubborn in his ideals; steel-like in his weakness, but no stronger in reality than unmelting ice.' And on 23 March 1930 Lord Sydenham of Combe, a former Governor of Bombay, wrote to Salisbury about the need to form an organisation to 'diffuse accurate information in regard to all matters affecting the welfare of the Indian Empire'.[30] Out of this correspondence and similar discussions was generated the

Indian Empire Society which quickly became the source of a stream of propaganda against the official policy towards India. It produced a regular monthly journal which Sir Louis Stuart edited and which was called the *Indian Empire Review*. The I.E.S. brought together Tory backbenchers, retired officials and the general public, but the Conservative Party does not seem to have had a regular backbench committee of its own devoted to Indian affairs until 1930 when one was established under the chairmanship of John Wardlaw-Milne, the M.P. for Kidderminster and a former member of the Governor of Bombay's Legislative Council and the Governor-General of India's Council as well as a former chairman of the Bombay Chamber of Commerce. At first, the interest in this committee seems to have been confined to the backbenchers whose military experience often presaged predictably die-hard opinions; but as the problem of India became more salient during 1930 and when it became intricately enmeshed with the leadership issue (for instance, in March 1931 during the St George's by-election campaign which overlapped with Irwin's pact with Gandhi, the cessation of civil disobedience, and the successful persuasion of the Congress Party to come to the second session of the Round Table Conference) the committee became a place of lively controversy and attendance rose accordingly.

Baldwin's own perception of the delicacy with which Indian affairs would have to be handled is revealed to some extent by his handling of the selection of the Conservative delegates to the Round Table Conference which was to open in November 1930. The publication of the Simon Commission's Report[31] in two volumes in June 1930 had again placed the Conservative leader in a difficult position. Although it seemed novel enough to many at Westminster, in India it received a very cool reception since it appeared, as the Indian *Daily Mail* (an organ of the Indian Liberal Party) put it, to be 'a rather badly-cooked rice pudding, strongly flavoured with the cinnamon of die-hardism.'[32] The Viceroy therefore needed to conciliate Indian opinion if the Round Table Conference was to be a success and he proposed to reiterate the British government's commitment to Dominion status (about which the Simon Report was silent) and to assure the Congress Party that future discussions would not be limited to the framework of the scheme of reform suggested by the report but that on the contrary the British government would be willing to make substantial modifications to the scheme.[33] This was too much, however, for the Conservative Party which, as occurred over the

Irwin Declaration, forced Baldwin to make its reservations about any such course plain to the Viceroy. A telegram was accordingly sent by Baldwin to Irwin on 3 July 1930 which started by asserting that Baldwin and his colleagues were 'most anxious' to support the Viceroy 'both on public and personal grounds' but confessed that they had 'feelings of grave anxiety at the way things seem(ed) to be shaping'. The telegram then went on to express the Conservative Party's opinion about the best course for Indian constitutional reform; its import is noteworthy because the party was to reverse its line when the National government took over for Indian policy:

> Further, since the Conference is to be free, it must be free, if Indians so desire, to discuss Dominion status and any of the schemes which Indians may put forward for its realisation. You will observe that the Simon Report offers no bar to such discussion or indeed to [a] declaration of Dominion status as [an] ultimate goal but it makes plain that [the] immediate realisation of [the] goal is impracticable and unthinkable and that it can only be reached by slow growth beginning in Provincial sphere, leading up through the creation of federal central government to ultimate solution. *In other words future Indian constitution must be a natural growth as in Dominions and United States and cannot be creation of a single act of Parliament or be reached till many existing difficulties have been overcome.*[34]

It seems fairly clear from the correspondence that Baldwin's hand was to some extent forced by Salisbury (who in a letter to Austen Chamberlain written on the next day underlined the particular importance of the topic of law and order and its sketchy treatment in the Simon Report; he also rather acidly commented that it was a pity that so few of his colleagues had read the report for the meeting which discussed the telegram).[35] But the core of many of the arguments which the opponents of the Government of India Bill were to use was foreshadowed in the telegram's insistence that the evolutionary and gradualist approach to Indian institutions was the correct one, and that this approach was 'vital to the whole scheme of the Simon Report' and its acceptance 'essential to the continuation of the all-party agreement on Indian policy'.[36] The Simon Report had made a profound impression; the limits on Indian political progress had been set; and everyone at Westminster would be happy so long as the framework designed by the Commission was maintained.

As Baldwin probably guessed, however, the exigencies of political accommodation in India meant that the principles outlined in
the Simon Report could not set limits on the Round Table negotiations. To underline the point Simon was not to serve on the
Conference for, as Simon explained to Austen Chamberlain,
Ramsay MacDonald and Irwin were both convinced that 'certain
quarters' in India would assume that the Conference was preju-
diced if Simon were present. Simon, though somewhat bitter, decided to accept the decision.

Other difficulties arose, however, in relation to the Conservative nominees for the Conference. Baldwin had initially
thought of asking Austen Chamberlain, Lord Peel, Lord Hailsham and Samuel Hoare to serve at the first session, and he wrote
to this effect to Lord Salisbury on 2 August 1930. Unfortunately –
as Austen Chamberlain had in fact warned Baldwin – there was
some doubt as to whether Salisbury would approve of
Chamberlain's participation because his conduct of the Irish
negotiations had alienated a section of the party. Baldwin pointed
out to Salisbury that Austen Chamberlain was very sensitive to
criticism in this matter and was therefore anxious to have
Salisbury's personal approval before accepting the nomination.
Salisbury, however, declined to give such an endorsement and a
rather embarrassed Baldwin had to convey the reason to Chamberlain. He wrote thus to Chamberlain on 9 August 1930:

> I regret very much that your apprehension was correct. He
> takes the view that you are too important a man not to be
> regarded as the leader of our quartette and he says with great
> reluctance that your Irish record is a handicap and that he does
> not feel the confidence that he would desire.[37]

Chamberlain was not apparently surprised by the reaction of
Salisbury, since he had already felt such an attitude 'clearly indicated' both in previous conversations and in what Eyres-Monsell
had told him about the state of feeling in the die-hard section of
the party.[38] Both Chamberlain and Baldwin realised that there
would be enough problems from that section of the party when
the substantive issues of the Conference were identified and that
it would be courting internal disagreement at this stage to send
there someone whose position was inherently suspect in the quarters which would have to be won over.

Throughout 1930, therefore, the concern with which Indian
developments were viewed increased, and the sensitivity of the

Conservative leadership to the potential divisions within the party was heightened. The Round Table Conference opened in November 1930 and the ten week session's achievements were debated in the House of Commons on 26 January 1931. Although the quality of the debate was somewhat marred by the fact that the House had been given only a very short period to digest the lengthy report of the Conference, what quickly became apparent was that the main Conservative spokesmen were determined to try to preserve the all-party unity which had previously marked the handling of Indian affairs.[39] Indeed Samuel Hoare, who spoke immediately after the Prime Minister, and who had been one of the Conservative representatives at the Round Table Conference, revealed how far the Irish conflict still dominated party thinking about the appropriate way to handle imperial difficulties:

> I should shudder to see this question become the pawn of party politics . . . I should be very sorry to see the Indian question go the way of the Irish question. I should be very sorry to see one party definitely pledged to one line of policy, and the opposition definitely pledged to reverse it.[40]

In Hoare's opinion there were three main features of the various sub-committee's of the conference's work which had emerged and which would be the focal point of future discussions. First, there was the idea of an all-India federation; secondly there was the agreement that responsible government should be granted to the provinces; and thirdly there was the fact that both the British and the Indian members of the Conference accepted that some safeguards would have to be built into any constitutional scheme, although as Hoare admitted, there was still 'much difference' on what the actual safeguards were to be.

Sir John Simon added a slightly discordant note to the debate when he pointed out that in some of the most intractable areas of the Indian problem – such as the question of communal representation – no advance had been made at all; and he gently chided the government on the treatment accorded to his own report (which had never been debated in the House) by thanking his colleagues on the Statutory Commission for the help which they had given him. It was Churchill's speech, however, which really broke the apparent unity of all parties on the question and which warned the House of opposition ahead. Churchill expressed his conviction that the handling of Indian affairs during the previous eighteen months had been 'most unfortunate' and had led already 'to results which will be long lamented'.[41] Why, asked Churchill, had the work of the Simon Commission been altogether ignored? Was it because the Viceroy had determined on his pronouncement, thus prejudicing the Simon Report even before its publication? Since 1929 there had been in Churchill's opinion a 'landslide' towards the extremists; and the Princes, by offering to enter an all-India federation, had thereby given not so much an assuring gesture of faith in the future of India but a signal of their fear that the Raj and British protection were crumbling. To argue that such a federation would mean the spread of liberty and democracy was nonsense: no assembly, however cleverly constructed, could represent the masses who would be delivered to the mercies of 'a well-organised, narrowly-elected, political and religious oligarchy and caucus'. The language of sturdy, old-fashioned imperialism echoed around the Commons as Churchill reiterated his belief that the British government should not forget the 300 million people who were Britain's duty and trust and who depended for their livelihood on the peace and order which British justice had brought to India.

Eloquent though Churchill's speech was it failed to convince the House of Commons and on the same day Churchill sent Baldwin his resignation from the Opposition Business Committee.[42] The split was the beginning of almost a decade in the political wilderness for Churchill, but the rationale of the act seemed clear enough at the time. Free of the restraints which being a party to Baldwin's overall opposition strategy imposed, Churchill could make use of those personal enemies of the Conservative leader – such as Lord Rothermere – who were anxious to exploit the Indian question and give it publicity in their newspapers. The Indian Empire Society and other prominent critics of dismantling the structure of British rule in India – such as Lord Lloyd – were naturally pleased to have acquired so forceful a champion in the Commons and felt that their position was aided by the resignation since it enabled a more public campaign to be planned.[43] And Churchill must have hoped that by setting the lead he would encourage the majority of M.P.s in his own party to force Baldwin to dissociate himself from the government's policy. Even if the middle of the road backbench Tory member would not do this for reasons of personal conviction, Churchill and his associates hoped that they might be persuaded to turn against the proposals for constitutional advance if they were made aware of a strong antipathy to such changes on the part of the electorate.

Churchill's resignation thus marked a new phase in the battle, as he saw it, to save the empire from itself. It should perhaps be remembered that the readers of the popular press had been bombarded with propaganda and exhortation in support of another ostensibly 'imperial' cause – that of Empire Free Trade – over the past eighteen months. Perhaps the readers had long ago learnt to discount it or to live with it, but many politicians would have felt that the response of the general public to Lord Beaverbrook's campaigns was evidence that the voters cared about the empire. So Churchill was probably justified in thinking that a campaign to mobilise the electorate against the 'betrayal of India' would stand a relatively good chance of succeeding. From the electoral point of view there seemed to be two areas where the Indian question might cause special concern: the home counties and Lancashire.

The home counties were likely to be politicially important for any campaign based on a cause which was 'die-hard' or 'right-wing' in character because of the large numbers of retired military and imperially-connected families – whether from commerce or public service – who lived there. (Orwell's characterisation of the Blimpish middle classes in 'England, Your England' was not without truth.) They would probably be members or officers of different sorts of voluntary associations including, of course, the local Conservative associations, so that as well as being likely to hold views sympathetic to the position of Churchill they were also likely to have, even if only to a very small extent, some experience of organisation and pressure group activity.[44]

Lancashire, however, was a completely different case. The area was experiencing in the interwar period severe economic distress because of the decline of a number of staple British industries located there. One such industry was, of course, the cotton industry and it was in relation to that industry that Churchill thought the impact of any extension of Indian independence would be significant. Since the First World War and the fiscal autonomy convention of 1919 India had had the right to regulate her own tariffs, although what this meant in practice to the conduct of the British cabinet in London varied from administration to administration and from secretary of state to secretary of state. Montagu, for instance, had used the convention to underline the British government's powerlessness to come to the aid of Lancashire in 1921, but Peel, in contrast, had made it clear to the government of India that he considered that the British government had the right to make 'representations' to her in relation to fiscal policy which affected

British interests.[45] The Labour government of 1929–31 seems to have been in difficulties over this question. It would obviously have been alert to the increase in unemployment which might follow a rise in the import duties on cotton, and Tom Jones noted that in 1930 the whole cabinet felt it necessary to bring the serious condition of the Lancashire cotton industry to the Viceroy's notice when such an increase was proposed, although Wedgwood Benn emphasised that the final decision lay in Delhi and not in Whitehall.[46] The cabinet records, however, reveal that in 1931, when a new Indian surcharge of 5 per cent on imported cotton piece goods was proposed, the Secretary of State refused to make representations to the Viceroy against it.[47] It was therefore somewhat tempting for those who opposed the British government's approach to the Indian question to suggest that a direct link between Lancashire's recession and India's autonomy existed and that the effect on Lancashire trade would be even greater if any further independence were accorded to the sub-continent. Indeed it might be true that British exporters feared that further import duties – which might be imposed by a nationalist India for political rather than economic or revenue raising purposes – would have a deleterious effect on their (and their employees') prosperity; but too often the British exporters also used the Indian situation to mask the fact that their trade was being lost to Japanese and American rivals.[48]

In addition to this economic dislocation, Lancashire was also going through a political transformation, as the two major parties fought to win seats which were passing out of Liberal hands, and the Conservative Party therefore had a direct interest in not seeming to neglect Lancashire's needs. The literature and tactics of the Churchillian rebels all reflect their hopes of being able to mobilise Lancashire in their campaign, and indeed the Tory leadership throughout the struggle also seemed afraid that Lancashire M.P.s and voters would side with the die-hards. The fact that both suppositions in the event proved ill-founded does not reduce their signifcance in the calculations of both sides at the time.

The formation of a National government and the general election of 1931 which resulted in a landslide towards its supporters meant that from that the success of any Indian policy depended upon the attitudes of the Conservative Party and the extent to which the Tory leader could contain any rebellion over the issue. It was perhaps with relief as well as from necessity that Baldwin rejected any portfolio and, as Lord President of the Council, devoted himself the problems of party management. India was clearly likely to (and did) take up a good deal of the time of that Parliament, and there was bound to be substantial backbench opposition to any measure of reform.

The new government had determined to keep the broad approach to Indian policy of its predecessors and Baldwin's choice as Secretary of State for India was Samuel Hoare. The first open clash between the government and its supporters came when MacDonald took the opportunity of the closure of the second session of the Round Table Conference to summarise to the House of Commons the progress already made. Hoare explained to the House that the objective of the National government's policy was an all-India executive and legislature, clearly designed for the purpose of carrying out federal duties; and in the provinces there would be autonomy designed to provide as much scope for individual development as possible. The whole structure, he told the House, would be buttressed by safeguards which would ensure that India's credit as well as the functions of law and order could ultimately be guaranteed by British supervision.

Churchill forced the House on the second day of the debate to consider an amendment designed in part to rekindle the ashes of a debate in the previous week on the Statute of Westminster (in which fifty backbenchers motivated by concern for Ulster's position had defied the whips and voted for an amendment put down by Colonel Gretton) but calculated also to draw attention to economic and political disadvantages which would follow from continuing the policies initiated by a Labour government. Forty-three backbenchers voted for Churchill's amendment, but although their numbers were tiny it was noticeable that many familiar figures on the backbenches – such as Colonel Gretton, Henry Page Croft and Sir Archibald Boyd-Carpenter – were opposing the government, as were some of the new intake such as Alan Lennox Boyd, the future Colonial Secretary. Their number however, was, to grow during the following four years and when Henry Page Croft came first in the private member's ballot in February 1933 and used the opportunity to draw attention to the deteriorating Indian situation, he got a relatively sympathetic reception in the House. The government had taken the precaution of putting the Whips on in this debate and, although only forty-two actually dared vote against the amendment which had been put down by the government, some 245 backbenchers, as the voting figures revealed, had defied the Whips and abstained.[49] It was this group of uncommitted backbenchers who might yet be converted to the die-hard cause if reform looked popular in the constituencies and if the government could not give the required assurances in relation to defence, law and order and, of course, British trade.

The vote on Page Croft's motion stimulated further activity inside Parliament. The interest which it had aroused made him think that it was worthwhile forming a committee to watch over the direction of Indian policy. On 11 March the manifesto of an India Defence Committee appeared in the press and drew attention to the spontaneous upsurge of feeling on the issue in the constituencies and to the passage of resolutions hostile to government policy by a number of Conservative associations. The Committee claimed that its view rather than the government's one reflected the true state of public opinion:

> We are reinforced in the belief that we represent ninety-five per cent of the Conservative Party in the country, possibly a majority of Liberal electors, and a great many workers in Lancashire and elsewhere, who normally vote Socialist but who realize that the Government's policy if persisted in may mean their complete ruin.[50]

The Committee held its first meeting in the House of Commons on the following Tuesday – 14 March – and sixty-four members attended. The invitations sent out had clearly stated the outlook of the group and most of those who attended may be reckoned to have come for reasons of sympathy rather than curiosity. Sir Alfred Knox was elected Chairman of the Committee and both Churchill and Page Croft were elected to a small executive of M.P.s; the committee then proceeded to stimulate and coordinate the parliamentary opposition to the government's policy.

The extent of the concern which the activities of this group caused Hoare may be judged from the cabinet records and Hoare's letters to the Viceroy (who from 1931 was Lord Willingdon, not Irwin who had returned home but remained interested in Indian affairs and played a prominent role in the cabinet's India Committee).[51] It had been decided to introduce a single comprehensive measure to deal with both the federal and the provincial levels of the problem, and now that the Secretary of State had decided upon the procedure to be followed he was anxious to get the whole question of the floor of the House and into the hands of the Joint select committee which would investigate the bill in detail.[52]

The government's proposals – on which the discussion of the joint select committee was to be based – were published in March 1933.

In general terms the White Paper envisaged a federal executive and a federal legislature which would together exercise power over both the provinces of British India and the States. The federal executive was to be in the hands of the King, represented, of course, by the Viceroy, and would be 'aided and advised' by a Council of Ministers. In the provinces, the Council of Ministers would be able to tender advice on the whole range of subjects; but at the centre the White Paper proposed that certain matters – defence, external affairs and what was called 'ecclesiastical administration' – would remain the personal responsibility of the Governor-General. The federal legislature was to be bi-cameral and each chamber would possess identical powers except that money bills and votes of supply would have to originate in the lower house. Of the 375 members of the lower chamber, 125 would be appointed by the rulers of the States and the remaining 250 would be directly elected representatives of British India, although the seats would be distributed among both the provinces and the communities. The upper chamber, or Council of State, could have a maximum of 260 members and 100 of these would be appointed by the rulers of the States. The British Indian members (150 in all) would for the most part be elected by the members of each provincial legislature by the method of a single transferable vote, although special treatment was envisaged for minority groups such as Anglo-Indians and Indian Christians. The Governor-General was given, in addition, the power to nominate extra non-official members to provide an opportunity for adding elder statesmen to the chamber. Specific proposals for allocating seats among the States had not been worked out by March, so that this section of the proposals was necessarily vague. Similarly the franchise for the lower chamber could only be given in general terms – though clearly education and property were to remain important qualifications for the franchise.

It was perhaps to be expected that these proposals – as any proposals would have done – came under attack from both the Indians, who found them disappointingly hedged by safeguards, and the die-hards, for whom any advance upon the Simon Commission's recommendations was foolhardy. Hoare thus found himself the 'isolated target of a plunging fire from two flanks', and he recognised that, even after the three-day debate on the proposals in the House of Commons in which the government had a substantial majority, he had been given 'an unmistakable warning of the die-hard determination to continue the fighting to the bitter end'.[53]

The die-hard fight was, however, removed from the parliamentary arena by the appointment of the joint select committee. A number of critics of the proposals, such as Churchill, Wolmer and Page Croft, refused to serve on this committee since they thought that its composition had been unfairly weighted in favour of the government. As Page Croft put it in a letter to Hoare:

> I would remind you that the present House of Commons was elected for a certain definite purposes and no single member [was] elected with a mandate to abandon British rule in India, and this fact I should have thought would have caused His Majesty's Government to take special pains to see that at least 45 per cent of the Select Committee should represent those who believe that India can be preserved for the Imperial Crown and that reforms should be instituted 'step by step' as indicated in the Government of India Act.[54]

But Salisbury, whom Hoare had originally hoped to persuade to chair the committee, did agree to serve. When the joint committee actually started its hearings, the diehards altered their tactics and concentrated their propaganda on the rank and file of the Conservative Party and the general public.

It has already been seen that the Indian Empire Society and the India Defence Committee originated at rather different stages of te campaign against the government's Indian policy and attracted a rather different audience. Thus by March 1933 the die-hards had at their disposal at least a rudimentary form of organisation at both the parliamentary and the grass roots level and contact had already been made with a number of Conservative local associations which had, as the *Indian Empire Review* regularly recorded, passed resolutions hostile to the reforms and had afforded aid to the die-hard cause in a number of ways. The propaganda distributed by the die-hards was obviously more sensational in character than the official reports and arguments in Parliament on which the government had to rely to make its case heard. But Hoare wanted some more effective counter-action to be taken against these pressure groups, which after all had access to the popular press in a way which the government did not and which might have an electorally damaging potential. J. C. C. Davidson, the former chairman of the Conservative Party and the man whom

Baldwin had asked to chair the States Enquiry Committee in 1932, had, it appears, been discussing with Gower at Conservative Central Office the idea of forming a pro-government pressure group since the Conservative Party Conference at Blackpool in 1932.[55] Baldwin, though he was not directly involved in the project, was kept informed of the subscribers to the finances of the campaign. In May 1933 the group – which was given the title of the Union of Britain and India (hereafter called U.B.I.) – announced in its first published statement an intention of supporting the general policy reform represented by the government White Paper and of combating the campaign of 'ill-informed propaganda on Indian affairs'.

The men who acted as the sponsors of this organisation (which of course both the government and Central Office knew would be more effective if the group could be made to appear as a spontaneous manifestation of informed interest in the debate rather than as a 'front' for government propaganda) were all men with long records of association with India. Prominent among them were Sir Edward Villiers and Sir John Thompson. R. A. Butler, who had been chosen to succeed Lord Lothian as Under-Secretary of State when the Samuelite Liberals left the National government, also became intimately involved in the affairs of the U.B.I. – although he remarks in his autobiography that the organisation had some difficulty in finding people to join it.[56] When a list of supporters of the U.B.I. was finally published, it did indeed contain many distinguished officials of British India but the die-hard cause – with the aid of the *Daily Mail* and *Daily Express* and, on a different level, the *Morning Post* – still made most of the running in the fight for the soul of the Conservative Party and in the struggle to convert a wider section of the public to its views.

In the struggle which both sides mounted to educate the nation in their arguments and to convert the extra-parliamentary Conservative Party to one or other views of the Indian situation, the Indian Empire Society had been proving less than satisfactory in organisational terms. Much of its work overlapped with campaigns which individual M.P.s like Churchill had been running independently; it had for some time been felt that more efficient co-ordination of resources was necessary. As the public campaign entered its final and most intensive phase with the dispatch of the White Paper to the joint select committee, the Indian Empire Society decided to move from its old headquarters to a new address at 48 Broadway in Westminster. From that address ostensibly separate bodies – the Indian Empire Society (with its *Indian Empire Review*) and the India Defence League – were to conduct an integrated campaign against the government.

The India Defence League was formally founded *after* the U.B.I. made its first public appearance, but of course the genesis of the body can be seen in the work of the Indian Empire Society and the India Defence Committee. In its first public statement in June 1933 the India Defence League claimed that it had come into being as the result of widespread apprehension in the House of Lords and the House of Commons as well as in the constituencies that the proposals for India's future would lead to disaster. The I.D.L. (which offered members of the Indian Empire Society honorary membership without further subscription) could now include both members of Parliament and the general public in its popular campaign. Lord Sumner, the president of the Indian Empire Society, accepted the presidency of the I.D.L. while Colonel Gretton and the young Patrick Donner became the treasurer and secretary, respectively. The chief organiser was Vice-Admiral C. U. Usborne, but he was later dismissed for inefficiency and replaced by Oliver Locker-Lampson. Apparently the M.P.s who were members of the I.D.L. each contributed £50 to the organisation's finances and larger sums were given by the Duke of Westminster and Jack Courtauld – a relation by marriage of R. A. Butler and the M.P. for Chichester.[57]

The India Defence League had initially decided against forming local branches, but when strong local committees began to enroll members – sometimes in areas which had hitherto not expressed much interest in the Indian question such as the North east – the I.D.L. saw that there might be advantage to be gained from publicly displaying that not all the I.D.L.'s support came from the home counties. This grass-roots support was eventually used to embarrass the U.B.I., which found that it could not easily counter the technique of securing the passage of constituency resolutions and publicising them widely. (Thus when Lord Brabourne tried to persuade his local Conservative association of the merits of the White Paper and attempted to have a resolution to that effect passed, it was so strongly opposed from the floor that it could not even be put to the gathering.) Unfortunately, as Sir John Thompson pointed out to his U.B.I. colleagues, the pro-government forces could not even counter this local I.D.L. activity with independently sponsored U.B.I. meetings because the propaganda effect of such meetings depended on their having good chairmen who were well-known in the area. Yet finding such characters was an almost insuperable obstacle:

> ... as in the class of provincial society from which powerful chairmen could be recruited, there is generally so strong a die-hard atmosphere that even professed well-wishers hesitate to come out in the open presumably because they do not wish publicly to profess political views which may introduce social complications into their local circles.[58]

Indeed it was only in 1934 that the U.B.I. started to organise local bases at all seriously and then it formed committees which could act as outlets for government propaganda rather than branches which assumed a larger number of members and activities. The U.B.I., however, made a virtue of this necessity by claiming that it did not want to form branches because that would mean it was copying the organisation of the I.D.L., and on the contrary it wanted its committees to be a marked contrast to the 'more social composition' of the I.D.L. Even then there were members of the U.B.I. Council such as Sir Charles Stead and Sir Laurie Hammond who thought that in their respective areas (Gloucestershire and Kent) the feeling against the government was so strong that it would be impossible to form any kind of representative local committee. Nevertheless, rudimentary countrywide committees were eventually created, but of course the U.B.I. continued to rely heavily on its central organisation and its area organisers for the conduct of campaigns.

By February 1934 the I.D.L. looked very strong indeed in terms of its support in the country. It had by that date published over twenty pamphlets (some of them with rather lurid names such as 'The White Paper with the Black Border'), and it recorded a doubling of recruits in the last three months of 1933. Its activities had certainly heightened the consciousness of the rank and file of the Tory Party on the subject, and the party managers had to face a concerted attack from the die-hards at virtually every meeting of the Central Council between 1932 and 1935, at every annual conference of the National Union and at the annual gatherings of the various areas and specialist offshoots of the Conservative organisation, such as the women's section, the Junior Imperial League and the Primrose League. The die-hards never succeeded in winning any of these confrontations, but they often came very close to doing so. Thus, at the Central Council meeting on 28 February 1933 a vote on a strong motion put forward by a representative of the West Essex Unionist Association was defeated by only 189 votes to 165 – although Sir Louis Stuart, who edited the *Indian Empire Review*, claimed that the public had been deprived of the opportunity for knowing the plain speaking that ensued because the chairman had bowdlerised the debate! The embarrassing closeness of the count caused *The Times*, which of course was lending all its aid to Baldwin and the official policy, to comment of the delegates:

> They do not, of course, represent the Conservative Party but they include delegates from all over the country, chosen as a rule for the ardour of their party spirit and infected with all the enthusiasm of irresponsibility.[59]

And in October 1934 (in what Page Croft called his 'last great effort' to rally the National Unionist Association to his cause) in a resolution, blocked as was customary by an official amendment, the Bristol annual conference of the National Union voted for the government by only 543 votes to 520. But as Sir Alfred Knox commented in a letter to Page Croft, although it was plain that the I.D.L.'s strength lay in the National Union, he did not believe for one moment that any demonstration of feeling there would modify the White Paper in any significant manner.[60]

Knox was, of course, right and although, while the U.B.I. was planning its final activities (which were designed to publicise favourably the report of the joint select committee and which were to be co-ordinated, it appears, by a joint committee of U.B.I. and Central Office officials), the I.D.L. was still recruiting new members and forming additional branches, it became obvious that the impact which it was having on the country was out of proportion to the impact it was having on M.P.s. With the publication of the joint select committee's report (which had been delayed by Churchill's accusation of breach of privilege against Hoare and Derby) the campaign acquired an unrealistic air; the battle had shifted back to Parliament.

The joint select committee's report modified the government's White Paper in three substantial respects only. In the first place, as a result of some pressure from Austen Chamberlain who was a member of the joint select committee, indirect election was substituted for direct election of the Central Assembly.[61] Secondly, the provisions against terrorism had been strengthened; and thirdly, further restrictions were devised to prevent India from discriminating against British trade for political reasons. The report itself was debated in Parliament on 10, 11 and 12 December 1934, and it was a measure of the advance which the die-hards had made in Parliament (although they had, as already mentioned, reached a plateau in this respect by 1934) that the motion approving the report was passed with 127 M.P.s voting against. And on the second reading of the bill the die-hards increased their numbers to 133. Thus, although the die-hards had convinced a sizeable proportion of their colleagues to join them in voting against the government, that proportion was by no means sizeable enough. Perhaps the general attitude was that of Viscount Knebworth, the M.P. for North Hertfordshire, of whom his father records that 'his sympathies were undoubtedly with the school that regarded the White Paper policy as one of surrender, but the more he studied the subject, the more difficult he found it to support this attitude with his reason.'[62] The bill passed its third reading by 386 votes to 122 and passed its stages in the Lords relatively easily thereafter. The whole bill received the Royal Assent on 24 July 1935. Ironically, however, the massive piece of legislation was still-born. Intrigue at home and in India prevented the Federation from coming into being at the target date of 1937, and the advent of war so changed the situation that even this measure of independence was deemed inappropriate in 1945.

What seems significant about the period of the controversy in retrospect is thus not so much what it revealed about the likely future of India (although the Act of 1935 did leave some legacy there), but what it revealed about the attitudes towards the empire in the interwar years. Thus, although the government and the majority of Conservative M.P.s were forced to acclimatise themselves to the notion that the Raj was not a permanent monument to an eternally guaranteed British position in the world, and that pragmatic changes would have to be made if India was even to be kept in the Commonwealth, a sizeable section of the Conservative backbenchers, the extra-parliamentary party, and the country found it painful to adjust to this change. Indeed many of them had so far failed to grasp the nature of it that they thought it could be effectively resisted. Perhaps the key to understanding why some could reappraise the empire rationally and others could not lies in the age factor (the eighty or so backbench M.P.s who consistently opposed the reforms were on average older than their fellow Tory M.P.s) or perhaps in some other decisive experience, such as military service. No answer can be given dogmatically. But in those few years British society like British politicians were confronted with an issue which was to be raised again in relation to the whole decolonisation process after the Second World War. Perhaps it is tribute to party discipline and the determination of the executive not to be swayed in its policies that the British Empire's road to becoming one with Ninevah and Tyre was not littered with more casualties.[63]

Notes

1. There were almost as many groups concerned with India operating in Britain in the interwar period as there were factions in Indian politics. Some of the most notable ones were the Indian Home Rule League, the Britain and India Association, the Parliamentary Committee on India and Krishna Menon's India League.

2. The standard work on the development of anti-imperial feeling in Britain is A. P. Thornton, *The Imperial Idea and Its Enemies* (London, 1959). For the *New Statesman*'s attitudes see E. Hyams, *The New Statesman: The History of the First Fifty Years* (London, 1963) and C. H. Rolph, *Kingsley: The Life, Letters and Diaries of Kingsley Martin*. (London, 1973). For George Orwell's attitudes see *Burmese Days* (London, 1935) and the essays, 'England Your England' and 'Shooting An Elephant', both of which are reprinted in *Inside The Whale and Other Essays* (London, 1962).

3. For an account of the components of the Conservative Party's creed on the eve of the First World War see Lord Hugh Cecil, *Conservatism* (London, 1912).

4. The Junior Imperial League was the forerunner of the Young Conservative movement. It was abolished after the Report of the Palmer Committee (1943–4).

5. The Primrose League was an organisation founded in memory of Disraeli; it held a romantic and imperialist view of the Conservative Party and had earlier been used by Lord Randolph Churchill in his campaign to win power in the party by exploiting his influence with the extra-Parliamentary wing of the party.

6. For a brief account of the relationship see M. E. Chamberlain, *Britain and India: The Interaction of Two Peoples* (London, 1974).

7. Geoffrey Moorhouse, *Calcutta*, 2nd ed. (London, 1974) p. 87.

8. For an account of the growth of nationalist sentiment in India see Anil Seal, *The Emergence of Indian Nationalism* (Cambridge, 1971).

9. For a summary of the role of the Congress Party in this period see Pattabhi Sitaramayya, *History of the Indian National Congress*, Vol. I: *1885–1935* (2nd ed. Bombay, 1946). For an account of the constitutional developments see E. Thompson and G. T. Garratt, *The Rise and Fulfilment of British Rule in India* (London, 1934) and R. Coupland, *The Constitutional Problem in India*, vol. I (Oxford, 1942). Also R. J. Moore, *The Crisis of Indian Unity 1919–1940* (Oxford, 1974). I am at present involved in a doctoral study of the Conservative Party's attitudes to imperial affairs in the 1930s.

10. Birkenhead to Reading, 4 Dec 1924, *Reading Collection*, MSS, Eur., E.238/7.

11. The other members of the Commission were Viscount Burnham, Lord Strathcona and Mount-Royal, Edward Cadogan, George Lane-Fox, Stephen Walsh (who was replaced by Vernon Hartshorn) and Clement Attlee.

12. Simon to Geoffrey Dawson, 12 Jan 1929, quoted in *History of The Times*,

vol. IV, parts 1 and 2 (London, 1952).

13. Birdwood to Worthington-Evans, 5 Jun 1929, *Worthington-Evans Mss.*

14. Irwin to Hailey, 10 Dec 1928, *Halifax Collection*, MSS Eur., E.220/14B.

15. On this see S. Gopal, *The Viceroyalty of Lord Irwin* (Oxford, 1957); R. J. Moore, op. cit.; R. C. Watts, 'The Development of British Policy Towards India and the Viceroyalty of Lord Irwin' (Oxford, D.Phil. thesis, 1974) and G. R. Peele, 'A Note on the Irwin Declaration', *Journal of Imperial and Commonwealth History* (May, 1973).

16. Davidson to Irwin, 9 Nov 1929, quoted in Robert Rhodes James, *Memoirs of a Conservative* (London, 1969) pp. 308–10.

17. James, 4th Marquess of Salisbury. I should like to record my gratitude to the late Marquess of Salisbury for discussing his father's role in the Indian episode with me and the present Marquess for extending me permission to quote from the Salisbury MSS at Hatfield House.

18. Irwin to Salisbury, 3 Dec 1929, *Salisbury Mss.*

19. Geoffrey Dawson wrote to Salisbury on 7 Jan 1930, however, that he had a letter from Irwin 'some weeks ago' predicting that the Congress Party would 'have nothing to do with the London Conference and would generally kick over the rails'; and despite the support which *The Times* was to give Baldwin and the British Government over Indian policy he confessed '. . . I remember writing in *The Times* when the famous announcement was made that its authors were impenitent optimists – but it was backed by such strong consensus of expert opinion that it was useless to be critical.' *Salisbury Mss.*

20. Patrick Hannon was the M.P. for Moseley and a close associate of Lord Beaverbrook. For a full account of his activities in this connection see Hannon and Beaverbrook MSS in the House of Lords Record Office.

21. See *The Times* for July 1929.

22. I should like here to thank Mr Martin Gilbert for the enormous amount of help which he has given me in my attempt to understand Churchill's role in the Indian revolt.

23. For an interesting account of the divisions in the Conservative Party at a slightly earlier date, see M. Cowling, *The Impact of Labour* (Cambridge, 1971).

24. Crid. 4268, 1933.

25. *The Economist*, 1 Jul 1933, quoted in Neville Thompson, *The Anti-Appeasers* (Oxford, 1971) p. 18.

26. Henry Pelling in his one-volume biography of Churchill comments on this facet of Churchill's character but does not really give any explanation for it. Henry Pelling, *Winston Churchill* (London, 1974).

27. See Churchill to Beaverbrook, 23 Sep 1930, *Beaverbrook Mss.* Churchill commented in the letter that in 1930 'we have written ourselves down as a second Naval Power, squandered our authority in Egypt, and brought India to a position when the miserable public take it as an open question whether we should not clear out of the country altogether.'

28. Pelling, op. cit. p. 404.

29. Pelling, op. cit., p. 347.

30. Lord Lloyd's comments are taken from Viscount Lee of Fareham, *A Good Innings*, ed. Alan Clark (London, 1974); for Sydenham's letter see Sydenham to Salisbury, 23 Mar 1930, *Salisbury Mss.*

31. Cmd 3568.

32. Quoted in *The Times*, 11 Jun 1930.

33. See the draft of the telegram sent by Baldwin to Irwin, 3 Jul 1930, *Austen Chamberlain Mss*, AC.22/3/7.

34. Ibid.

35. Salisbury to Austen Chamberlain, 4 Jul 1930, *Austen Chamberlain Mss*, AC.22/3/10.

36. *Austen Chamberlain Mss*, AC.22/3/7.

37. Baldwin to Chamberlain, 9 Aug 1930, *Austen Chamberlain Mss*, AC.22/3/17.

38. Chamberlain to Baldwin, 11 Aug 1930, *Austen Chamberlain Mss*, AC.22/3/18.

39. H. C. Debs., 26 Jan 1931.

40. Ibid.

41. Ibid.

42. Churchill promised, however, not to let the feelings of friendship he had for Baldwin be altered by policy differences and he underlined his intention to continue giving Baldwin whatever aid was within his power to defeat the Socialist government. Baldwin replied that, though he regretted Churchill's decision, he thought it right in the circumstances and that their friendship was now too deeply rooted to be influenced by differences of opinion whether temporary or permanent.

43. Public meetings had already been held on the issue in the City of London and a series of mass demonstrations was by this stage being organised for the Manchester area.

44. I am treating this theme more extensively in my doctoral thesis. There is also much relevant material in the Stuart papers in the Bodleian Library Oxford.

45. For Montagu's attitude see E. J. Turner, 'The Fiscal Autonomy Convention', memorandum in the *Hirtzel Collection*, MSS, Eur., D.713; For Peel's see the telegram from the India Office to the Government of India, 16 Jan 1924, *Baldwin Mss*, vol. 193.

46. See Thomas Jones, *Whitehall Diary*, vol. II (Oxford, 1969) pp. 242–3.

47. 28 Jan 1931, P.R.O., CAB.23/66.

48. See for example Lord Lloyd's remarks on Japanese rivalry at the annual dinner in 1929 of the British Cotton Growing Association. *Cotton Factory Times*, 11 Oct 1929.

49. For a discussion of this incident see Henry Page Croft, *My Life of Strife* (London, 1948) p. 216 *et seq.*

50. *The Times*, 11 Mar 1933.

51. For the details of the discussion of the Cabinet's India Committee see CAB.27/520, which covers the forty-two meetings of the committee from 16 Mar 1932 to 12 Feb 1935. For Hoare's comments to the Viceroy see Templewood Collection and Templewood MSS in the India Office Library and the Cambridge University Library, respectively.

52. For the arguments for and against a single bill and the development of the timetable see P.R.O., CAB.27/520, meeting no. 2 (12 May 1932) and meeting no. 3 (26 May 1932).

53. See Lord Templewood, *Nine Troubled Years* (London, 1954) pp. 82–91 for a brief account of these difficulties.

54. Page Croft to Hoare, 4 Apr 1933, *Page Croft Mss*.

55. Most of the material relating to the U.B.I. is based on the Thompson Collection in the India Office Library.

56. Lord Butler, *The Art of the Possible* (London, 1971).

57. I should like to take this opportunity of thanking Mr Patrick Donner for discussing the India Defence League with me.

58. Draft (undated) of the comments by Sir John Thompson on a memorandum on the functions of local committees, *Thompson Collection*, MSS. Eur., F.137/5.

59. *The Times*, 1 Mar 1933.

60. Knox to Page Croft, 6 Oct 1934, *Page Croft Mss*.

61. For a discussion of the changes and the explicit recognition of the need to accommodate Chamberlain see P.R.O. CAB.27/520, meeting no. 34 (12 Apr 1934). Also the discussions in the *Salisbury Mss* and the *Austen Chamberlain Mss*.

62. The Earl of Lytton, *Antony* (London, 1935) p. 355.

63. The only general work dealing with the decolonisation process as a whole is R. Von Albertini, *Decolonisation* (New York, 1971); on the British side two works are of particular interest for this later period: D. Goldsworthy, *Colonial Issues in British Politics* (Oxford, 1971) and J. D. B. Miller, *Survey of Commonwealth Affairs: Problems of Expansion and Attrition* (London, 1974).

6 The Politics of Violence

JOHN STEVENSON

The unemployed did not quietly suffer their degradation and poverty. They were hungry; their wives and children were hungry; they marched on the streets with mighty protest demonstrations, and savage battles were fought from day to day in one town after another against the police who were ordered to suppress these militant activities. If history is to be truly recorded our future historians must include this feature of the 'Hungry Thirties'.

W. Hannington[1]

Prior to 1914, periods of economic depression in Britain had often been accompanied by serious social unrest and radical political agitation. It was not surprising, therefore, that the onset of mass unemployment in the interwar years, and especially in the thirties, seemed to many people to pose a major threat to the political stability of the country. Amongst these contemporaries was Harold Macmillan, who considered that after 1931 'something like a revolutionary situation' had developed.[2] A similar view was expressed by Stafford Cripps at the Labour Party Conference in 1931 when he declared his belief that 'the one thing that is not inevitable now is gradualness.'[3] Many modern historians have taken up this theme: Professor Marwick, for example, has characterised the thirties as a decade in which 'Men of moderate political opinions, or of none, began to talk the language of revolutionary violence.'[4] With the sources now at our disposal, however, it is possible to assess more clearly the actual threat of a substitution of 'revolutionary violence' for the conventional procedures of parliamentary politics. Up to now it has been the activities of the British

146

Union of Fascists, Mosley's blackshirts, which have occupied the attention of historians concerned with this problem. But in the worst years of the depression, in the immediate aftermath of the financial and political crises of 1931, it was not the blackshirts who seemed to offer the most alarming prospect of organised political violence, for their major campaign of marches and meetings came after 1933; rather it was the programme of 'hunger marches' and demonstrations organised by the most important left-wing movement of the unemployed in the thirties, the National Unemployed Workers' Movement.[5] The intention here is to examine the role and attitude of the N.U.W.M. in the unemployed demonstrations of the early thirties and, in particular, its part in the largest national demonstration of the unemployed in that period, the 'National Hunger March' of 1932.

The N.U.W.M. had been founded in 1921 as a militant organisation to campaign on behalf of the unemployed. From the beginning it was dominated by Communists, many of them drawn from the engineering unions. Its national organiser and effective leader was Wal Hannington, a tool maker and former shop steward from London. Its history during the twenties was one of persistent agitation for relief work and improved benefits, using the techniques of mass demonstration and hunger marches. For a time in the mid-twenties the N.U.W.M. was recognised by the T.U.C., but by the end of the decade both the T.U.C. and the Labour Party regarded it with considerable suspicion as a Communist Party organisation with which they could have no .official dealings. None the less the N.U.W.M. retained an influence out of all proportion to its actual membership and its support from traditional labour leaders, derived from its almost exclusive championship of the rights of the unemployed as a whole and the rapid worsening of the unemployment situation after 1929.

By August 1931 the number of registered unemployed had reached a total of almost two and three-quarter millions, primarily concentrated in the old industrial areas of coal mining, cotton clothmaking, iron and steel production, and shipbuilding. By 1931 it was clear that there was considerable discontent amongst some sections of the unemployed, not only because they were out of work, but also because of the rates and operation of unemployment relief. Agitation on the issue of relief rates and their administration provided the background to the riots and disturbances of 1931–2; the introduction of the means test provided the immediate context for the national hunger march of 1932. The government's attitude to unemployment relief was dictated by the view that the Unemployment Insurance Fund, out of which unemployment benefit was paid, should be self-supporting. By the autumn of 1931 the fund was already deeply in debt because of the unexpectedly heavy incidence of unemployment during the twenties. As a result, when the National Government came to make its round of economy measures in the aftermath of the financial crisis of August 1931, one of the main targets was the level of unemployment benefit, which was reduced by an average of 10 per cent whilst the levels of contributions were raised. It was at this point that the government introduced the means test. This limited the period for which unemployment benefit could as of right be drawn to twenty-six weeks. After this period those requiring relief had to apply for 'transitional payments' which were financed by a special grant from the Exchequer and paid through the local Employment Exchange. But before qualifying for these transitional payments the applicant had to undergo a means test carried out by the local Poor Law authority, the Public Assistance Committee, who would then notify the Employment Exchange of the circumstances and the rate of relief which should be given, up to a ceiling. Any form of income, savings, or possessions could be set against the scale of relief and of necessity the operation demanded a close scrutiny of each family's financial circumstances.[6] Not surprisingly a great deal of ill-feeling and resentment was generated amongst the unemployed, not only at the procedures adopted, but also at the levels of relief which were eventually granted. In Lancashire only 16 per cent of the unemployed received the full level of transitional payment whilst a third were disallowed relief altogether. By January 1932 over 900,000 people were registering for transitional payments, and complaints about the operation of the means test began to become increasingly common.[7]

In this context the N.U.W.M. under the leadership of Wal Hannington began to have a serious impact upon affairs. By the autumn of 1931 the N.U.W.M. was the only group which openly urged militant action by the unemployed in the face of the means test. The Labour Party and T.U.C. were opposed to the setting up of organisations of the unemployed as a whole because individual trade unions claimed to represent their own unemployed members. At the same time the still firmly-held belief in financial orthodoxy inhibited many Labour Party and trade union leaders from campaigning actively against measures which seemed to be dictated by a world-wide crisis. Equally the undoubted Communist orientation of the N.U.W.M. meant that it was shunned by the official leadership of the Labour movement, at least at the national level. The actual position of the N.U.W.M. in relation to Comintern was ambiguous. The organisation received instructions and directives from Moscow; nonetheless it retained considerable autonomy and frequently drew the condemnation of Comintern for its 'trade union legalism', when instead of pursuing a policy of confrontation and mass polarisation it concentrated upon dealing with the technicalities of unemployment relief and particular cases of hardship. But during the worsening situation of 1931 the N.U.W.M. increased its membership from 20,000 to 37,000 within six months and under pressure from Moscow set out to build up the movement through a programme of demonstrations and marches.[8] As a result the autumn and winter of 1931 witnessed a number of clashes between police and unemployed demonstrators, and this marked the beginning of the most serious phase of such violence in the thirties.[9]

Disturbances continued into 1932 as the N.U.W.M. kept up a programme of marches and demonstrations against local Public Assistance Committees. These were usually aimed at securing relief work, an improvement of relief scales, and the mitigation or abolition of the means test. As a result several violent clashes occurred between the police and N.U.W.M. demonstrators. In London the Chief Commissioner of Metropolitan Police banned the N.U.W.M. from holding its meetings outside Labour Exchanges and when this order was defied there were persistent disturbances as the police attempted to clear the demonstrators away with baton charges. In January 1932 fighting broke out between the police and demonstrators in Keighley and Glasgow, and three days later army reservists were called out to protect the town hall at Rochdale against unemployed demonstrators. Further disturbances took place in the spring and summer of 1932, reaching a new climax in September when very severe disturbances broke out in Glasgow, Belfast and on Merseyside, especially in Birkenhead where there were several days of rioting.[10] These clashes led to a number of questions in the House of Commons: two men had been killed in Belfast and there were complaints about police behaviour in Birkenhead. By the beginning of October further clashes in London forced the Home Secretary, Sir John Gilmour, to clarify the government's attitude towards the situation. In the House of Commons on 19 October, Gilmour, in reply to a question about disturbances in London on the previous day, commented:

> I want the House to realise that the demonstration yesterday was no spontaneous movement. It is quite clear . . . that the National Unemployed Workers' Movement, a Communist organisation, or in the main a Communist organisation has been the root, and the instigator, of these difficulties. It is well known as a Communist organisation, but its membership is not entirely confined to Communists. There are some quite respectable and decent men who are members of it.

He remarked upon the 'very material connection' between Moscow and the demonstrators and the similarity in aims expressed by Comintern, the *Daily Worker*, and the N.U.W.M. In particular he singled out for attention a passage from the *Daily Worker* for 18 February which stated: 'By mass struggle in the streets and by tremendous pressure on the public assistance committees we must compel the authorities to abandon the operation of the means test.'

Gilmour replied to criticism of police tactics in the same vein. Accepting that the dispersal of crowds by baton charges had become necessary in some cases, he said:

> On the other hand, it is worthy of noting that at Birkenhead the technique of street fighting which has been advocated by the Communist International has been considerably developed. For instance, the police found at Birkenhead that trip wires – barbed wire in one case – had been stretched across the road about a foot from the ground, lamps had been extinguished, and manhole covers removed. These examples which I quote are constantly referred to with approval in the Communist Press.[11]

These remarks were of particular relevance because whilst he was speaking the N.U.W.M. was in the midst of its greatest effort of its campaign of 1931–2. Eighteen contingents, making up what the N.U.W.M. called the 'Great National Hunger March against the Means Test', were making their way towards London for 27 October where, with the unemployed of the capital, they were to present a mass petition of a million signatures against the means test and undertake what *The Unemployed Special* described as 'an invasion of Westminster'. The Scottish contingent had already been on the road for three weeks when the Home Secretary spoke in the Commons on the 19 October.[12] Other contingents had only just started off. The Norwich constabulary described the orderly departure of the East Anglian marchers on 16 October; they bore a placard of a human skeleton with the words, 'Mr. Chamberlain says we must cut to the bone.'[13] In all about 2000 marchers were involved, mainly drawn from the N.U.W.M. The T.U.C. and the Labour Party officially opposed the march because of its N.U.W.M. sponsorship, but at the local level the marchers often received sympathetic support from Labour supporters and trade unionists, as well as from some purely philanthropic bodies. The government was highly suspicious of the march; Gilmour referred to the petition as only the 'ostensible object' of the demonstration. This seemed justified when the progress of the contingents through England was attended by a certain amount of violence, even before they reached London. The N.U.W.M. had decided to demand overnight accommodation in the workhouses of the towns through which they passed, but were not prepared to accept the normal 'casual' relief which was given to vagrants and other casual users of the workhouse. As a result there were a number of incidents when the marchers claimed a better provision from local workhouses than the strict letter of the regulations said they were entitled to. At Burton-on-Trent on 17 October there was a tense confrontation in the town centre between the women's contingent, supported by local unemployed demonstrators, and the police because of the attempt to impose upon the marchers the 'casual' regulations. Eventually the marchers were allowed into the workhouse on more or less special terms. At Stratford on 20 October the Lancashire contingent was involved in a serious disturbance with the heavily reinforced local constabulary in similar circumstances. When questioned about the government's attitude to the marchers, the Home Secretary refuted claims that he had given special instructions to the local police forces to deal harshly with them. He made two points: first, that he had no direct responsibility for law and order in the localities and secondly, that both he and the Commissioner of Police in London would use every means to avoid clashes, for it 'is not our desire to cause hardship'. In fact, on 29 September the Home Office had advised local police forces and Health authorities to maintain strictly the principle of 'casual' relief and advised Chief Officers of Police to make 'all necessary arrangements' to deal with any disturbances which might arise from enforcing these regulations.[14]

The somewhat tougher official line taken by the Home Secretary was symptomatic of the seriousness with which the march was viewed by the government. In fact, judging from the thoroughness of their preparations to receive the marchers in the capital, they appeared to be quite seriously alarmed. The Metropolitan Police sent out requests to local constabularies for information about the marchers, particularly about those with a record of involvement in disturbances or demonstrations. In response, lists of prominent marchers were sent in with descriptions, details of past criminal or political activities, and in one case with photographs to ease recognition of the marchers when they reached London. A fairly typical entry from the Glamorgan constabulary read:

> T.W.P. * * * 28 years of age, height 5'6", brown hair, brown eyes, dark complexion. A single man and dresses respectably. He is a very dangerous agitator and is very defiant when he has come into contact with the Police. He refuses to acknowledge any kind of law and order and has been convicted on several occasions for assaulting the Police.[15]

In addition the Metropolitan Police were supplied with information about the behaviour and attitude of the marchers en route. The Chief Constable of Oxford reported on 24 October that the 230 men of the Lancashire contingent had behaved in an orderly fashion whilst in the city, but he believed that they were armed with cudgels which they had kept hidden during their stay.[16] In addition the N.U.W.M. was thoroughly infiltrated by police informers who kept up a steady flow of information to the authorities, which found its way into the Metropolitan Police files.[17] According to this information the N.U.W.M. were expecting the demonstrations in London to be the largest ever known, and after rallies in Hyde Park the plan was to present the petition to Parliament on 1 November. Some of the information was very alarmist: there was talk of the police being sympathetic towards the marchers and of the marchers arming themselves with a variety of weapons, including darts, vitriol, cudgels, and firearms.[18] On the basis of this information the Metropolitan Police prepared for the worst. They were determined to prevent any mass lobby of the House of Commons and were prepared to enforce strictly a prohibition on mass demonstrations within a mile of Westminster.

The police prepared for nearly 2000 men, including mounted detachments, to be on duty, with a reserve of 600 'specials'. The Coldstream Guards were held in readiness in case they were required. What most exercised the mind of the authorities was the prospect that the ranks of the marchers would be swollen once they arrived in London. One informant had already told the police that the N.U.W.M. were confident of having enough people to force a way into Parliament if necessary.[19] The authorities were aided by the attitude of the media; for example, the B.B.C. offered to broadcast messages dissuading people from attending the demonstrations if this became necessary. The press largely ignored the march, both *The Times* and the *Manchester Guardian* made no mention of it at all in the week preceding its arrival in London.[20]

Apprehensions of this kind seemed borne out by the immediate background to the arrival of the marchers. On 24 October there were clashes with the police at County Hall, Westminster, when a deputation of London unemployed organised by the N.U.W.M. presented a series of demands for improved relief scales and work schemes at T.U.C. rates.[21] On 25 October a speaker at a meeting in Hackney claimed that riots had forced concessions on relief scales in other parts of the country. In addition several handbills had been found in London, asking the police to display solidarity with the unemployed to defeat cuts in their own pay, but ending with an ominous pledge that 'If you attack us, we shall know how to defend ourselves, how to fight back.'[22] However, the contingents arrived peacefully in London on the evening of 26 October and were accommodated in a number of institutions and halls in the inner suburbs. On the morning of 27 October the contingents marched to attend a welcoming rally in Hyde Park, accompanied by large numbers of police. Shortly after two o'clock the marchers and their supporters began to arrive in the park until several thousand people filled it. Hannington estimated the number at 100,000, though the police report claimed there were between 10,000 and 25,000. Nonetheless it was an impressive number and all went well until about four in the afternoon when fighting broke out around the Marble Arch entrance to the park. Hannington in his account of the disturbances blamed the inexperienced special constables for starting the incident, but the police report claimed that they had acted to control a group of 500 or more who had broken away from the main body. The exact truth is almost impossible to discern, but the result was a confused mêlée in which both mounted and foot police were called in to disperse the crowds. Several baton charges were made and twelve people arrested before the fighting died down between four-thirty and five o'clock. According to police reports seventy-seven people were injured, nine of them policemen and the rest demonstrators.[23] Three days later on Sunday, 30 October, there was a very large demonstration in Trafalgar Square, probably involving more people than the Hyde Park demonstration. Though there was sporadic fighting on the fringe of the crowd as the police tried to clear roadways on the edge of the square, the meeting proceeded without major interruption.[24]

The major event, to which these demonstrations had only been the preliminary, was the presentation of the N.U.W.M.'s million-signature petition asking for the abolition of the means test, the abolition of the Anomalies Act, and the restoration of the 10 per cent cut in unemployment benefits. The tactics in regard to presenting the petition were later described by Hannington in the following terms:

> On achieving this target [a million signatures] we had decided not to ask a Member of Parliament to present the petition but to claim the right for it to be presented by a deputation from the Hunger Marchers. We claimed this right under an ancient Law entitling Commoners to appear for such purpose at the Bar of the House of Commons.[25]

The Special Branch's 'Precis of Further Information re Hunger Marchers' was in no doubt that Tuesday, 1 November, was to be the 'big day' when the N.U.W.M. intended to force their way to the House of Commons and present their petition. As they had been forbidden from petitioning en masse, it was expected that this would cause violent clashes with the police and informers forecast 'real bloodshed on that day'. It was reported that the marchers would use diversionary tactics to break through the police cordon around the House, by creating disturbances in restaurants and in the suburbs 'to keep the police on the move'. Reports claimed that seamen and dockers in the East End had been canvassed and asked to attend the demonstration, bringing with them their hooks for handling bales. At least 15–20,000 were expected at the demonstration and the Special Branch warned that if the petition was refused or received an unsatisfactory answer, 'there will be much window smashing, looting, etc.'[26]

There was serious alarm about what was going to happen and

the *Daily Telegraph* was in little doubt about who was to blame:

> How long is London to be subjected to the indignity of having
> its police forces – regular and special – mobilised to deal with
> the Communist HANNINGTON and his Marchers, but in reality
> with HANNINGTON and the revolutionary riff-raff of London?
> Ninety per cent of the Marchers may well be dupes, pawns in a
> Communist game directed by the master-intriguers of Moscow
> . . . The abolition of the Means Test is a pretext. The present-
> ation of a Petition is a blind. Hannington, the professional or-
> ganiser of these marches, is conceited indeed, if he supposes
> that his communist riff-raff could make a revolution, but that
> they could do incalculable damage by loot and pillage in an
> hour or two of mob excitement is undeniable, and that
> bloodshed would ensue is certain.'[27]

The Times had already made its position clear about the march
when under a headline of 'Liberty or Licence', it asked:

> Is there to be no limit to the right of the workless to hamper the
> workers? The evil will grow if it is not checked. There are plenty
> of ways in which legitimate discontent may be rationally
> expressed. The government must seriously consider whether
> the spurious importance which these mass marches are bound
> to be given at home or abroad should not be countered by
> special restrictive measures.[28]

On the morning of the first *The Times* urged the marchers to go
home at their own expense and to stop being 'the dupes of political
propagandists who believe in violence as the proper instrument of
policy'. The *Manchester Guardian* took a similar line; it accused the
Communist Party of 'exploiting the unemployed'.[29]

The N.U.W.M. was not only confronted with a largely hostile
press; it had very little support from Labour members of Parliament and was completely cut off from official T.U.C. backing.
Even the few sympathetic Labour members were finally alienated
by the N.U.W.M.'s refusal to present the petition through the
normal procedures and their attempt to conduct a mass petition of
the House of Commons. On the morning of 1 November the police
acted. They raided the headquarters of the N.U.W.M. at Great
Russell Street, seized a large number of documents, and arrested
Wal Hannington. At Bow Street police court he was charged with
'Attempting to cause disaffection among members of the Metropolitan Police contrary to the Police Act, 1919'. The evidence

against him consisted of notes taken by the police of his speech at Trafalgar Square on 30 October when he had urged the police to refuse to act against the hunger marchers. Almost more important than the charge itself, bail was refused, and he was taken immediately to Brixton prison.[30] Nonetheless the march organisers went ahead with the plans for the evening, and by the late afternoon demonstrators were moving towards Westminster. But as they reached the vicinity of the House they were met by both mounted and foot police who broke up the large bodies of demonstrators using the main streets. By about seven o'clock something like 3000 demonstrators had arrived in Trafalgar Square via side streets. In the meantime the mass petition, which was the point of all this activity, had been taken by taxi and lodged by the N.U.W.M. leadership in Charing Cross railway station cloakroom so that it could easily be taken to the House of Commons. By now the crowd had gathered around the station entrance and the police had made several baton charges already in an attempt to disperse them. The petition, which was in several large bundles, was being moved out of the station by some of the leaders of the N.U.W.M., including Emrys Llewellyn and Sid Elias, when the Superintendent of 'E' division of the Metropolitan Police approached them and said, 'If you take this petition through the streets with the crowd in their present condition it will be likely to provoke a riot.' The Superintendent admitted that he did this to gain time until his superiors were aware of what was happening. The Superintendent then directed Emrys Llewellyn to return the petition to the cloakroom, which was done, though 'with some demur'. He reported, however, overhearing some of the committee saying that they could easily bring it out again when the police had gone. This was not to be, for about an hour later the Superintendent entered the cloakroom and took possession of the petition, which was immediately taken to Bow Street. With this, the focal point of the demonstration if not of the whole march had been frustrated. It remained to be seen whether the police's 'arrest' of the petition would create the disturbance which they had sought to avoid by seizing it. Fierce fighting broke in several different places as news of the arrest of the petition spread. The laconic police statements tell their own story: '. . . more of the disorderly element returned to Trafalgar Square and it became necessary to disperse them . . .'; 'Westminster had to be cleared . . .'; 'The West London contingent of about five hundred was broken up by police as it was about to become disorderly in Edgware Road.' At nine o'clock the police called out their reserves to deal with several disturbances, some of them far from the centre of the city as Shepherds Bush, where a crowd of 800 was reported to have been dispersed at eleven o'clock. A determined attempt to force a way across Westminster Bridge was prevented only with difficulty by the police. By ten o'clock there was sporadic fighting going on in Parliament Square, Whitehall, Trafalgar Square, the Strand, Charing Cross Road, Victoria Street, along the Embankment and on Westminster Bridge Road. The area was not entirely quiet until about one-thirty in the morning by which time about forty people had been arrested and about fifty injured.[31]

Following these events the marchers prepared to leave London on 5 November. The petition was reclaimed by the N.U.W.M. on the fourth and a receipt signed for it by an N.U.W.M. member at Bow Street. The contingents of marchers were escorted to their respective railway stations by the police and left for their destinations without incident. A number of court cases remained to be settled in the aftermath of the demonstrations. The most important was of Hannington himself, who was tried at Bow Street on 8 November and convicted on the charge of causing disaffection, for which he received three months' imprisonment.[32] A number of other offenders were dealt with in the days following the demonstrations. Four men were given six months for their part in the Hyde Park disturbances, one three months, and two others small fines. In addition five men were given six months for their part in the Trafalgar Square disturbances of 1 November.[33] The police had also drawn up charges of conspiracy against three men who were accused of trying to convey to Hyde Park a van loaded with sticks with nails driven through them. Information was given against two of the men by an ex-I.R.A. man from Manchester who had turned police informer after his arrest in 1921. A devout Catholic himself, he claimed they were 'Communists and atheists' and that he had heard one of them make 'violent and inflammatory' speeches in Manchester. The police obviously hoped for a conviction on these men, but they were disappointed. The solicitors reported that the men appeared 'before a bench not very happily consisting of Mr. P***** the Chairman, and two other justices with, we believe, strong labour tendencies'. Only one of the men was convicted, but on a lesser charge of vagrancy, for which he received two months hard labour. The solicitors commented that 'it is at least a very good thing to have obtained a conviction of this man, Q*****, as he is undoubtedly a very hot-headed agitator.'[34]

It is now appropriate to try to put the events described above into some sort of perspective. The 'Great National Hunger March' of October–November 1932 marked the culmination of the most violent phase of demonstrations on the issues of unemployment and unemployment relief in the 1930s. But in some respects one of the most surprising things about this campaign was that it was not more vehement. The whole phase of agitation in 1931–2, mainly conducted by the N.U.W.M., is indeed remarkable not for its scale and viciousness but for its lack of it given the contemporary descriptions of social conditions in the depressed areas and the undoubted hardships caused both by unemployment and the operation of relief, especially the means test. The issue of how the unemployed in general perceived their condition and their consequent attitudes towards it is too great a one to be dealt with fully here. It is plain, however, that militant and violent discontent was never very widespread on the issue of unemployment or the means test. Various general explanations have been put forward for this. W. G. Runciman has suggested that the overriding fatalism of the unemployed came from a sense of powerlessness in the face of a crisis which seemed almost beyond human control. Much of the literature of the depression expressed this view; the titles speak for themselves: 'The Riddle of Unemployment', 'What is Unemployment?', 'Is Unemployment Inevitable?' and so on. Moreover, these were views which were largely shared by the traditional leaders of working-class communities, the Labour Party and the trade unions. Runciman also suggests that because whole communities suffered in common, there was less of the ill-feeling and resentment which might have been evident had the unemployed felt themselves to be 'starving in the midst of plenty'.[35] Thus, the very concentration of unemployment in the old industrial areas acted as a check upon the expression of violent discontent. A. J. P. Taylor, on the other hand, has stressed the point that such discontent as there was, concentrated upon the issue of relief scales rather than anything more fundamental and that the presence of basic relief at all, however minimal, prevented the erection of barricades in Britain between the wars.[36] Both these points are credible and help to explain why the N.U.W.M. was never able to become a mass movement; on Hannington's own admission the organisation never captured more than 10 per cent of the total number of unemployed at any one time. He added his own reasons for this, for he believed that relatively few workers were prepared to regard unemployment as anything other than a temporary predicament and therefore took no steps to organise themselves.[37] Above all the N.U.W.M. found itself unable to break the dominance of traditional labour organisations in the depressed areas, and the hostility and suspicion with which it was regarded by both the Labour Party and the T.U.C. meant that it was fighting an uphill struggle against entrenched attitudes and influence.

Thus even when the N.U.W.M. marched they did so not in thousands, with the backing of trade unions and other representatives of organised labour, but in contingents of a hundred or more each, as a rather suspect minority organisation. The total number of marchers involved in 1932 was about 2000, impressive in its way, but only a fraction of the numbers which might have been commanded with the support of organised labour. Though the marchers staged two fairly large demonstrations in London between 27 October and 1 November 1932, at which probably 25–30,000 people attended, many of their demonstrations were much smaller, and were certainly well below the figures which Hannington claimed. If the whole campaign of 1931–2 is examined, the question again arises, of not why there was so much violence, but why so little. In all the N.U.W.M. campaign over the two years led to about thirty disturbances, mainly of a very minor scale of fighting and a few scuffles. The most serious in terms of casualties were the disturbances in Belfast in October 1932 when two people were killed. Elsewhere casualties were of a lesser degree. During the demonstrations in London in October and November of 1932 there were probably a handful of serious injuries, and a number of minor ones. The total estimate of the damage compiled by the police came to just over £200, mainly consisting of broken windows, one of which alone cost £120.[38] This was scarcely violence on a revolutionary scale. It is worth, too, looking at the intentions of the N.U.W.M. in so far as they can be determined from police evidence and the statements of Wal Hannington. There can be little doubt that the N.U.W.M. mounted a determined and militant campaign in 1931–2 against the means test and for better relief scales. In doing so they were prepared to defy the law when they saw it as obstructing their purpose; indeed, they saw this as a means of drawing attention to their cause. As Hannington himself said in the dock at Bow Street at his hearing:

I have led the unemployed in what might be described as an agitational war against starvation. I believe that is why I am in this dock this morning, and if my crime is that I have led the unemployed efficiently in the war against starvation, then I am quite proud to admit my guilt in that respect.[39]

But how much further did the intentions of Hannington and the N.U.W.M. go? On the evidence, it does not seem very far. Even the most alarmist police informers confined their speculations to the prospect that the N.U.W.M. might undertake a mass lobby of Parliament. Moreover, what is more interesting is the attitude of the N.U.W.M. itself, for throughout its public statements and Hannington's memoirs it is plain that the public face of the N.U.W.M. was militant, but non-violent. In every case, Hannington and other participants in hunger marches put the blame for violence upon the police. This might seem an obvious thing to do, but it must be remembered that in some countries a virtue would have been made out of violence in the circumstances of mass unemployment. Rather the N.U.W.M. chose to act within the traditional British restraints upon the use of overt violence. In that respect they were far more constitutionally minded than Mosley's blackshirts. Moreover, their use of the monster petition to Parliament speaks volumes for their acceptance of traditional, indeed almost antiquated modes of political expression.

The events of 1 November 1932 bear some remarkable ressemblances to the situation faced by the Chartist leaders at Kennington Common in 1848. Like them the N.U.W.M. had put its faith in a mass petition to Parliament, backed up by a massive show of force by their supporters, but it was also faced with a very similar dilemma. When it came to the point of forcing their way to the House of Commons in the face of strong opposition by the authorities, they like the Chartists declined and allowed their petition to be returned to Charing Cross Station cloakroom and ultimately to be removed. Police records themselves provide further evidence that the N.U.W.M. were unprepared for a violent challenge to the authorities on 1 November. When Hannington was arrested a mass of documents were seized; amongst them were the responses of the various contingents to the idea of carrying sticks during the demonstrations. Of the contingents only three were in favour of carrying sticks or cudgels, even after the violence of 27 October. The general feeling was that they would not carry sticks on 1 November but have them nearby for use if they were attacked.[40] This essentially passive reaction by contingents of marchers who were supposed to contain some of the most violent and dangerous agitators in the country makes it clear that there was no revolutionary intent in the events of October to November 1932. Thus in common with many earlier movements the N.U.W.M. could be said to have fallen prey to the 'politics of violence'. They were already in the position in autumn 1932 of being accused of stirring up violence and disaffection. They had two alternatives. They could cold-bloodedly embrace that course of action but risk repression by the authorities and the alienation of moderate support. On the other hand, they could act as they in fact did, militantly but cautiously, and risk being ineffective. Arguably the N.U.W.M. was in the worst of all possible worlds during its campaign. It was regarded not only by conservative voices, but also by many Labour supporters, as being a subversive organisation, so that support was consistently withheld from it by the official leadership of the Labour Party and the trade union movement. At the same time it received constant and often disruptive attention from the police: it was kept under constant surveillance both by the Special Branch and by informers inside the organisation, its leader was eventually arrested at a critical point in the campaign, its demonstrations were certainly dealt with in a fairly tough manner, and its offices were searched and its documents and papers confiscated, an action for which the N.U.W.M. was later awarded damages in court. The N.U.W.M. was branded with being the cause of the violence which attended the demonstrations, something which was unlikely to win them much moderate support, but a week of sporadic and rather futile violence in the capital still left the stated purpose of the march uncompleted, the presentation of the mass petition. Ironically, it was because the N.U.W.M. leadership had no wish to precipitate a wholesale battle around the House of Commons that the petition had not been presented. In fact, the N.U.W.M. had fallen between two stools; they had been unable to achieve their purpose by overawing the authorities by a show of force and determination; nor had they been able to win general sympathy for a peaceful and disciplined series of demonstrations.

It is hard to resist the conclusion that the N.U.W.M. hunger march of 1932 was something of a failure. None of the points on the petition were adopted as a result of the march and, although the march received publicity, a good deal of it had been unfavourable. In this the N.U.W.M. suffered because of its isolation from official T.U.C. or Labour Party support. As a result the N.U.W.M. had no significant group of M.P.s within Westminster to turn their agitation into effective action. The results of the 1932 march stand out in striking contrast to the later agitation against the Unemployment Act of 1934. Here, an Act which set out ostensibly to raise relief levels by centralising the functions of the local Public Assistance Committees, in fact reduced many recipients' relief scale. Uproar resulted not only outside Parliament but inside it, where according to one commentator 'the Government was under heavier parliamentary criticism from all sections of opinion than at any time in the inter-war period.'[41] Michael Foot has described it as 'the biggest explosion of popular anger in the whole inter-war period, second only to the General Strike itself'.[42] This agitation was effective, a standstill order was introduced and nobody's unemployment relief was reduced. The reasons why this agitation was successful, and that of the N.U.W.M. in autumn 1932 was not, are significant. In 1934-5 the N.U.W.M. marched and demonstrated as it had in 1932, but this time there were also demonstrations and marches organised by the Labour Party and the trade unions. Moreover, there were M.P.s on both sides of the House of Commons who were prepared to take up the issue of the Unemployment Act. This was a much broader agitation which mobilised a good deal of moderate opinion, both inside and outside Westminster. As a result the agitation remained 'respectable', organising demonstrations and marches but without the clashes with the police seen two years earlier. The effect was, if anything, even more formidable. *The Times* spoke of the 'spirit of 1926' being abroad once again.[43] Because much middle ground was captured and moderate supporters were not alienated by violence, the agitation proved effective. It was able to channel its agitation into parliamentary action, in a way which the N.U.W.M. had been quite unable to in 1932, through the M.P.s for the depressed areas. The success of this agitation and the failure of the N.U.W.M. showed clearly how violence was no substitute for influence in the context of British politics in the 1930s. Extraparliamentary agitation was very weak unless it could secure the support of groups like organised labour and effectively translate popular pressure into votes within the House of Commons.

It is instructive, too, to look at the N.U.W.M.'s activities in comparison with the most famous of the hunger marches, the Jarrow march of 1936. Many people still regard it as the epitome of all hunger marches and it is frequently referred to as the symbol of the plight of the unemployed in the thirties. But in many ways this is rather curious. The Jarrow March consisted of about 200

people. It took place at the same time as a national march by the
N.U.W.M. which was much larger in terms of numbers, but
which attracted far less attention. There were many reasons for
this. One was that Jarrow seemed to encapsulate the desolation of
a one-industry town which was crippled by the closure of its ship-
yard. Its unemployment rate was one of the highest in the country,
though not the highest. Moreover, it had in Ellen Wilkinson a
public relations representative of genius. But it does in no way
belittle the Jarrow Marchers to suggest that they captured public
sympathy at least as much for the ultra-respectable way in which
the march was planned and conducted as for anything else. From
early in October 1936 Ellen Wilkinson, with other town officials,
was in contact with the Metropolitan Police, making arrangements for the marchers to present their petition to the House of
Commons. The march organisers accepted the stringent conditions laid down by the police that they should not undertake a
mass lobby but attend in small groups to individual M.P.s whose
names had to be given in advance. Because the marchers were prepared to accept these conditions, the Home Office ruled that the
marchers would be allowed to have tea in the House, 'since the
Marchers show every sign of being orderly, it would be a good way
of encouraging and placating them.'[44] Moreover, the Special
Branch was encouraged by the 'non-political' nature of the march
and reported that the N.U.W.M. and Communist Party had
tried, unsuccessfully, to gain the Jarrow Marchers' co-operation.
It was even reported that one man had been expelled from the
march en route because he was a Communist. Equally when the
marchers arrived in London they refused to allow any Communist
speakers to share their platform.[45] One result was that the Home
Office allowed Movietone News to take some film of the Jarrow
Marchers' rally in Hyde Park, when they had always refused permission to do this in the past.[46] The Jarrow Marchers peacefully
attended the House of Commons, were entertained to tea by sympathetic M.P.s and taken on a sight-seeing trip down the river.
When they returned they found that their petition had been presented in their absence.[47] Nonetheless the Jarrow Marchers
scored a tremendous publicity success, their march and the plight
of the town drew much greater press coverage than the much
larger rally of the N.U.W.M. a week later at which the police estimated that 12,000 attended.[48] The Jarrow Marchers became a
folk legend, and they did so at least in part because they obeyed
the rules. As a result they received much sympathy from the

media and the 'establishment', and through them from the public at large.

In conclusion, it is clear that there was little chance of a revolutionary situation developing from the organisers of the unemployed during the thirties. Partly this was because the N.U.W.M. was unable at any time to command the sort of support which might have made it a really significant force in British politics. At the same time its isolation from both the Labour Party and the T.U.C. meant that it was deprived of the sort of grass-roots support and access to the House of Commons which would have enabled it to be more effective. Moreover, looking at the way the N.U.W.M. acted in 1932, one can easily understand why a certain element of disenchantment was evinced in Moscow at their behaviour and attitude. Even when the N.U.W.M. set out on its campaign of mass demonstration and protest against the means test there is little evidence of serious revolutionary intent. On the other hand, such violence as occurred was sufficient to taint the N.U.W.M. as a dangerous and possibly subversive organisation. In fact, the N.U.W.M. seems to have had no clearly worked out attitude to the use of political violence in the context of the thirties and as a result they were more often the losers than the beneficiaries in the 'politics of violence'.

Notes

1. W. Hannington, *Never on Our Knees* (London, 1967) p. 246.

2. H. Macmillan, *Winds of Change* (London, 1966) p. 288.

3. *Report of the 31st Annual Conference of the Labour Party*, p. 205.

4. A. Marwick, *Britain in the Age of Total War* (London, 1970) p. 226.

5. See R. Benewick, *The Fascist Movement in Britain* (London, 1972) and 'The Threshold of Violence', R. Benewick and T. Smith, *Direct Action and Democratic Politics*; for official attitudes to the 'hunger marches' see M. Turnbull, 'The Attitude of Government and Administration towards the "Hunger Marches" of the 1920s–1930s', *Journal of Social Policy*, vol. 2 (1973).

6. B. B. Gilbert, *British Social Policy, 1914–1939* (London, 1970).

7. See N. Branson and M. Heinemann, *Britain in the Nineteen Thirties* (London, 1971) Chapter 3.

8. H. Pelling, *The British Communist Party* (London, 1958) pp. 63–5.

9. W. Hannington, *Unemployed Struggles 1919–1936* (London, 1936), pp. 219–43.

10. Ibid., pp. 230–43.

11. *Hansard*, fifth series, vol. 269, cols 275–7.

12. Hannington, op. cit.; *The Unemployed Special* (Sep 1932).

13. Public Record Office, Metropolitan Police Records (hereafter Mepol), ser. 2, vol. 3064, item 25N, information from Norwich constabulary.

14. *Hansard*, op. cit., cols 279–80; W. Hannington, op. cit., pp. 243–68; Home

Office Records, ser. 158, vol. 28, p. 167.

15. Mepol 2, 3064, item 28A, Commissioner Metropolitan Police to local constabularies, 24 Oct 1932; Mepol 2, 3064, items 25N, 25K, replies for Scottish, North East, South Wales and East Anglian contingents. Name and address of subject withheld.

16. Mepol 2, 3064, item 25K, report of Chief Constable of Oxford, 24 Oct 1932.

17. For a fuller discussion of this, see R. Hayburn, 'The Police and the Hunger Marchers', *The International Review of Social History* (1973).

18. Mepol 2, 3064, items 20D, 22J, and 25R information on marchers, 21–6 Oct 1932.

19. Mepol 2, 3064, item 20D, information to police; Mepol 2, 3065, items 6N, 6P, report on police preparations.

20. Mepol 2, 3064, item 27A.

21. Hannington, op. cit., pp. 245–7.

22. Mepol 2, 3064, item 27B, report on marchers, 31 Oct 1932.

23. Hannington, op. cit., Mepol 2, 3065, item 3C, report on Hyde Park demonstration; *The Times*, 28 Oct 1932.

24. Hannington, op. cit., pp. 250–1.

25. Hannington, *Never on Our Knees* (London, 1967) p. 267.

26. Mepol 2, 3064, item 26A, report on N.U.W.M.

27. *Daily Telegraph*, 1 Nov 1932.

28. *The Times*, 28 Nov 1932.

29. *Manchester Guardian*, 1 Nov 1932.

30. Hannington, op. cit., pp. 269–70.

31. Ibid., pp. 270–2; Mepol 2, 3066, items 6A and 6B.

32. Ibid., pp. 273–7.

33. Mepol 2, 3065, item 7B; Mepol 2, 3066, item 5R.

34. Mepol 2, 3067, items 2A, 5B, 5C, 5D, 7A, 7B. Names withheld.

35. W. G. Runciman, *Relative Deprivation and Social Justice* (London, 1966) pp. 63–5.

36. A. J. P. Taylor, *English History, 1914–1945* (Oxford, 1965) p. 149.

37. Hannington, *Unemployed Struggles, 1919–36*, op. cit., p.p. 32–3.

38. Mepol 2, 3065, item 6S.

39. Hannington, op. cit., p. 265.

40. Mepol 2, 3067, item 5K.

41. Runciman, op. cit., pp. 65–7.

42. M. Foot, *Aneurin Bevan* (London, 1962) i, 201.

43. Ibid., pp. 201–2; Hannington, op. cit., pp. 278–97; Branson and Heinemann, op. cit., pp. 30–1.

44. Mepol 2, 3097, item 29C, Special Branch report on Jarrow March, 6 Oct 1936; Mepol 2, 3067, item 28B, regulations governing access to the House of Commons.

45. Mepol 2, 3097, item 28A, Special Branch report on Jarrow March, 6 Nov 1936.

46. Mepol 2, 3097, item 28C.

47. Mepol 2, 3097, item 28A.

48. See *The Times*, 2 Nov 1936; Mepol 2, 3053, items 16A, 22A, 22B, reports on Means Test demonstration on 8 Nov 1936.

7 Liberals, Labour and Local Elections

CHRIS COOK

The rise of Labour and the downfall of the Liberal Party have long been themes which have fascinated historians. The historical debate has so far tended to focus on three main periods: the years of the Liberal government, 1906–14; the period of wartime politics, 1914–18; and the six years from 1918 to 1924, which saw the Lloyd George coalition, the split in the party, and the final blow dealt by the minority Labour government that followed the 1923 general election. Few historians have examined the Liberal Party after 1924; fewer still after 1931. Indeed, the period from 1931 to 1945 has yet to see a serious and scholarly published study of the Liberal Party.

This neglect is hardly surprising. Even the hardiest of enthusiasts would find in the abject and pathetic Parliamentary Liberal Party after 1931 little to excite or enthuse. Outside Parliament, however, the disintegration of the party at the grass roots was an important political event with lasting consequences for British political development.

At this local grass-roots level the Liberal Party had not been entirely destroyed by 1929 or even 1931. In the borough councils, even though hardly a city remained in Liberal control, the Liberals still occupied (often in alliance with Conservatives) an important place in many councils. Before Labour could finally reduce municipal politics to the two-party battle that dominated parliamentary politics, the Liberals had finally to be destroyed.

Whilst the Labour Party languished nationally in the 1930s, at local level this final battle with the weakened ranks of the Liberal

Party was won. By 1945 the Liberals had been driven by Labour from the council chambers. It is with this last electoral battle of Liberals and Labour from 1929 to 1945 that this essay is concerned.

The study of electoral change in Britain between the wars has to a very large extent been concentrated on studies of voting behaviour in general elections.[1] Published studies of municipal politics have by comparison been very much the poor relation. There is at present no comprehensive study of municipal elections for the period 1918 to 1945, whilst even individual case studies are few in number.[2] For the 1930s this generalisation is even more marked. Whilst some work has been done on the decline of the Liberal Party at municipal level for the period 1918 to 1929, the decade after the formation of the second Labour government remains almost entirely untouched.[3]

This lack of serious study of municipal electoral activity after 1929 is a sad neglect. The varying success of Liberals at local level, the number of candidates fielded, the degree of success achieved by Labour candidates, the emergence of local anti-Socialist 'pacts' – all these are themes in which municipal evidence can provide much that explains or corroborates the national political scene.

In many aspects municipal politics in the decade after 1929 saw a fairly undisturbed continuation of the main themes that had dominated local politics in the 1920s. Three main developments had overshadowed local elections in the decade after 1918: the advent of an intensive Labour challenge for municipal office, which developed in intensity as the party progressed nationally; an almost total and uninterrupted decline of the Liberal Party, especially in the larger cities, which continued even when Liberalism nationally (as in 1923 and 1927–8) enjoyed a revival; and, finally, the rise of anti-Socialist 'Municipal Alliances' in a whole variety of towns in which the Labour challenge threatened the older parties.

The increased Labour challenge for municipal office, spurred by the 1918 Constitution and the evolution of a national party with constituency organisation in virtually every borough, also benefited from the expansion of the local government franchise in 1918. This measure approximately doubled the number eligible to vote in municipal elections.[4] These two factors together ended the era in local government when municipal elections had often gone largely uncontested.[5]

The advent of Labour brought municipal politics to the fore-front of the party political battle. It was, indeed, Labour rather than either of its main opponents that launched the largest chal-lenge for local government elections. In terms of the number of candidates fielded, Labour's challenge grew steadily and relent-lessly after 1919 (see Table 7.1).

TABLE 7.1   *Candidates for Municipal Election, 1921–9*

Year	Con. (%)	Lab. (%)	Lib. (%)	Ind. (%)	SAMPLE
1921	31·0	35·1	18·6	15·2	1772
1922	31·8	37·7	17·7	12·8	1701
1923	30·3	34·6	17·3	17·8	1833
1924	31·3	38·5	17·0	13·2	1676
1925	29·6	38·9	15·0	16·5	1856
1926	30·6	43·4	15·6	10·4	1861
1927	29·2	42·8	13·7	14·3	1596
1928	29·8	40·1	12·6	17·5	1770
1929	27·5	44·3	12·4	15·8	2044

These figures demonstrate very clearly the contrast between the Labour and Liberal performance. In 1921 the Liberals had fielded 18·6 per cent of the sample of candidates. By 1929, after an almost uninterrupted decline, this figure had fallen to only 12·4 per cent. In direct contrast, the Labour attack gradually expanded, so that by 1929, 44 of every 100 candidates for municipal office were being put forward by the party.

A particularly strong municipal challenge was fielded by Labour in November 1926. For the first time Labour contested every seat in such towns as Nottingham.[6] In such cities as Edin-burgh Labour achieved a breakthrough in 1926 which had eluded them earlier.[7] Labour continued this heavy pressure in succeeding years, whilst the Liberals, even at the height of their parlia-mentary revival in 1927 and 1928, continued to field an increas-ingly weaker municipal challenge.

The same pattern of Liberal decline and rising Labour strength can be seen in the gains and losses of the parties each November. The most dramatic result occurred in the first postwar municipal election in November 1919, when Labour won an electoral land-slide.[8]

After 1919, with the exception of 1922 when Labour failed to hold some of its remarkable 1919 victories, the party scored a net gain of seats in each successive year up to 1929 – whilst the Liberals (as Table 7.2 demonstrates) suffered exactly the reverse. Liberals lost seats in every year (except for 1922), with substantial losses in the period 1923–6.

TABLE 7.2 *Labour Gains and Liberal Losses in Municipal Elections, 1921–9*

	(a) Liberal				(b) Labour		
Year	Gains	Loss	Net Loss	Year	Gains	Loss	Net Gains
1921	16	60	44	1921	78	42	36
1922	33	11	(+ 22)	1922	5	168	(– 163)
1923	12	36	24	1923	66	38	28
1924	18	42	24	1924	51	31	20
1925	11	33	22	1925	73	26	47
1926	8	61	53	1926	160	14	146
1927	14	33	19	1927	115	20	95
1928	12	27	15	1928	123	12	111
1929	13	28	15	1929	112	12	100

The period of Labour's most spectacular advance (except for 1919) was from 1926 to 1929 – a period when many of the former Liberal industrial seats in Yorkshire and the Northeast fell to Labour.

In the face of this intensive Labour challenge, Liberal representation had by 1930 been very much reduced in the councils of many major boroughs. In some, indeed, Liberals had been completely removed. By 1930 not a single Liberal councillor or alderman remained in such boroughs as Preston, Barrow or Smethwick. Only a solitary Liberal remained in Wigan and Birkenhead. Liberal representation in Birmingham, a city where the Liberal cause had been dying for a generation was down to 5 in a council of 121. Meanwhile in Leeds, where Liberals had in happier days been a powerful force, only 5 remained in a council of 78. In Blackburn, a Lancashire town that was once a Liberal stronghold, only two Liberals survived on a council of 53.

Outside these towns in which municipal Liberalism was almost extinct, Liberals had often been able to survive only by joining forces with their traditional opponents, the Conservatives. After the 1919 Labour municipal victories, local anti-Socialist parties were organised in a variety of towns. Sheffield saw the creation of the Progressive Party; in Hull a 'Hull Municipal Alliance' was formed. Similar titles were used in Bristol, Reading and Southampton. In virtually all the towns of the Northeast (and in South Wales) anti-Socialist candidates fought as 'Moderates'. By 1930 there were very few towns in which, once Labour had secured a majority on the council, the older parties had not united against them.

Even where Liberals had not amalgamated to form a municipal anti-Socialist party, a 'pact' with the Conservatives left them enjoying full co-operation. Such towns as Coventry and Wolverhampton provide models of this form of anti-Socialist alliance.[9]

Thus, by 1930 Liberal municipal politics in many large boroughs had suffered one of two fates: amalgamation with the Conservatives – either by a 'pact' or by complete fusion in a new party – or virtual elimination at the hands of Labour.

There were, however, especially in the West Riding of Yorkshire, in parts of Lancashire, and in the old radical towns of the Midlands, areas where Liberals even in 1930 still possessed a strong base in many councils. The chart below sets out the areas of Liberal strength after the municipal elections of November 1930:

(1) *Boroughs where Liberals in control*	Huddersfield (37/60)
(2) *Boroughs where Liberals still largest single party*	Tynemouth (18/36); Cardiff (17/52); Halifax (26/60); Keighley (10/24); Middlesbrough (15/44)
(3) *Boroughs where Liberals still second largest party*	Bradford; Burnley; Bury; Burton; Doncaster; Exeter; Northampton (= with Labour); Portsmouth; Wallasey; Sunderland; Swansea; West Hartlepool; Wolverhampton (= with Labour); Worcester.

Thus, as the above figures show, by 1930 Liberals had lost control of all the major provincial boroughs, with the sole exception of Huddersfield. Elsewhere in the West Riding, the Liberals remained the largest single party in Halifax and Keighley and had additional areas of strength in the Northeast (Middlesbrough and Tynemouth), South Wales (Cardiff and Swansea), parts of Lancashire and certain of the Midland towns.

However, whilst the Liberal decline had left the party without overall control of any borough except Huddersfield, Labour's advance had not, even by 1930, brought them control of more than a handful of the really large towns. Of the 80 major provincial boroughs, Labour's control after 1930 was limited to those listed below.

Provincial Boroughs Controlled by Labour after 1930 Municipal Elections

Barrow (Lab. 22, Con. 9)
Birkenhead (Lab. 33, Con. 24, Lib. 1, Ind. 2)
Bradford (Lab. 44, Con. 19, Lib. 25)
Derby (Lab. 38, Con. 18, Lib. 7, Ind. 1)
East Ham (Lab. 27, Civic Party 13)
Merthyr (Lab. 23, Ind. 7)
Norwich (Lab. 32, Con. 24, Lib. 7, Ind. 1)
Sheffield (Lab. 57, Prog. 37, Ind. 2)
Stoke (Lab. 59, Anti-Soc. 53)
West Ham (Lab. 56, Civic Party 8)
Wigan (Lab. 40, Con. 15, Lib. 1)

Of the largest cities neither Birmingham, Bolton, Bristol, Cardiff, Coventry, Leicester, Liverpool, Manchester, Newcastle or Nottingham had been won for Labour by November 1930. Although many boroughs were captured by Labour after 1932, many still eluded the party's grasp until 1937 or even 1945.[11] Thus, Bristol and Coventry went Labour for the first time only in 1937. Others, such as Nottingham and Wolverhampton, only fell in 1945.

An important stumbling block in Labour's advance to municipal power was the persistence of Liberal strength at council level. Even though Liberal strength survived only because of an alliance with Conservatism, it still prevented Labour winning working-class wards essential to its bid for power. Labour's vital achievement after 1931 was to bring about the final and absolute destruction of any remaining Liberal strength in the provincial boroughs. In this sense the decade after 1929 constituted the last act in the drama of Labour and the downfall of Liberalism.

Labour's success, in the years after 1929, in destroying municipal Liberalism is an overlooked theme for most historians. Indeed, even Labour's recovery at local level from the débâcle of 1931 has so far lacked a serious study. This neglect is a double pity, for Labour's municipal recovery is a phenomenon of far more than local significance.

Indeed, there is a fundamental divergence in British politics in the period after 1931 between Labour's performance in general elections and its performance in municipal voting. After the disaster of 1931, a débâcle at municipal as well as parliamentary level, Labour's recovery at local level was rapid, dramatic and complete. Yet in by-elections and in the 1935 general election Labour's recovery was both patchy and uneven, and of nothing like the same magnitude.

The municipal disaster of November 1931 was the worst-ever electoral performance for Labour in municipal inter-war elections. A year earlier the election of November 1930 provided the first check for eight years to Labour's municipal advance. In line with the parliamentary by-election performance of the party, the check was substantial. As the *Yorkshire Post* commented, the Conservative gains were sufficiently emphatic to indicate a direct swing of the political pendulum. Labour gained only 27 seats, losing 92. This net loss of 65 seats was sufficient for Labour to lose control of Leeds, Hull, Swansea, Barnsley and Blackburn – in this latter borough 10 of the 11 Conservative candidates swept the board. The Conservatives enjoyed a net gain of 69 in the large boroughs, whilst the Liberals, despite this anti-Labour swing, still suffered a net loss of 8 seats. Neville Chamberlain, Chairman of the Conservative Party, saw in the results 'a striking failure of their (i.e. Labour) complete failure to cope with the distress under which the country is now suffering'.

Such a statement was a little ingenuous. The results were partly a natural swing back from 1927, partly a protest at the govern-

TABLE 7.3   *Municipal Elections, November 1931*

Party	Candidates	Successful	Gains	Losses
Con.	465	350	149	5
Lib.	154	107	26	5
Lab.	709	149	5	206
Com.	50	—	—	—
Ind.	258	154	46	10
	1636	760	226	226

ment, but perhaps as much as anything due to a renewal and extension of Conservative–Liberal municipal pacts – as in Sheffield, where for the November 1930 elections the anti-Labour parties combined under the label 'Municipal Progressive'.[12]

By the time of the elections of November 1931 the political situation in the country had undergone a drastic upheaval. After the formation of the National government, and the Labour disaster in the 1931 general election, Labour no doubt expected a major setback in 1931; the results fulfilled their worst expectations. In the 80 largest boroughs only 149 of the 709 Labour candidates were successful. Labour gained a mere 5 seats for the loss of 206. The statistical details of the massacre can be seen in Table 7.3.[13]

Even worse than these national figures were the performances in individual boroughs. Not a single Labour candidate was elected in Birmingham, Bradford, Birkenhead, Stockport or Middlesbrough. Only one was returned in Salford and Cardiff. Only 2 of the 31 Labour candidates in Liverpool secured election, 2 of the 12 both in Swindon and Derby, and a mere 3 out of 14 in Coventry. Only Leeds, Sheffield and Manchester (each electing 7 Labour councillors) escaped the worst of the holocaust.

To some extent the Labour losses were exaggerated by the combination of Conservative and Liberals. But no excuse could entirely hide the scale of the disaster. A mere twelve months later, however, a reversal of Labour's fortunes at municipal level had very suddenly occurred.

Compared to 1931, the number of Labour candidates fielded, and their success, can be seen in Table 7.4.

TABLE 7.4

1931	Candidates	Elected	1932	Candidates	Elected
Con.	465	350	Con.	490	218
Lib.	154	107	Lib.	174	87
Lab.	709	149	Lab.	836	458
Ind.	308	154	Ind.	329	106

Labour won 458 seats (52.7 per cent of the sample) in 1932, one of its highest success rates to date. Although, compared with 1929, Labour only gained a net tally of 15 seats, this was a gain over one of its previous best years. The size of the Labour recovery compared to 1931 can perhaps best be gauged from Table 7.5.

The exact extent of Labour's recovery in 1932, in terms of swing since 1931, is difficult to determine. An analysis of comparable contests, shown in the table 7.6, gives an indication not only of the enormous swing, but of the fact that this is clearly a return of the Labour faithful.

TABLE 7.5   *Labour Candidates Elected, 1931–2*

	1931 Candidates	*1931 Elected*	*1932 Candidates*	*1932 Elected*
Birmingham	24	0	26	13
Birkenhead	14	0	13	9
Bradford	22	0	20	11
Derby	12	2	16	9
Liverpool	31	2	32	15
Manchester	21	7	28	16
Reading	11	1	11	7
Salford	14	1	14	8
Sheffield	24	7	20	15
Southampton	13	2	13	9
Stockport	13	0	10	7

The rapidity of the Labour recovery in 1932 has perhaps not been sufficiently emphasised in existing accounts of the politics of the early 1930s. This rapid recovery by Labour, especially in areas where the issues of unemployment and the means test were most explosive, may well explain the subsequent failure of the

TABLE 7.6   *Swing to Labour in Municipal Elections, November 1931–November 1932*

Borough	*Comparable Contests*	*Swing*	*% Increase Lab Vote*
York	5	9.3	15.0
Leeds	18	13.5	3.5
Salford	13	14.0	19.3
Gateshead	7	14.2	32.1
Barrow	6	3.8	14.2
Lincoln	6	13.2	26.5

Communist and N.U.W.M. challenges. It also questions the extent to which Labour really lost its working-class vote in the 1931 general election.[14]

Labour's recovery, already marked in 1932, reached new heights in 1933. In municipal terms 1933 was one of the best years the party ever enjoyed. In the urban district council elections Labour appeared to have regained, and probably surpassed, its previous high water mark. Sweeping Labour gains in the November elections brought Labour to power in such cities as Sheffield, Norwich, Leeds, Bootle, Swansea and Barnsley – adding to the 15 boroughs controlled prior to November 1933. In 7 boroughs in 1933 Labour gained a council majority for the first time. In 4 others Labour moved up to a position of strength equal to the combined forces of its opponents (Barrow, Lincoln, Newport, Oldham), whilst in such towns as Canterbury the party won its first-ever seats.

With 181 gains and only 5 losses, with 444 of its 880 candidates successful, and with Labour winning control of a variety of boroughs never before controlled, the party had achieved a goal that would have seemed impossible in the wake of MacDonald's actions two years earlier. Neither Conservatives nor Liberals had any crumbs of comfort from 1933 – the Conservatives gained 6 seats, losing 112; the Liberals picked up 5 for the loss of 33.

The elections of November 1934 provided Labour with its third successive year of widespread gains. Labour, attacking the seats lost in the débâcle of 1931, secured 203 gains for a loss of only 8. Conservative and Independents suffered a net loss of 165, the Liberals a net loss of 30. Heavy Labour gains in Derby, Stoke and Hull gave Labour control of councils lost in 1931. Five Labour gains won Labour control of Burnley for the first time. Elsewhere in Lancashire (one of Labour's best areas) the party won Oldham and secured a tie of councillors in Birkenhead. Persistent Liberal losses to Labour were the order of the day.

The first comfort – or so it appeared – for the Conservatives came with the municipal elections of November 1935 – held within the shadow of the general election on 14 November. On balance Labour suffered a net loss of seats. Press Association figures gave Labour 36 gains and 60 losses, the Conservatives 50 gains and 18 losses. This relatively tiny turnover of seats (compared, for example, to the previous years) was nonetheless much used to bolster the National Government's General Election campaign. Ramsay MacDonald welcomed the results as 'a pointer to

the results of the General Election' whilst Lord Jessel claimed
they were 'a good augury'. On the Labour side, Morrison admitted that the results were 'somewhat unexpected'.

In fact, Labour's setback was exaggerated by the results from
the West Midlands. Fifteen of Labour's net loss of 24 seats were
concentrated in three West Midland centres.[15] In the 1935 General Election, Birmingham and the Black Country continued this
regional trend.[16]

Apart from the West Midlands, Labour's most serious result in
1935 was Leeds, where 4 Conservative gains gave them control of
the council. Despite these reverses Labour nonetheless still did extremely well in 1935 (with 167 candidates alone returned unopposed, and 366 of a field of 898 successful in contested elections).

If in 1935 Labour had slipped only slightly from their high
watermark of 1933–4, by November 1936 the tide was flowing
much more strongly against them. Labour, having to defend its
1933 gains, suffered a net loss of 81 seats (47 gained, 128 lost) in
1936. Conservatives (and their independent allies) secured a net
gain of 81; the Liberals, even with Labour on the defensive, still
suffered a small net loss.

By November 1937 the turnover of seats had settled after the
landslide victories of the early 1930s. Indeed, the municipal elections of 1937, which appeared to suggest a slight Labour setback,
were in fact distorted by a variety of cross-currents. Whilst the
Conservatives secured a net gain of 36 seats (71 gains, 35 losses),
Labour had 67 gains and 72 losses. The key here was the Liberals,
whose net loss of 28 was almost entirely to Labour. In addition,
Labour's performance appeared worse because of a variety of
reverses for local reasons in Merseyside.[17]

Very similar national results occured in November 1938, the
last municipal elections before 1945. Labour again lost a little
ground to the Conservatives, who secured a net gain of some 20
seats. Once again Liverpool and parts of Lancashire made
Labour's reverse appear worse than it really was.[18] After 1938
Labour slipped back from its position as largest single party in
Burnley, Bristol, Hull and Sunderland, but gained a prize with
the capture of Gateshead.

Thus, after 1931 Labour's recovery had been dramatic until
1935; it had then evened out on a plateau, suffering slight setbacks
made worse by important regional variations and local issues.
Meanwhile, whilst this battle for control of the major provincial
boroughs was thus being fought between Conservative and

Labour, the Liberals remained virtually consigned to the shadows. For the Liberals the decade after 1930 saw a continuous and almost uninterrupted decline. By 1938, despite an occasional stronghold in Yorkshire and Lancashire, the party had almost ceased to be represented on many borough councils; the municipal elections of November 1945, with their sweeping Labour gains, finally ended what remained of the old Liberal Party.

Two trends that had dominated municipal Liberal politics in the decade from 1918 to 1929 continued after 1930: a slow but persistent fall in the number of candidates brought forward, and an equally uninterrupted and persistent net loss of seats each November.

The fall in the number of Liberal candidates for the decade after 1929 is set out in Table 7.7.

TABLE 7.7   *Candidates for Municipal Elections, 1929–38*

Year	Con. % of Total	Labour % of Total	Liberal % of Total	Ind. & others % of Total	Total Candidates in sample
1929	27·5	44·3	12·4	15·8	2044
1930	30·3	42·5	11·9	15·3	2022
1931	28·4	43·3	9·4	18·8	1636
1932	26·8	45·7	9·5	18·0	1829
1933	24·0	43·1	9·3	23·6	2942
1934	23·6	43·2	7·8	25·4	2168
1935	26·5	45·7	7·9	19·8	1963
1936	26·0	45·1	6·5	22·3	2383
1937	25·9	44·3	6·1	23·7	2302
1938	26·1	44·8	5·6	23·5	2481

The percentage of Liberal candidates, which had stood at 18 per cent in 1922, had fallen to 12½ per cent by 1929. By 1931 the total had fallen below 10 per cent; by 1935 it was down to 7.9 per cent and by 1938 to a mere 5.6 per cent. No doubt many erstwhile Liberals had found a home in the ranks of the Independents during the 1930s, for the Independents tally of candidates rose from 16 per cent in 1929 to 23 per cent a decade later.

The reduction in the number of Liberal municipal candidates, in itself a symptom of the malaise afflicting the party, was mirrored in the net loss of seats suffered each November. In every year (apart from the anti-Labour landslide of 1931) Liberals suffered a net loss of seats.[19] Perhaps a better indication than this was to be found in the *share* of seats won by Liberals each November, as set out in Table 7.8.

TABLE 7.8

Year	Sample	Won by Liberals	%
1931	760	107	14·1
1932	869	87	10·0
1933	919	93	10·1
1934	1078	98	9·1
1935	936	94	10·0
1936	1342	103	7·7
1937	1084	62	5·7
1938	1185	85	7·2

In 1931, 1 in 7 council seats was won by a Liberal; by 1935 this was down to 1 in 10, and by 1938 to 1 in 13.

These overall figures of gains and losses to a certain extent disguised a significant change in the type of seats won by Liberals during the 1930s. During this period Liberals lost steadily and persistently to Labour in a variety of Midland and Northern industrial districts, whilst themselves picking up isolated gains from the Conservatives in a few seaside and middle-class resorts. Thus, in 1934 Liberals lost their last remaining seat on Wigan Council to Labour, and suffered heavy losses in Lancashire and the Midlands.[20] At the same time they picked up occasional Conservative seats in Bath and Bournemouth.[21]

Throughout the 1930s the temptation of hard-pressed Liberal councillors to join forces with the Conservatives in an anti-Socialist 'municipal alliance' continued to increase. Each November it was possible to detect another borough where the anti-Socialist forces had joined ranks. Thus, in 1932 it was the turn of Plymouth. Conservatives and Liberals united for the first time, 8 Labour seats were gained, and only 4 out of 18 Labour candidates emerged successful. In 1934 the Liberals and Conservatives in Doncaster (where some form of co-operation had existed for a long time) were now combined in a 'Progressive Non-Party Group'. Similarly, at Ipswich a 'People's Party' was brought about by a merger of Conservatives and Liberals.

In the late 1920s earlier anti-Socialist pacts had often provoked division and dissent within the Liberal ranks, especially from the more radical Young Liberals.[22] During the 1930s no such revolts occurred. Indeed, one of the most consistent features of municipal Liberalism in the 1930s was the absolute lack of any attempt to provide an independent Liberal challenge.

Thus, in Hull no independent Liberal ever challenged the united forces of the Hull Municipal Alliance; in Coventry no challenge came forward against the Progressives; in Bristol, even with the municipal 'general election' of 1936, not a single Liberal ever ventured to do battle with the Citizens Party. These examples can be multiplied many times. The phenomenon was as true in Reading as in Rotherham; in Newcastle as in Plymouth. Any attempt at an independent Liberal challenge in these towns was conspicuous only by its absence.

It was symbolic of the new era of two-party politics that Liberalism should finally have surrendered its independence in the spiritual home of radicalism and Free Trade – Manchester. In 1931 Liberals and Conservatives entered into a 'pact' at municipal level which marked the end of the road for the party.[23]

This Liberal decline after 1931 was nowhere greater than in the old radical towns of the Midlands, cities where prior to 1914 Nonconformist Liberalism had reigned supreme.

Four towns epitomised these old radical Midland Liberal strongholds: Nottingham, Leicester, Coventry and Northampton. All were towns in which, even in the 1920s, Liberals had won, or come close to winning, parliamentary seats.

At local level in these four towns, prior to 1930, Liberals had sought municipal salvation in a variety of ways. In Coventry the Liberals had entered into a formal agreement with the Conservatives to oppose Labour. Despite an occasional protest the agreement was wholeheartedly maintained.[24] In Leicester much tacit co-operation of Liberal and Conservative took place, but in certain years Liberals and Conservatives had come into marked conflict.[25] Certainly the Liberals in Leicester had not completely abandoned their independence by 1930. In Nottingham Liberals had co-operated with the Conservatives rather more often than in Leicester, although such wards as St Ann's (a noted Nonconformist stronghold) proved difficult.[26] Elsewhere, despite Conservative co-operation, the Liberals in Nottingham displayed little life. In Northampton, in marked contrast, the Liberals after

1922 were more or less fighting as an independent party.[27] A few wards organised agreements with the Conservatives, but three-cornered contests were a fairly regular occurrence.

Thus, in different ways municipal Liberalism had still survived in these four Midland towns by 1930. Liberal representation in these boroughs after the November 1930 elections is set in Table 7.9.

TABLE 7.9   Representation by Party in Midland Boroughs, 1930

	Con.	Lab.	Lib.	Ind.	Total
Coventry	25	17	18	—	60
Leicester	21	29	13	1	64
Nottingham	27	27	10	—	64
Northampton	22	13	13	—	48
	95	86	54	1	236

Thus, by 1930 none of these towns was controlled by Labour (although Labour had briefly gained Leicester in 1928), whilst in Coventry and Northampton Labour had not overtaken the Liberals as the second largest party. Although much reduced from their former strength, Liberals still retained 54 of the 236 seats compared to 95 Conservative and 86 Labour.

By the end of the decade a transformation had occurred (see Table 7.10).

TABLE 7.10   Representation by Party in Midland Boroughs, 1938

	Con.	Lab.	Lib.	Ind.	Total
Coventry	16	36	12	—	64
Leicester	28	26	8	2	64
Nottingham	34	28	2	—	64
Northampton	24	15	8	1	48
	102	105	30	3	240

By 1938 Liberal strength had fallen to 30 of a total of 240. Labour had supplanted the Conservatives with the largest aggregate total, having made heavy gains at Coventry (winning control in 1937) and having broken Liberal strength in Leicester, Nottingham and Northampton. Except in Coventry the Conservatives had *also* improved their position. The only losers had been the hapless Liberals.

The causes of the disastrous Liberal decline after 1930 varied from town to town, but an examination of municipal politics in each of the four towns reveals certain basic factors.

In Nottingham the Liberal collapse after November 1930 was both dramatic and complete. From a council strength of 10 in 1930, Liberal representation had slumped to 4 by 1934. The explanation was not that the Liberals had fought and lost; by and large they had simply failed to fight at all (see Table 7.11).

TABLE 7.11   *Municipal Election Contests in Nottingham, 1933–8*

Year	Contests	Con. v. Lab.	Lib. v. Lab.	Con. v. Lib. v. Lab.	Others*	Unopposed
1933	12	10	2	—	—	4
1934	15	12	—	2	—	2
1935	13	11	1	—	1	3
1936	12	10	2	—	—	4
1937	11	9	1	1	—	5
1938	13	9	1	—	3	3
	76	61	7	3	4	21

* These contests were: 1935: Lab. *v.* Nat. Lab.; 1938: Con. *v.* Ind.; 2 Lab. *v.* Citizens' Association. Fringe candidates who intervened in straight fights have been excluded.

Thus, in 76 contested elections, Liberals had fought a mere 10 contests, only 3 against Conservative opponents. Not a single straight fight occurred between Conservative and Liberal. Labour, fighting 75 of the 76 contested elections, were faced with a single Conservative or Liberal opponent in 68 of these contests. Thus, though three parties remained represented on Nottingham Council, the era of three-party politics had long since passed. It was perhaps symbolic that in the last prewar municipal elections, in November 1938, of 53, 144 votes polled Labour secured 25,884, Conservatives 23,042, the newly-formed Citizens Association 2785, and the Liberals a mere 1433. The accommodation with Conservatives, which had aided Nottingham Liberals in the 1920s, was of no avail in the later decade. Without a single council stronghold and with no fighting spirit left, municipal Liberalism had all but died in Nottingham by 1939.

The demise of Nottingham Liberalism was closely paralleled in Leicester. In the 1920s both towns had witnessed similar anti-Socialist deals, although the Leicester Liberals in such years as 1924 or 1926 had provoked three-cornered contests in some wards. Both in numbers and in fighting spirit the Liberals in Leicester were a slightly hardier plant than their somewhat withered neighbours on the Trent.

TABLE 7.12   *Liberal Representation on Leicester Council*

Year	Con.	Lab.	Lib.	Ind.	Total
1930	21	29	13	1	64
1934	26	26	11	1	64
1938	28	26	8	2	64
1945	23	28	2	—	63*

*1 vacancy

Liberalism had not merely remained stronger in Leicester up to 1930 than in Nottingham; its subsequent decline was neither so dramatic nor complete. Two main features, however, were the same – a declining strength on the council (Table 7.12), and an increasing reluctance to field candidates, especially against Conservatives (Table 7.13).

TABLE 7.13   *Municipal Election Contests in Leicester, 1931–8*[28]

Year	Contests	Con. v. Lab.	Lib. v. Lab.	Con. v. Lib. v. Lab.	Others
Nov 1931	8	1	5	—	2
Nov 1932	12	7	5	—	—
Nov 1933	12	6	6	—	—
Nov 1934	16	7	8	—	1
Nov 1937	16	12	2	1	1
Nov 1938	14	12	1	—	1

As Table 7.13 indicates, only 1 Liberal gave battle in a three-cornered contest after 1931, and this only because of a specific

local factor.[29] Not a single Conservative–Liberal straight fight occurred. Prior to the municipal 'general election' of April 1936 –
the elections that really marked the end of municipal Liberalism
in Leicester – Liberals had shared fairly equally in the anti-
Socialist battles but in the last two pre-war municipal elections of
1937 and 1938, only 3 Liberals entered straight fights against
Labour, compared with 24 Conservatives. Another feature of the
weakening of Liberalism was its diminished number of unopposed returns (see Table 7.14).

TABLE 7.14   *Unopposed Returns in Leicester, 1919–35*

	Con.	Lib.	Lab.
(a) 1919–26	22	18	11
(b) 1927–35	31	5	21
	53	23	32

Only two wards, Abbey and Belgrave, allowed an unopposed Liberal to be returned after 1927. A further feature was the defection
of sitting Liberals to the Conservatives (as with Councillor Cave in
Westcotes in 1937) and Liberal-held seats which lapsed by
default. All these factors combined meant that by 1938 Leicester
had joined Nottingham as a lost cause for the Liberal Party.

With municipal politics in Coventry the elections after 1930
can be quickly recounted. Not a single Liberal ever did battle
with the anti-Socialist 'Progressive Party' during this period. The
two anti-Socialist parties remained locked in an alliance, each
gradually losing seats to Labour, who won control of Coventry for
the first time in 1937. The Liberals, utterly reliant on the Conservatives, with no safe seats of their own, and with their aldermanic numbers much reduced after 1937, had become by 1939 a
mere appendage to the Progressive Party. Liberal representation
in Coventry was purely nominal; the Liberals fought only under
the Progressive banner; it is doubtful if any Liberal could have
secured election without the Progressive label, and indeed even
with this support they were hard put to win seats. No Parliamentary Liberal fought Coventry in 1931 or 1935. When a Liberal ventured to fight Coventry East in 1945, he obtained 5 per

cent of the poll, finishing fourth behind the Communist candidate. It was an appropriate epitaph for Coventry Liberalism.

As if to illustrate the variety of Midland politics – and the diverse fate of municipal Liberalism – Northampton provides a rather different example. Northampton municipal politics in many ways had closely followed parliamentary politics. From 1919 to 1922 coalition with the Conservatives had been the order of the day; from 1923 to 1929 Liberals had generally mounted an independent challenge, losing heart as Labour consolidated its hold on the working-class wards. After 1929, like the Liberals in Parliament, the party locally went in no clear direction, gradually growing weaker until disaster overtook it.

Up to 1930, however, in Northampton Labour had failed to become the second largest party and a fairly active Liberalism was still in existence. During the 1930s the position changed with a vengeance (see Table 7.15).

TABLE 7.15   *Council Comp. in Northampton, 1931–45*

Year	Con.	Lab.	Lib.	Ind.	Total
1930	22	13	13	—	48
1934	24	12	12	—	48
1938	24	15	8	1	48
1945	16	26	4	2	48

Although the Liberal decline was general, the crucial year was 1937 – the same year that Labour swept to control in Coventry. In that year all 5 Liberal retiring councillors were defeated, Labour capturing 2 seats, the Conservatives 3. As the local paper commented, 'never before can an established party have suffered so crushing a defeat at a municipal election in Northampton'.[30]

The balance of politics at municipal level was transformed: for the first time in a generation Conservatives obtained a clear majority on Northampton Council, whilst for the first time ever Labour supplanted the Liberals as the second largest party.

In a sense 1937 merely confirmed what had long been becoming more apparent: the removal of the Liberals to the sidelines of Northampton politics. Once again, as in Nottingham and Leicester, Liberals were hardly ever to be seen challenging a Conservative, whilst their own anti-Socialist challenge grew gradually weaker.

Thus, in 1933 only 1 Liberal had come forward in the 12 contested wards (to oppose a Labour candidate). In 1934 there was still no three-cornered contest. Labour faced 6 Conservative and 5 Liberal challengers. In 1935, 6 Liberals were in the field, but none was to be found opposing a Conservative. A solitary three-cornered contest in 1936 preceded the Liberal rout in 1937. The outcome of 1937 proved that, when attacked by Labour and Conservative, independent Liberalism was virtually defenceless. Northampton, too, had seen the final eclipse of local Liberalism.

Thus, by 1938 Liberal representation in these four Midland boroughs had fallen from 54 in 1930 to only 30, a figure still exaggerated by aldermanic strength. Even this last vestige of an older order fell – both in the Midlands and nationally – in 1945.

The municipal elections of November 1945, the first since 1938, and the first to be held under the principle of universal adult suffrage for the local government vote, completed the elimination of Liberal strength from most councils. It proved the final end of the road for the Liberals who had managed to survive the interwar period. The success achieved by the parties is set out in Table 7.16.

TABLE 7.16

Party	Candidates	%	Elected	%
Labour	2074	46·2	1372	62·8
Conservative	1105	24·6	384	17·6
Liberal	360	8·0	92	4·2
Others	952	21·2	337	15·4
	4491		2185	

Labour, with 2074 candidates for the seats at stake, saw 1372 (66·1 per cent) of their standard bearers successful. Only 384 Conservatives (some 28·0 per cent of the Labour total) were successful. A mere 92 Liberals (4·2 per cent), from a tiny field of 360 candidates, were elected. In the 148 largest boroughs, according to Press Association calculations, Labour gained a massive 972 seats (for the loss of 22), whilst Conservatives and Independents suffered net losses of 473 and 340 respectively. The Liberals gained 5 seats for the loss of 134.

Labour's gains were sweeping and nationwide, but nowhere

was their progress greater than in the former Liberal strongholds of Lancashire, Yorkshire and the Northeast. In Lancashire Labour gained 16 seats in Blackburn, 17 in Bolton, and 12 in Bury. In Yorkshire Labour gained 14 seats in Bradford, 20 in Leeds, 12 in Doncaster, and 10 in Huddersfield. In the Northeast Labour took 14 gains in Sunderland and 10 in Newcastle.

Such sweeping gains removed the last Liberal councillors in a variety of centres. In Wolverhampton heavy Labour gains left the town without a single Liberal councillor. In Birmingham, where a massive field of 59 Labour candidates had come forward, the last three Liberals were swept away, in many cases in total humiliation.[31] In Leeds only a solitary Liberal was left on a council of 104.

In the Midlands the Liberals, who still remained on the councils of the four boroughs analysed earlier, were a pitiful remnant (see Table 7.17).

TABLE 7.17   *Party Representation in Midland Boroughs, 1945*

	Con.	Lab.	Lib.	Ind.	Total
Coventry	13	31	4	—	48
Leicester	23	38	2	—	63
Nottingham	25	36	1	2	64
Northampton	16	26	4	2	48
	77	131	11	4	223

Labour, who had won control of Leicester, Nottingham and Northampton in 1945, had all but obliterated the Liberals, who could muster only 11 representatives.

The provincial boroughs where Liberals now retained a separate and strong identity had virtually all vanished. In none of the 80 largest county boroughs were Liberals in overall control. Only in Huddersfield did the Liberals just remain the largest single party. Otherwise Liberals were now the second largest party only in three towns – Burnley, Halifax and Keighley.[33]

Elsewhere Liberals had temporarily survived either by amalgamation with the Conservatives (as in the Citizens Party in Bristol, the Progressives in Sheffield, the Municipal Alliance in Reading, or the Municipal Association in Hull) or by fighting as 'non-party' independents. Even this latter channel became increasingly unsafe in the post–1945 period as the 'independent' in municipal politics found it increasingly difficult to survive. For all but a remnant of Liberals the end of the road had come.

It was perhaps fitting that 1945, the year when Socialism achieved its first majority in Parliament, should mark the final and unremitting demise of the party of Gladstone, Asquith and Lloyd George. The last representatives of the age of Asquith had disappeared with the advent of the age of Attlee.

Notes

1. Some useful studies of interwar elections are: Michael Kinnear, *The Fall of Lloyd George: The Political Crisis of 1922* (London 1973); Chris Cook, *The Age of Alignment, Electoral Politics in Britain, 1922–1929* (London, 1975); E. A. Rowe, 'The General Election of 1929' (Oxford B. Litt. thesis); C. T. Stannage, 'The General Election of 1935' (Cambridge Ph.D. thesis). See also M. Kinnear, *The British Voter* (London, 1968) and Chris Cook and John Ramsden (eds), *By-Elections in British Politics* (London, 1973).

2. A welcome exception is the important study of Wolverhampton. See G. W. Jones, *Borough Politics: A Study of Wolverhampton Borough Council* (London, 1969).

3. On this theme, see Cook, *The Age of Alignment*, pp. 49–87.

4. Figures for the proportion of the population who possessed the local government franchise before 1914 varied from town to town. The figures in 1911 were Leicester (19·6 per cent), Sheffield (18·5 per cent), Manchester (17·1 per cent), Leeds (19·7 per cent), Bristol (18·3 per cent), Cardiff (14·8 per cent) and Swansea (16·2 per cent). After 1918, these proportions approximately doubled. Compiled from *London County Council: Comparative Municipal Statistics* (London, 1912–13) vol. I, pp. 124–5. See also B. Keith-Lucas, *The English Local Government Franchise* (Oxford, 1952).

5. Between 1919 and 1926, 72 per cent of the wards falling vacant each November in Nottingham, 61 per cent in Leicester, 82 per cent in Northampton, 93 per cent in Leeds and no less than 98 per cent in Bradford, were contested.

6. *Nottingham Guardian*, 2 Nov 1926.

7. Prior to 1926, Labour's representation on Edinburgh Council had grown to only 6 by 1925. Eight gains in 1926 brought its representation up to 14.

8. Outside London, Labour gained around 400 seats. This estimate is based on figures in G. D. H. Cole, *A History of the Labour Party*.

9. For Coventry see Cook, *The Age of Alignment*, pp. 58–60. For Wolverhampton, see G. W. Jones, *Borough Politics*.

10. Labour had, in fact, lost control of five boroughs as a result of the 1930 elections. These were: Leeds, Hull, Swansea, Barnsley and Blackburn.

11. The first boroughs to be captured by Labour after 1932 were (in 1933) Sheffield, Norwich, Bootle, Swansea, Barnsley, Ilkeston, Willesden, Leeds, Wallsend, Barking, Lincoln. In 1934 Labour added to its tally Stoke, Oldham, Hull, Derby, Burnley, Birkenhead.

12. *Yorkshire Post*, 2 Nov 1930.

13. Figures taken from Press Association, quoted in *Times*, 2 Nov 1931.

14. This theme will be discussed in more detail in the book I am currently writing (with John Stevenson) on British society and politics in the 1930s.

15. Labour lost 6 seats in Stoke (very probably a reaction to regaining control in 1934), 6 in Birmingham and 3 in West Bromwich.

16. See Cook and Stevenson, op.cit.

17. In Liverpool, where Labour lost control of the council with 8 losses, the fight had centred on the issue of a 75 per cent grant to aid Roman Catholic schools. This revival of sectarian politics undoubtedly weakened Labour's chances.

18. Conservatives took a further 7 seats from Labour in Liverpool, 4 in Burnley and in Bury, and 3 in Stockport.

19. Liberal gains and losses each year (with losses in brackets) were: 1930, 9 (17); 1931, 26 (5); 1932, 14 (20); 1933, 5 (33); 1934, 4 (34); 1935, 10 (12); 1936, 11 (16); 1937, 3 (31); 1938, 14 (16).

20. Labour gains from Liberals in 1934 included Burnley (2), Bury (1), Coventry (2), Derby (2) and Leicester (4).

21. It is tempting to see in Liberal strength in seaside towns and resorts a forerunner of the 'New Liberalism' of the 1950s and 1960s. Equally, in suburban London the rapid rise of 'Ratepayers Associations' (not merely Conservative fronts) provides a certain preview to 'Orpington man' a generation later.

22. See, for example, Young Liberal protests in Wolverhampton. These are discussed in *Jones*, op. cit.

23. *Manchester Guardian*, 2 Nov 1931.

24. For details of this agreement, see Chris Cook, *The Age of Alignment*, pp. 58–60.

25. Ibid., pp. 62–4.

26. Ibid., pp. 61–2.

27. Ibid., pp. 64–5.

28. A municipal truce took place in November 1935 prior to a municipal 'general election' in April 1936.

29. The retiring Liberal councillor for Westcotes ran in the same ward as a Conservative. The Liberals then fielded a candidate who came a relatively poor third.

30. *Northampton Chronicle and Echo*, 2 Nov 1937.

31. The retiring Liberal Councillor in Erdington Ward secured 419 votes (4·8 per cent of the votes polled), to Labour's 5323 and the Conservatives 3004. *Birmingham Mail*, 2 Nov 1945.

32. The council composition of these West Riding towns was:

	Lib.	Con.	Lab.	Ind.	Total
Huddersfield	25	12	23	—	60
Burnley	11	10	27	—	48
Halifax	21	15	23	1	60
Keighley	10	10	14	6	40
	67	47	87	7	208

8 Patriotism under Pressure: Lord Rothermere and British Foreign Policy

PAUL ADDISON

During the National government of 1931–40 the Conservative party included a substantial, if fluctuating, right wing. Sometimes the Right attacked the government, as over India, and occasionally they applauded it, as over Spain, but they seldom determined policy. Neville Chamberlain, the dominating mind in foreign affairs, was no more influenced by the Anglo-German Fellowship, the society for Hitler's fellow-travellers in Britain, than Labour governments by Red Clydeside. But as the history of the Labour party requires an understanding of socialism, so the Right merits attention as a component of Conservatism. Perhaps the Right could be defined by their feeling for nationalistic values: at home, the belief that nationality should override sectional claims, and abroad, advocacy of strength and intransigence. If so, the rise of Nazi Germany revealed a loss of self-confidence on the Right since the previous German challenge of the period before 1914. Moreover, the Right were now confused. In traditional John Bull terms, the new Germany posed a threat to British greatness, but on the social plane the Nazis were announcing Germany as the guarantor of Western Europe against Bolshevism. Which, then, was the true enemy, Germany or Russia? The Right tended to split over the question, a division acutely reflected in the activities of the proprietor of the *Daily Mail*, viscount Rothermere (1868–1940), an erratic amateur politician who was both pro- and anti-German at once, a vocal apologist for Nazism, and a strident alarmist in the campaign for rearmament. After the outbreak of war in 1939, Rothermere published a book entitled *My Fight to Rearm Britain*. Churchill, as first lord of the admiralty, contributed a preface in which he said:

> When the present régime in Germany was new you were indeed
> one of the few voices warning Britain of her need for an over-
> whelming air force and a modernised navy. I know how
> ungrudgingly you have spent time, energy, and money in your
> endeavours to make the nation aware of its danger and its need
> to rearm.[1]

How can the paradoxical Rothermere be explained?

When Northcliffe died in 1922, his press empire, with the
exception of *The Times*, passed into the hands of his brother
Harold Harmsworth, Viscount Rothermere. The two brothers,
self-made millionaires sprung from the suburbs, had started up
business together in 1888. Fleet Street held that in the construction of the Harmsworth empire, Northcliffe provided the
journalistic flair, Rothermere the financial wizardry. In 1926
Rothermere's private secretary estimated that his employer was
worth some £26 millions.[2] Wickham Steed observed:

> His instinct for moneymaking amounted almost to genius. Nor
> did he apply it only to newspapers. He 'went into' businesses of
> many kinds, such as cattle-farming and fruit-growing. Few men
> could ever boast that they had got the better of him in a 'deal',
> and everything he touched seemed to turn if not into gold at
> least into a profitable investment.

This indeed was Wickham Steed's charge against Rothermere –
that he was not concerned with profit in order to maintain the
credit and influence of his newspapers, but with excessive profit
pursued for its own sake, the press being just another industry.[3]
Rothermere would not have understood this. He was proud that
his family had made millions, and no visible sense of guilt accompanied his numerous public benefactions and generous private gifts.

'He is a heavy man', wrote the journalist Collin Brooks on first
meeting him in 1935, 'with a face that seems almost brutal in his
rugged personality, but his aura is young and he is very forceful
and direct in both speech and movement.'[4] Rothermere was no
man for delicate touches of irony, humour, or imaginative colour.
His prose was a steam-roller, apt for road-building but just as
likely to be driven imperturbably down the garden path. His
mind, in fact, had a stodgy texture. It was well-stocked with information, not only about the details of his business operations, but

in European history and various literary and cultural enthusiasms. But when it came to ideas about politics and society, Rothermere had few, and those he had he overworked. In business a shrewd and decisive man who could wield power by issuing instructions to employees, Rothermere was ill-attuned to the political arts of manipulating his equals. In 1917 he was made the first Minister for Air, but it was the only political office he ever held. He plotted his way gauchely to resignation in five months. He lacked, Baldwin's biographers point out, 'the redeeming virtue which Beaverbrook shared with Churchill, a naive delight in his own machinations'.[5] This was associated, no doubt, with the powerful current of ennui in his character. An inveterate globe-trotter, he would even pace the London streets before breakfast, as though in search of fresh sights and scenery to protect him from boredom. His women friends were many, and seldom mattered very long. Lloyd George once complimented him at dinner on the young lady he thought Rothermere was planning to take with him to Europe. 'Oh,' said Rothermere, 'it isn't *that* one. It's another one.'[6] Gloom developed, projected usually on to the world scene. Brooks wrote:

> His prevailing mood was politically one of the deepest pessimism, and personally of almost uproarious satirical mirth. He was convinced that Britain had entered a phase of decline, had lost her old militant virtues, and, in her softness, was lusting after strange idols of pacifism, nationalisation, and everything which would continue to sap self-reliance . . . His family had all been at one time nominal Liberals, but he amongst them was a temperamental Tory of the Johnsonian school.[7]

Rothermere belonged in spirit to the Lloyd George era of 1916–22, and he never quite appreciated that it was over. In Lloyd George's heyday politics had the atmosphere of an intensely personal struggle among a handful of masterful gamesters. The political parties, it seemed at times, were merely suits of cards, the dog-eared clubs or diamonds which went to make up a winning hand. On the assumption that the press was powerful – and it was so long as politicians believed that it was – press lords expected to be admitted to the game. After the fall of Lloyd George the party system reasserted itself. The idea that some backstairs *fronde* of big politicians and press magnates could shake the system became increasingly out of date. But Rothermere, Lloyd George and others still acted on the assumption: so did Baldwin. Furthermore, in the days before opinion polls it was imagined that the popular press could sway millions of votes virtually overnight. Rothermere, therefore, was in the habit of conducting himself like a kingmaker. After the fall of Lloyd George he demanded from Bonar Law, as the price of his newspapers' support at the election, an earldom for himself and Cabinet rank for his twenty-four-year-old son Esmond. Bonar Law called his bluff, and Rothermere was obliged to support him without strings.[8] Once Bonar Law was Prime Minister, however, Rothermere was soon talking in his previous vein. He wrote to Beaverbrook: 'If Bonar Law places himself in my hands I will hand him down to posterity in three years as one of the most successful prime ministers in history, and if there is a general election I will get him returned again.'[9] So it went on for the rest of the 1920s. Conservative party managers continued to exaggerate the power of the press and treat Rothermere as a power in the land.

There were times when Rothermere appeared to have a vested interest in prophesying doom, for it was usually in the role of Cassandra that he carried on his political manoeuvres. But the attitudes of the Right deserve to be taken seriously: Rothermere certainly believed in his own prophecies, and his campaigns to stir up trouble in the Conservative ranks were a genuine, if egocentric, attempt at statesmanship. His first major initiative was the anti-waste party of 1919–21. The theme was that if the government went on spending so much ('squandermania'), there would be an economic collapse. The first anti-waste M.P. to be elected was Esmond Harmsworth; eventually others followed and the Lloyd George coalition buckled before widespread pressure for economy in 1921 and appointed the Geddes committee to make the cuts.

Rothermere's second venture was organised in partnership with Beaverbrook, the proprietor of the *Daily Express*, in 1930: the United Empire Party. Although Beaverbrook's aim was 'Empire Free Trade' Rothermere was disturbed more by the Indian problem; he argued that the loss of India would bring 'immediate economic ruin to this country'. The income of every man and woman in Britain would fall by at least four shillings in the pound. There would be between four and five millions unemployed. In India itself there would be communal massacres, and the 'untouchables' would be abandoned to all the cruelties of the caste system. The United Empire Party came within an ace of driving Baldwin from the leadership of the Conservative Party.[10]

But then a major and decisive setback took place in the fortunes of Beaverbrook and Rothermere.

In the armoury of British politics the weapon of moral anathema, devastating in the hands of the skilled practitioner, was lying unused. Gladstone had wielded it for Liberalism; Lloyd George had thrown it away. Baldwin annexed it. With the same dexterous flick of the wrist with which he later decapitated Edward VIII in the Abdication crisis, Baldwin castigated Rothermere and Beaverbrook: 'What the proprietorship of these papers is aiming at is power, and power without responsibility – the prerogative of the harlot throughout the ages.' After the St George's Westminster by-election of March 1931 Beaverbrook and Rothermere were headless wonders, but they continued to run about unconscious of the fact. Rothermere probably never understood. Perhaps Beaverbrook learned the lesson in 1945.

Rothermere had one optimistic, even utopian, cause to champion. In the mid-1920s he encountered the princess Stefanie Hohenlohe-Waldenburg, a lady of Viennese origin, who had married and divorced a Hungarian magnate. For reasons best known to herself, she persuaded him to take up the unlikely cause of the revision of Hungary's frontiers. As one of the defeated nations at the end of the First World War, Hungary had lost territcry by the Treaty of Trianon to Czechoslovakia in the north, Rumania in the east, and Yugoslavia in the south. In June 1927 Rothermere inaugurated a campaign in favour of 'justice for Hungary' with an article in the *Daily Mail*: 'Hungary's Place in the Sun'. The hierarchy of Hungary, an autocratic state under the rule of the Regent, Admiral Horthy, jumped to the conclusion that Rothermere was a power behind the English throne. He was built up as 'the little father of Hungary': avenues, parks and squares were named after him. A memorial of thanks, containing one and a quarter million signatures bound in twenty-five volumes, was organised and presented to him. In the course of 1928 three approaches were made to Rothermere by Hungarian supporters who wished to enlist his support in a campaign to make him king. His son Esmond paid a quasi-royal visit in 1928 and was acclaimed almost like Bonnie Prince Charlie. But in the end Rothermere decided not to throw his hat, (or rather his crown), into the ring.[11] Now, however, he felt himself to be something of a figure in the fortunes of central Europe. In 1932 he began to employ the princess Stefanie in exploratory efforts to restore the Hapsburgs and the Hohenzollerns, communicating through her with Admiral Horthy and the ex-Crown Prince of Germany.[12]

Such was the light operatic prelude to Rothermere's part in the conflicts of the 1930s. The rise of Nazi Germany placed him in the classic dilemma of the die-hard Right. As one of the richest men in Europe, in common with some of his fellow plutocrats, he admired Fascism as a bulwark against Bolshevism. (He had, of course, praised Mussolini in the 1920s.) But as a pillar of the British empire, an upholder of the 'civilising mission' of the British in India, and a patriot of the traditional school, he was bound to fear that Hitler would undermine Britain's position. He grieved still for the loss of two sons killed in the First World War, and found it emotionally difficult to face the cost of another war in human lives. Many on the Right were so eager to bury their heads in the sand that they trusted Hitler's protestations of peace and friendship for Britain. Rothermere admired him but knew that he could not be trusted, and this in itself reveals a rare quality of insight in him.

On one level he was soon falling for Nazism. As he saw things, Britain was running down. With the slump had come the National government of 1931: the true fires of Conservatism were burning low under the steady drizzle of Ramsay MacDonald's premiership; and India was being given away by a Labour ex-pacifist in unholy alliance with Baldwin. The rituals of parliamentary politics provided no answer to the slump and no action. There was too much talk and not enough authority. 'The Indian proposals', Rothermere told his readers from his ship in Colombo harbour,

> are simply proposals to govern by talk. They are in direct defiance of the whole trend of modern democratic movement. European peoples, such as the German, Italian, Polish and Portuguese, ballot with full knowledge of the futility and folly of the ballot box. Politicians are turning from Government by talk to Government by authority.[13]

In July 1933, six months after Hitler's assumption of power, Rothermere addressed his readers from 'somewhere in Naziland' in an article entitled 'Youth Triumphant'. In Germany, said Rothermere, vigorous and idealistic youth had taken the helm with splendid results. In Britain, too, the old men (he admitted that he was old himself) should give way to youth.

> Our 'parlour Bolsheviks' and 'cultured Communists' have started a campaign of denunciation against Nazi 'atrocities',

which, as anyone who visits Germany quickly discovers for himself, consist merely of a few isolated acts of violence such as are inevitable among a nation half as big again as ours . . .

. . . In the last days of the pre-Hitler regime there were twenty times as many Jewish Government officials in Germany as had existed before the war. Israelites of international attachments were insinuating themselves into key positions in the German administrative machine . . .

. . . It is from such abuses that Hitler has freed Germany.[14]

Later in the year Rothermere was arguing that Hitler must be supported for fear that if he failed the Communists would seize power in Germany. As early as 1934 he maintained, in the course of arguing that Germany must be given elbow room, that Tanganyika, the Cameroons and Togoland, all ex-German colonies, should be handed back to Germany.[15] In many respects Rothermere was already the fully-fledged ultra-appeaser. George Ward Price, his veteran European correspondent, did indeed produce later on the classic text of appeasement, from the pure, undefiled wells of Fascist public relations: *I Know These Dictators*. Everything is there: the Nazi social miracle, Hitler the peacemaker, the 'explanation' of the Jewish problem, the encirclement of Germany by Reds, the stupidity of some of the British press in its provocation of Hitler, Hitler's pleasure in the company of the Mitford sisters, 'those typical young Englishwomen of today'.[16]

Hitler and Rothermere began a lengthy correspondence in 1934. Perhaps Hitler, like the Hungarians, thought that he was a power behind the throne. Through the good offices of the princess Stefanie Hohenlohe-Waldenburg, Rothermere was invited to meet Hitler in December 1934; she escorted him to the Fuhrer's presence, this time at Berchtesgaden, in January 1937. There can be no doubt that Rothermere was impressed. He also understood Hitler well, describing him as a practical mystic, 'the rare combination of dreamer and doer', who meant to raise Germany to the standing of a world power of the first class.[18]

Throughout the 1930s Rothermere was haunted by the ghost of Northcliffe and the atmosphere of Britain before 1914. That was the great age of Germanophobia, with its spy stories, armaments and invasion scares. Northcliffe had helped to build up this ethos. In 1905, for example, he commissioned the novelist William le Queux to write a serial for the *Daily Mail* depicting the German invasion. This, felicitously as it may seem, had been planned by the Germans to pass through several major population centres in England where the *Daily Mail* had hopes of building up its circulation. The German invaders were reluctant to give notice of their next port of call, but here Northcliffe gave them a helping hand by publicising the fact that they would be invading Colchester tomorrow. Le Queux turned his serial into a successful book, *The Invasion of 1910*.[19] In 1914 the *Daily Mail* published a booklet reproducing its own warnings and called (ironically) *Scaremongering*.

In the 1930s there was similar alarmist literature, this time portraying the horrors which would overwhelm Britain when her towns were bombed. One of the root causes of appeasement was the exaggeration of the scale of damage and suffering which would be caused by air attacks. Prophetic novels on this theme included McIlraith and Connolly's *Invasion from the Air* (1934) and Nevil Shute's *Ruined City* (1938). McIlraith and Connolly dedicated their story to Baldwin, quoting his speech of November 1932 which included the chilling pronouncement: 'The bomber will always get through.' Rothermere helped to popularise the conception that Britain might be defeated by an aerial *blitzkreig*. In November 1933 he told his readers: 'If we fail to fill this fatal gap in our national defences it is quite possible that many of us will live to see our country confronted at a few hours' notice with the choice between acceptance of a humiliating ultimatum and virtual annihilation from the air.'[20]

Rothermere really feared that Hitler might launch a surprise air attack on Britain. 'I have the belief that this war will start some time next year when it is least expected', he wrote in October 1934 to Baldwin's confidante J. C. Davidson. 'It looks as though the blow may fall next year,' he informed the Secretary for War. To the First Lord of the Admiralty he wrote of 'Hitler's coming war against the West . . .'[21]

The only deterrent against a surprise attack would be an immense bombing fleet which could inflict retaliation on Germany. 'We Need 5,000 War Planes', he told his readers in November 1933, and in May 1935, 'Wanted: 10,000 Aeroplanes'. To stir up agitation he depicted bombing in the most lurid fashion. As the electors of Lowestoft were in the midst of a by-election campaign he produced an article, 'If Lowestoft were bombed':

> There would probably be a rush for the open broadland country behind the town. But those who ventured out would

run into even more immediate peril than those who waited to be blown up or burnt in their own houses. Suffocating gas; sneezing gas; weeping gas; blistering, burning gas, would be flooding the streets. A few breaths would be enough to reduce the strongest man to a helpless, twisted form, vomiting, writhing, and screaming in the agonies of a slow but certain death.[22]

An armaments scare might have been no more than a means of stirring up mischief in the Conservative Party. This was certainly one of its functions in Rothermere's eyes, but he was perfectly serious and obsessive about the air danger. He commissioned the Bristol Aeroplane Company to produce a fast aircraft suitable for adaptation to military purposes and presented it as a gift to the Air Ministry in August 1935. It was called the 'Britain First' and was used as a prototype in the development of the Blenheim bomber.[23] Rearmament in the air was always, in Rothermere's mind, a defensive strategy to protect British isolationism. Hitler would only be tempted to attack if Britain were weak; if she were strong he would be obliged to get on with his mission of eradicating Bolshevism. 'Britain First' was a Fascist slogan.

For six months, beginning in January 1934, the *Daily Mail* gave editorial support to the British Union of Fascists, led by Sir Oswald Mosley, and generous coverage was accorded to its activities. Once upon a time Rothermere had coined the slogan, 'Hats off to France'. Now it was 'Hurrah for the Blackshirts'. It is not easy to judge what Rothermere was doing. Was he prepared to go over to Fascism in the belief that it would triumph? Or did he see in the B.U.F. one more device, like the anti-waste party, for reshuffling the parliamentary pack in the hope of a royal flush? The latter seems more likely. Some phrases of Rothermere's can be read as approving the importation of Fascism, but he was very vague and never committed himself to any of the distinctive Mosley planks. He preferred to disguise the fact that Fascism was involved at all by referring to the B.U.F. as the 'blackshirts', and portraying them as though they were a vigorous branch of the young Conservatives. He denied to his readers that the Mosleyites were antagonistic to Jews or bent on dictatorship. Thus he turned a blind eye to the character of the movement.[24] Many Jews did not. According to Mosley (and standard Fleet Street lore) it was Jewish advertisers who brought pressure to bear on Rothermere to abandon his public connection with Mosley. They agreed to exchange letters. Rothermere wrote that he could not support anti-semitism, dictatorship, or the corporate state, and that no movement calling itself Fascist would ever succeed in Britain. Nevertheless, he expressed the hope that Mosley would ally with the Conservatives at the coming election.[25] Most likely Rothermere's aim was to make the Fascists junior partners in the die-hard Right's triumph over MacDonald and Baldwin. That seems to be the tenor of a letter to Lloyd George, early in 1935, when Lloyd George was searching for support for his 'New Deal':

> The Labour Party does not need an ally. The rump of the old Liberal Party will never swallow your high tariffs. The only thing left for you is to attach yourself to the Die-Hard Conservative Party. I am quite sure that right-wing politics are going to rule this country very soon. The right-wing movement has captured Italy and Germany and is capturing France. Come out very strongly on India and air armaments and I believe at the end of a couple of years you will be the leader of the Conservative Party and once more Prime Minister.[26]

In 1934 Rothermere acquired the services of a new writer on the *Sunday Dispatch*, Collin Brooks. For five years Brooks and Rothermere were to be very close, and before he died in 1940 Rothermere made Brooks his literary executor and potential biographer.[27]

Brooks was a warm-hearted, vivacious figure with a typewriter which chattered constantly beneath his fingers; out poured his daily journalism, his series of standard guides to finance and the City, a string of thrillers (or 'shockers' as he preferred to call them), and a fluent diary of his rapid movements about Fleet Street: whom he met, anecdotes he wished to collect, gossip. Talk was his great delight as he dashed from one aperitif to another before dining at one of the large number of clubs he frequented. Brooks had grown up in the quiet Lancashire resort of Southport. His father, a salesman, was prominent in local Tory politics, which were dominated by the 'King of Lancashire', Lord Derby. Brooks left school with only an elementary education and went on to educate himself by voracious and untrammeled reading. He pressed his way forward into the throng of Lancashire Toryism, commerce, and journalism, and after a thorough apprenticeship in the latter arrived in Fleet Street as assistant editor of the *Financial News*. A man of the world, Brooks had, none the less, a vulnerable side to his personality. He felt himself always to be 'the little boy from the Bastille', wondering at his own presence among famous names, the stars of the literary, theatrical, and political worlds. Having adulated from afar, he retained a touch of hero worship even when he saw the great at their worst. Family tradition accounted for his political attitudes. He disliked bureaucracy, the advance of egalitarianism, and many of the Jews he encountered in the financial world. The old deferential Toryism was for him, with its idealisation of hierarchy, leadership, and aristocratic values.

Fascism intrigued him, and in June 1934 he went with a party of friends to the famous Olympia rally of the British Union of Fascists, which erupted into violence and led the government to introduce the Public Order Act. After the meeting Brooks wrote to an old Southport friend:

> The Fascist technique is really the most brutal thing I have ever seen, which is saying something. There is no pause to hear what the interrupter is saying: there is no tap on the shoulder and a request to leave quietly: there is only the mass assault. Once a man's arms are pinnioned his face is common property to all adjacent punchers.
>
> . . . It was also interesting to find Mosley beginning cock-a-whoop when an interrupter was battered out (thrown out is a misnomer) and growing apologetic as the psychological tone of the audience changed into disgust and personal fear, no man or woman knowing when he or she might not be either borne down in a wild mêlé or be mistaken as an interrupter.

At this juncture Rothermere was still publicly supporting the B.U.F. On 11 June Brooks noted in his diary:

> Rothermere (who is quite certainly a maniac of a mild brand) filled the *Sunday Dispatch* with justifications for the Fascists – justifications which missed the whole point. The point of the matter surely is that to answer Communist brutality by Fascist brutality in the middle of an orderly audience of peaceful citizens is to undermine the whole theory of the modern State . . .[28]

Brooks first met Rothermere in January 1935. They rapidly became favourite and patron. Brooks was at various times in the years 1935–7 feature writer, city editor, and editor of the *Dispatch*, and thereafter a freelance assistant to Rothermere. There was too big a gap between their relative positions and ages for them to become intimate friends, but they shared each other's company extensively, and Brooks accompanied his master on jaunts and business trips around the world. After one week's work for

Rothermere Brooks wrote:

> I found R more likeable and sane than ever I had anticipated.
> But the fact remains that with a dictator of this kind, on whose
> whim thousands of men depend for their livelihoods, a great
> business is conducted like a Byzantium Court and not an enter-
> prise nominally for the honest dissemination of news and views.
> There are too many sycophants, the tendency is to staff the
> place with ignorant men who will not challenge a line of policy
> by their knowledge or their principles – the whole community
> degenerates into a funk-ridden community of time-servers.[29]

Brooks found himself in January 1935 spinning round at high
speed in a right-wing merry-go-round. On the spur of the
moment, Randolph Churchill decided to fight a by-election on the
die-hard ticket against the official Conservative at Liverpool
Wavertree. The *Dispatch* gave him a good splash – on
Rothermere's instructions. Then there was Rothermere's
decision to found a National Air League consisting of pilots who
would tour the country warning against the peril from the air (and
provide yet another fifth column in the Conservative ranks). To
help finance the League Rothermere ordered Brooks to 'go and
get £10,000 from Lucy Houston'. Lady Houston, a rags-to-riches
eccentric, was the owner of the *Saturday Review*, a right-wing
patriotic weekly which reflected her private conviction that the
Prime Minister, Ramsay MacDonald, was in the pay of Moscow.
Brooks hastened to Rothermere's rooms at the Savoy to tell him
the news that Lady Houston would pay. Rothermere was in ebul-
lient mood. Kingsley Wood, a Conservative minister, had just
been to see him, fishing for support at the next election. 'I told
Kingsley Wood they'd no chance as things are,' Rothermere went
on, 'and even if I supported 'em they'd be licked.' Two days later
there was lunch at the Savoy so that Rothermere could introduce
to Mosley some of the young airmen who were to take part in the
Air League. Having publicly renounced their connection the two
were still hankering after an *entente*. At the end of January every
effort was made by Rothermere in support of Randolph Churchill
at Wavertree. Captain Norman Macmillan, the pilot who was to
be president of the Air League, investigated the Liverpool docks
and wrote a timely article in the *Mail*, 'If Liverpool were Bombed'.
Both he and Brooks spoke from Randolph's platform.[30]

Churchill obtained a large enough vote at Wavertree on 6
February to scupper the official Conservative candidate and give

Labour the seat. Brooks was invited, as Rothermere's go-between, to meet the Conservative Chief Whip, David Margesson, who was anxious to damp down the embers of revolt on the Right of the party. Margesson, however, had nothing to offer beyond apologies for the prolongation of the National government.

'What can we do?' he asked. 'We can't interfere with the auton-omy of the local committees. Take Samuel [Marcus Samuel, an anti-Mosley Conservative recently returned at the Putney by-election] . . . the local people want £1,000 a year spending there – that ruled out everybody but two possibles, of whom Samuel was the least impossible – from our point of view it is heart-rending – the safe Conservative seats held by these hopeless duds . . .'

'I tell you, Brooks, that your city men will give us money for the National Government but they won't give a penny for the Tory Party alone . . . We know that Ramsay is a liability, but what can we do . . .' We talked of 1931. He said Baldwin had then had to accept the Ramsay leadership because of Buck-ingham Palace, and that the same influence is potent in keeping Ramsay in office still.[31]

Much of Brooks's time in 1935 was absorbed by the National League of Airmen, which was enrolling its two classes of mem-bers, pilots and observers. Rothermere records that among its ac-tive supporters were the duke of Westminster, the Hon. F. E. Guest, Major-General Fuller (the military commentator and Fas-cist), Admirals Murray Sueter and Mark Kerr, the Marquis of Donegall, Flight-Lieutenant Guy du Boulay, Patrick Donner, M.P., and Commander de Haga Haig. Rothermere put £50,000 into the venture, and the League was particularly active in the general election of 1935, when it claimed the full support of Con-servative associations in 160 constituencies. Air parity with the largest air force in Europe, and the creation of a Ministry of Defence, were its main campaign cries.[32]

Rothermere liked to fish about in political waters and was highly flexible in his tactics. In the spring of 1935 the departure of MacDonald and a reshuffle in the National government were imminent. Rothermere decided that the Right should place its bets on a big crisis in the long run. Hence he was now for the mini-mum degree of reshuffle, a position which Winston and Randolph Churchill both contested vigorously. Randolph became very heated with Brooks:

> Here is my father – the greatest statesman of his time – and this
> old fool Rothermere says there isn't a man outside the Govern-
> ment worth bringing in – it's madness – Do you mean that if my
> Father was made Minister of Defence the Government and the
> country wouldn't be infinitely stronger . . .

On the eve of the new Baldwin premiership Churchill Senior appeared.

> He is intent on a thorough reconstruction, and had come to
> upbraid R. for advocating only a minor reshuffle. R's view is
> that after this change about, in a little while there will be a
> genuine war panic and a big reconstruction, and then Winston
> will be in an extraordinarily strong position.[33]

On 3 October 1935 Mussolini's armies invaded Abyssinia,
challenging the League of Nations and the doctrine of collective
security. The National government believed that it had to appear
to support the League for the sake of public opinion. The die-
hards were for letting the League collapse. On the eve of war
Brooks was dispatched to report the critical meeting of the Council of the League. Unless the League were ended, he wrote, it
would trap the younger generation into a war for a cause which
was no concern of theirs. 'It will make our sons into the hired mer-
cenaries of some unworthy race . . .'[34] Having won the general
election of November 1935 on the platform of collective security,
the government blundered into the Hoare–Laval pact of
December, an Anglo-French scheme for partitioning Abyssinia.
The *Daily Mail* welcomed the plan, but Hoare was driven from the
Foreign Secretaryship in a storm of Tory indignation, and
Anthony Eden replaced him. Rothermere's phobia of sudden
defeat had been briefly reawoken by the prospect of a descent by
the Italian air force on British battleships in the Mediterranean.

Germany was, of course, his predominant and enduring fear.
'My dear fellow,' he said to Brooks, 'I can't bear to think of your
children in London. This terrible war is coming. They will be in a
death trap. Why don't you take a cottage in Norfolk?' Thereupon
he offered Brooks a cottage near his estate in Norfolk, and a rise in
salary. 'Have some champagne, my dear fellow. You'll need a
tonic. Men with vivid minds like yours and mine cannot help
being depressed by what we know. Have a bottle of champagne.'[35]
Once, he sought Brooks's advice on what to do with £200,000,

'in the belief that Germany means war, and will be successful.'
Rothermere thought it might be wise to buy gold and store it in
Switzerland, or buy reichsmarks and store them.[36] When Hitler
marched his troops into the Rhineland in March 1936, he gave an
interview to the *Daily Mail* in which he threw up a smokescreen of
peaceful rhetoric and proposed a non-aggression pact: 'HITLER'S
HISTORIC STATEMENT TO THE DAILY MAIL'. Rothermere, however,
felt 'convinced that Hitler means conquest, but not at this juncture.' In February 1937 Brooks found his master 'more than ever
gloomy about the imminence of war over the German colonial
issue.'[37] He continued to bang the drum for air defence and in
1936 began to campaign for voluntary recruitment to the services.
This gave him a novel line to run in the abdication crisis of
December, which seemed to be a providential opportunity of
unhorsing Baldwin and the National government: 'Now that the
shortages of recruits has become a grave national emergency, the
King is the only human agency to whom we can look to make the
voluntary system a success. If he goes, conscription will be inevitable.'[38] The victory of the Left in the Spanish elections of
February 1936, and the French elections in April, sent shivers of
apprehension down die-hard spines. The Popular Fronts were at
once identified in the right-wing mind with Communism, and a
more positive drive to come to terms with Germany can be seen
emerging at about the time of the outbreak of the Spanish Civil
War in July 1936. Rothermere, now sixty-eight, was an autumn
leaf in the breeze. 'Get Together with Germany', he urged his
readers. Not since the Bolshevik revolution had the Left made
such rapid headway. The 'British mind' admired the orderliness
of the Nazi regime: 'And it is furthermore beginning to realise that
this powerful, patriotic, and superbly organised country con-
stitutes an element of stability amid those rising tendencies of disorder and disruption which are becoming increasingly and
seriously manifest in Europe.' As for the civil war in Spain, Britain
was dependent upon a friendly Portugal, and a 'Red' victory
'would mean the destruction of all that splendid work of national
development which has been done by the strong and enlightened
Government of Dr. Salazar.'[39]

Rothermere was now all appeaser. Czechoslovakia (February
1937) was 'a sham' and the Czechs 'a crafty race' who would 'rue
their evil doings' now that Hitler had risen as the champion of the
German-speaking Sudeten minority. He revived the idea (May
1937) that Britain should give back the ex-German colonies in

Africa. 'If Germany forces a way to the Black Sea,' he was writing in May 1938, 'some of us may not like it, but what has it to do with us?' Hitler was 'a man of rare culture. His knowledge of music, painting, and architecture is profound.'[40] When Hitler demanded and obtained the partition of Czechoslovakia by the Munich agreement of September 1938, Rothermere shed no tears. During the crisis he had done his best, a little pathetically, to use his 'influence' in Germany. On 26 September, Brooks recorded:

> R told me on the telephone that, with the assent of the Foreign Office, he had sent a telegram to Hitler, speaking as his friend and as a friend to Germany and as one who lost two of his three boys in the last war, asking Hitler to incorporate in tonight's speech some word of assurance to the many millions who fear war.[41]

Rothermere found a special source of private satisfaction in the Munich agreement. Poland had taken its share of Czechoslovakia; now it must be Hungary's turn to urge its claims. Rothermere had Ward Price draw up a *pronunciamento* to the people of Hungary, which Brooks read with amazement:

> It lamented at their failure to secure their lost territories now that Germany was being satisfied and was satisfying Poland, lamented that they had not secured foreign support for their claims, said that for 11 years R had not visited that hard hit country, but, as they knew, had never ceased to work for it, recalled Esmond's triumphal tour of ten years ago and concluded by saying 'Now I am ready to return and lay at the disposal of your Government my counsel and connections . . .' It was, in short, a bid for the Regency.

The manifesto was scrapped when Rothermere learned that the Hungarians were content to await the outcome of a four-power conference at Vienna. Ward Price and Brooks amused themselves by imagining the court of Lord Rothermere moved to Budapest, with Ward Price running foreign affairs and Brooks the Central Bank.[42] The Vienna conference awarded Hungary a substantial slice of Slovakia, and the Hungarian cabinet invited Rothermere to take part in the celebrations arranged to commemorate the return of the lost territories. He toured Hungary feasting on praise and applause, was received by Admiral Horthy and given a high decoration held only by two other non-Hungarians – Hitler and Mussolini. Wherever he was announced crowds gathered to chant

'Long live the Lord!'[43]

Rothermere's last years were troubled. He had handed over the conduct of the *Daily Mail* to Esmond at the beginning of 1938 and withdrawn from political dabbling. But Princess Hohenlohe-Waldenburg brought an action against him claiming breaches of agreements to employ her as his foreign political representative, and to clear her name from charges that she was 'a spy, or "vamp", and an immoral woman'. She lost the case, but it embarrassed Rothermere by lifting the curtain to provide a glimpse of his European activities in the 1930s. Moreover, the princess possessed photostats of some of Rothermere's political correspondence. By the time the case was heard war had broken out. It was not the happiest time for Rothermere to be in court recalling his letters to Hitler, and when the case was over he still worried that copies of his political correspondence would somehow leak out into publication. Brooks, going through the files at Rothermere's request, found for example a letter to Ribbentrop in which Rothermere denied that he had ever intrigued for the restoration of the German crown prince, and continued: 'You know I have always been a fervent admirer of the Fuhrer . . .'[44]

In the course of 1939 Rothermere had Brooks and Ward Price compile three volumes setting out the record of his activities over Hungary and Germany.[45] After the outbreak of war, perhaps because he was ailing and tired, he went through the motions of supporting the war with little inward conviction. Brooks noted on 9 September 1939:

> He has sent a window-dressing telegram to Winston [First Lord of the Admiralty] pleading with him to bomb, torpedo or capture the Bremen, but on the phone this morning he was positively exultant about the alleged German seizure of Poland, which he said was 'the quickest thing on record!' He is still englamoured by Hitler, and cannot believe that a nation which has not employed R. or Esmond in its counsels can possibly be any good or in any way prepared.[46]

Brooks was irritated by this kind of attitude. He himself had been a strong appeaser up to the outbreak of war. On the suggestion of Rothermere he had written a fierce condemnation in 1938 of the policies associated with Eden and anti-Fascism, *Can Chamberlain Save England?* But now that war had broken out Brooks was for fighting it through.

Rothermere went on his travels again in the winter of 1939–40 –

Venice, Delagoa Bay, Luxor. In March he was home again, but soon anxious to get away to the United States. The opportunity presented itself in May, when Churchill became Prime Minister and Beaverbrook Minister of Aircraft Production. Beaverbrook provided an honourable cloak for Rothermere's departure: an 'official mission' to report on the aircraft industry in North America.[47] Brooks, under the impression that a vital contribution to the war effort was at stake, abandoned his national savings job in London and accompanied him. Soon he discovered that Rothermere was too tired and depressed to achieve very much and longed only for tranquil sunshine. The battle of Britain was beginning, and Brooks returned home. In November Rothermere died in a hotel in Bermuda.

Having acquired a true affection for Rothermere, Brooks championed him in later years. In a broadcast during the London blitz he claimed that Rothermere was the first public figure to realise the danger from Hitler, even in advance of Churchill. It is true that Rothermere was a prophet of the blitz: no one else believed in the early 1930s that Britain was in *imminent* danger of air attack from Germany. Nothing, of course, could have been further from the minds of the Germans in 1934 or 1935 than an immediate air assault on Britain: Rothermere was the victim of a phobia. But it was a phobia rooted in fact, and he did something to build up the pressure for rearmament inside the Conservative Party. Churchill himself thought that Rothermere could make acute judgments, marred as they were by pessimism. 'My dear Harold,' he wrote to him in July 1936,

> . . . If, as you say, we are going to be vassals of Germany, I can only hope I shall not live to see it!
> You have been wonderfully right in your talks with me:
> 1. At Christmas predicting the violation of the Rhineland;
> 2. The collapse of the Abyssinian resistance; and
> 3. that Mussolini had squared Hitler about Austria.[48]

Rothermere sensed the predatory forces in the world and could hear them sliding through the jungle towards their prey. He could feel them closing in on Britain. But he lacked the moral energy to resist them. He could not think in terms of Fascism as a threat to civilisation; it seemed to him, if anything, more like a police force to protect the old way of life. He and his fellow die-hards had at first reacted to Hitler by emphasising the danger. By 1938, most of them had evolved into ultra-appeasers, afraid of war, defeat and

Russia: almost alone, Churchill preserved the robust nationalism of 1914.

A Note on Arms and Profits

Rothermere was not above mixing politics with business enterprise. Mosley records (*My Life*, p. 346) that Rothermere planned to go into cigarette production using the B.U.F. branches as distribution outlets, and ordered £70,000 worth of machinery before changing his mind. Rothermere declared that before beginning his campaign for rearmament he sold his aircraft shares, including shares in Rolls-Royce. The Brooks diary shows also that Associated Newspapers parted with Rolls-Royce shares when it was discovered that they were in the portfolio. Rothermere often discussed finance with Brooks, whose knowledge of the City was considerable, but never reflected on the impact of rearmament on investment. Rothermere's financial interests must have been affected at least indirectly by rearmament, but there is no sign that he thought in these terms. His business advisers on the *Mail* and *Dispatch*, and Beaverbrook himself, advised that alarmism was harming the profits of his newspapers by depressing readers. He pressed on. His one direct financial motive seems to have been the conviction that war would destroy the rich, a commonly held view in the 1930s.

Notes

1. Viscount Rothermere, *My Fight to Rearm Britain* (1939) p. vii.
2. Cecil King, *Strictly Personal* (1969) p. 73.
3. Wickham Steed, *The Press* (Penguin Books, 1938) p. 91 *et seq.*
4. Diary of Collin Brooks, 13 Jan 1935. I am grateful to the family of the late Collin Brooks for allowing me to read his diary and quote from it. It is a vivid document, dedicated to racy talk about the theatre, poetry and literature, and to vignettes of social history as much as to politics.
5. Keith Middlemas and John Barnes, *Baldwin* (1969) p. 257.
6. A. J. P. Taylor (ed.), *Lloyd George, A Diary by Frances Stevenson* (1971), p. 233.
7. Collin Brooks, *Devil's Decade* (1947) p. 144.
8. Robert Rhodes James, *Memoirs of a Conservative* (1969) p. 135.
9. A. J. P. Taylor *Beaverbrook* (1970) p. 207.
10. *Daily Mail, The Economic Crisis foretold by the Daily Mail 1921–1931* (? 1932); *Daily Mail Blue Book on the Indian Crisis* (1931).
11. Viscount Rothermere, *My Campaign for Hungary* (1939); Admiral Nicholas de Horthy, *Memoirs* (1956) p. 135.
12. In 1939, as related in the essay, the princess took unsuccessful legal action against Rothermere. The proceedings illuminate some of Rothermere's activities in the 1930s. They were reported in *The Times* between 9 and 16 Nov 1939.
13. *Daily Mail*, 17 Apr 1933.
14. *Daily Mail*, 10 Jul 1933.

15. *Daily Mail*, 13 Oct 1933.

16. George Ward Price, *I Know these Dictators* (1937).

17. *The Times*, 9 Nov 1939.

18. *Daily Mail*, 4 Jun 1935.

19. See I. F. Clarke, *Voices Prophesying War* (1966), Chapter 4.

20. *Daily Mail*, 7 Nov 1933.

21. Rothermere, *My Fight to Rearm Britain*, pp. 110–16.

22. *Daily Mail*, 6 Feb 1934.

23. Viscount Rothermere, *Warnings and Predictions* (1939) p. 59–62.

24. Robert Benewick, *The Fascist Movement in Britain* (1972) p. 98–104; *Daily Mail*, 22 Jan 1934, 2 May 1934.

25. *Saturday Review*, 11 Aug 1934; Sir Oswald Mosley, *My Life* p. 343–7.

26. Rothermere to Lloyd George, no date but early 1935. Lloyd George Papers, G/141/43/1. I am grateful to Dr John Campbell of Edinburgh University for supplying me with this reference.

27. Collin Brooks, *Tavern Talk* (1950) p. 37.

28. Brooks to Norman Watson, 10 Jun 1934, copy interleaved in the Diary; Diary, 11 Jun 1934.

29. Diary, 10 Jan 1935.

30. This paragraph derives from the Diary for 19 Jan to 3 Feb 1935.

31. Diary, 6 Mar 1935.

32. Rothermere, *My Fight to Rearm Britain* pp. 89–95. Brooks noted once, on 6 December 1935: '. . . the League is virile enough, but most of its supporters (as is inevitable) seem to be cranky mediocrities.'

33. Diary, 5 May, 28 May 1935.

34. *Sunday Dispatch*, 8 Sep 1935.

35. Diary, 9 Mar 1935.

36. Diary, 10 Apr 1935.

37. Diary, 13 Mar 1936, 8 Feb 1937.

38. *Daily Mail*, 7 Dec 1936.

39. *Daily Mail*, 25 Jan 1937.

40. *Daily Mail*, 12 Feb, 4 May 1937; 13 May, 20 May 1938.

41. Diary, 26 Sep.

42. Diary, 14 Oct.

43. Rothermere, *My Campaign for Hungary* pp. 172–89.

44. Diary, 2 Dec 1939.

45. *Warnings and Predictions, My Campaign for Hungary, My Fight to Rearm Britain*.

46. Diary, 9 Sep 1939.

47. Taylor, *Beaverbrook*, p. 422.

48. In 1935 at Rothermere's suggestion Brooks began a separate 'Brooks–Rothermere Diary', which was to tell the story of two men who realised that war was imminent in the setting of blissful ignorance surrounding them. The late Miss Rosemary Brooks allowed me to read through the diary, which includes Brooks's copying out of the letter from Churchill.

9 The Whitehall Factor: The Role of the Higher Civil Service 1919-39

MAX BELOFF

In any period of history the role of the civil servant is bound to attract less notice from the historian than the doings of statesmen. Statesmen fill the centre of the public stage; in modern times they face the electorate and seek to impress their personalities through the press. Their doings form the staple of contemporary chronicle, and after their retirement (and sometimes sooner) they publish memoirs or are the subject of biographies. The political history of an era is usually written first of all from the public record; only when the archives become available is it possible to write administrative history and even then the personal characteristics of civil servants which may well have affected the advice they gave and their patterns of work may well find little reflection in official papers that are written according to set forms and with some affectation, at least, of impersonality. Few civil servants in modern times are likely to have much time for personal correspondence and few are likely to be diarists. We are not likely to find that a twentieth-century Samuel Pepys has been occupying a Whitehall desk. In this, of course, civil servants differ from diplomats whose absence from their home base is more likely to encourage correspondence and even the keeping of diaries.[1]

Sooner or later, of course, administrative history comes to be written and we learn something at least of the rise and fall of departments and of the impact of departmental considerations upon public policy. But even then it tends to be the kind of history that is written by specialists for specialists and is not easy to integrate into the general narrative of events, or into the record of economic and social change.[2] It is arguable that this is still the case in respect of the period of British history falling between the two world wars and that until this lack can be remedied our understanding of that period must to some extent be distorted.[3]

The distortion is the more important in that in some respects the period is the one in which the higher civil service in Britain probably reached the height of its corporate influence. The work of government had been much increased by the pre-war emergence of the welfare state and the process was carried further by some of the legislation of the period itself. While most of the wartime controls had been dismantled, the extension of government activity brought about by the war was not wholly temporary. On the other hand the new or enlarged activities of government were still presided over by a very small number of higher civil servants, numbering by 1939 some 500 generalists with another fifty or so exercising more specialised functions.[4]

The importance of the small size of the administrative class at this time is further enhanced by the fact that it was only then that the trend towards the unification of that class reached its fulfilment. And one gets the consequent assumptions about the need for all-roundedness in administrators rather than for departmental specialists and for higher civil servants to be available for transfers between departments.[5] One tends too easily to forget that the Victorian civil servants like their predecessors in earlier centuries (and like most American civil servants) were recruited by and to particular departments. The belief that administration was itself the primary skill and that a good man could easily pick up the business of any department was a relatively new one. Criticisms of this view have been the commonplace of discussions on the British civil service in more recent decades. But in practice it may have had its advantages, and even the suggested uniformity of social origin, educational experience and general outlook may have had its advantages as well. The way in which the civil service was expanded in wartime by introducing newcomers from the universities and other walks of life without any notable breakdowns in the handling of business represents a not inconsiderable achievement, comparable in its way with the manning of the shadow factories upon which the production of armaments so largely depended. It is probable that the smoothness of the operation owed a good deal to the capacity of the permanent civil service to provide a framework within which the temporaries might operate and that it was eased by the fact that many of these newcomers had much in common with their colleagues, in that they were accustomed to the same basic techniques, spoke the same kind of language, and dare one add, belonged to the same clubs?

It is more difficult to find the appropriate criteria for judging governmental performance during the interwar period itself. The most salient fact about most of the domestic issues of the period is, of course, the priority attached to financial considerations and hence to the Treasury view. It is obvious that in this connection the fact that the unification of the civil service took place under the aegis of the Treasury and that throughout the period – from 1 October 1919 to 30 September 1939 – the same man, Sir Warren Fisher, was permanent secretary to the Treasury and in that capacity head of the civil service is highly significant.[6]

What this meant in practice was of the first importance, and how far individual civil servants, including Warren Fisher himself, should be regarded as responsible for the working out of policies for which historians usually give credit to the politicians constitutionally answerable for them is the most important of the questions one must ask. Unfortunately, it is also the hardest to answer. To some extent the more humdrum side of policy-making has been obscured by some of the more dramatic aspects of Fisher's term of office and, more particularly, by his attempt to bring the Foreign Office within the sphere of his jurisdiction.[7] The two departments had never worked closely together and the Treasury had always been reluctant to use financial policy as a method of forwarding objectives in foreign policy.[8] In the confused situation after the end of the war when Lloyd George took charge of the most significant parts of the peacemaking process, there was a great deal of friction arising from the suspicion on the part of the Foreign Office (and in particular of its irascible chief, Lord Curzon) that the Treasury was pursuing a line of its own in such questions as that of reparations. The situation in this respect was ameliorated after the departure of Lloyd George; and Baldwin in particular was insistent on keeping in touch with opinion in the Foreign Office and was very close to Sir William (later Lord) Tyrrell, the permanent under-secretary at the Foreign Office from 1925 to 1928.[9]

But questions of personnel continued to create suspicion of Fisher's role and intentions. It was suggested that when Fisher was made chairman of a committee of investigation into the 'francs scandal' of 1928 in which a member of the Foreign Office was the central figure, he used the occasion to further his own purposes. The fact that in the committee's report (Cmd 3037) members of the Foreign Office were referred to as 'civil servants' was taken as an indication that he had won an important victory.[10] And it has been shown that in 1930 it was he who against the wishes of the Foreign Secretary, Arthur Henderson, persuaded Ramsay MacDonald to appoint Sir Robert (later Lord) Vansittart as permanent under-secretary.[11]

In the 1930s the issue of rearmament and of Fisher's role in the debates on that topic have once again made some impact upon general historical writing, largely because it was again an issue connected with foreign policy in relation to which participants in the debate have felt much freer to air their views.[12] Although Fisher's role in this arena has not been fully examined, it has been brought into clearer focus because of the role of the other dominant civil servant of the era, Sir Maurice (later Lord) Hankey, who is unique among his colleagues in having a fully satisfactory biography devoted to him, in addition to the material in his own published diaries and other writings.[13] Already secretary of the Committee of Imperial Defence which was in abeyance in wartime, Hankey became the first Secretary to the Cabinet when the office was created by Lloyd George in 1916; he remained Secretary to the Committee of Imperial Defence when it was revived after the war and was from 1922 also Clerk to the Privy Council, retaining all three offices, as well as acting as secretary to a large number of imperial and international conferences between that year and his first retirement in 1938.[14]

The salience of an issue is what is most likely to throw light on the role of civil servants; yet it does not necessarily mean that issues of this kind are the most important from this point of view. For instance, much has been written (usually from a hostile point of view) about the alleged role of Sir Horace Wilson (another silent and largely unknown figure) during his period of secondment to the Prime Minister between 1935 and 1939, and in particular in respect of Chamberlain's foreign policy at the time of Munich. Yet by 1935 Wilson has already been a civil servant for thirty-five years. He was permanent secretary at the Ministry of Labour during the period 1921–30 with its major problems in the field of unemployment and industrial unrest, and the Government's chief industrial adviser from 1930–9 (a post which partially overlapped with his secondment to the Prime Minister). He was then to end his official career as Warren Fisher's successor at the Treasury and as head of the civil service from 1939 to 1942.[15]

One feels that there is here a lot more to explore. Or take Sir John Anderson (later Lord Waverley) whose role in the General Strike is alluded to in another chapter in this volume. By 1922, when Anderson became permanent under-secretary at the Home Office, he had held a variety of civil service posts, having begun (in the Colonial Office) in 1905. His ten years at the Home Office during which he served seven secretaries of state have been overshadowed by his later career as Governor of Bengal during a very difficult period and as a member of Churchill's war cabinet. They account for only 33 of the 409 pages of his official biography.[16] Yet given the fear of subversion and even revolution that underlay so much of the surface calm of British politics, one feels there must be more to tell.

It was perhaps the fact that Anderson was to play an important political role as much as his qualities as an administrator that assures him of his place in the history books; those who served only in Whitehall come off less well. It is hard for instance to find any issue involving financial questions in relation to which the name of Sir Richard Hopkins does not sooner or later appear in the documents. Yet Hopkins, who transferred from the inland revenue to the Treasury in 1927 and was second secretary from 1932 to 1942 when he succeeded Horace Wilson as permanent secretary for the last three years of the war, makes little impact upon the writers of general history.[17] It is hard not to believe that the Treasury's leading expert on fiscal matters and principal link with the Bank of England and its powerful governor (from 1920 to 1944), Montagu Norman, must have been more important in his own right than many cabinet ministers.

It is important that we should know the facts about the role of the senior civil servants in this period not only in order better to understand how policy was made but also for a more precise reason. In domestic political history, as other essays in this volume show, it is the period in which the Labour Party replaced the Liberal Party as the alternative party of government. For the first time a party dedicated to a socialist transformation of society held office, even if only within minority governments. It was not altogether unreasonable for some adherents at least of the socialist creed to argue that while civil servants might impartially advise and execute the wishes of successive ministers of different parties but all basically dedicated to the preservation of the *status quo*, they could not be expected to feel the same about the newcomers whose class origin and general outlook would also be less familiar to them. The first two Labour governments were much more genuinely 'labour' in the social sense than their successors.

It must also be remembered that in answering this question in relation to the senior civil servants we have already mentioned, and some others of considerable importance, we are dealing with men whose basic training and experience predated the rise of Labour. Hankey was born in 1877, Vansittart and Fisher in 1879, Hopkins in 1880, Horace Wilson and Anderson in 1882; all of them were thus adults and already embarked on their careers before the election of 1906 which may be said to inaugurate Labour's rise to power. Thomas Jones, who as deputy secretary of the cabinet from 1916 to 1930 and afterwards as the *éminence grise* of more than one politician was also a figure of some influence in the interwar period, was even older, having been born in 1870. The question of generations must surely also be of some significance here. How far did these men instinctively sympathise with those wishing rather to put a brake on the progress of collectivism than to accelerate its progress?

In other spheres also it was a period of much novelty. Britain was still an imperial power; yet of a very different kind to what had been the case before 1914. The autonomy of the 'old Dominions' was conceded; India was beginning to tread the same path; the leadership of the 'Mother Country' was less and less automatically recognised. Did someone like Hankey resent the need to pander to what might appear to be the ill-informed prejudices of Dominion statesmen far removed from the cockpit of Europe?[18] On the other hand the Colonial Office was trying somewhat intermittently and inconsistently to carry out some of the older ideas of Joseph Chamberlain about turning to good account the 'underdeveloped estates' of Britain's possessions overseas. What would be the civil service and in particularly the Treasury attitude to any departure from the old assumptions that the colonies must pay for themselves and that there must be no subventions by the home taxpayer.[19]

In questions of high policy or of general principle it is difficult to separate the role of the advisers from that of the ministers themselves, except on the rare occasions when a sudden change in personnel gives a clue to a serious and unbridgeable difference of opinion, as when Vansittart was 'kicked upstairs' on January 1938 to give way to Sir Alexander Cadogan at the height of Chamberlain's drive for appeasement. But much policy particularly in domestic matters is not as easily resolved into questions of 'either/or' as is the case in external relations or occasionally in the planning of defence. Policy often takes the form of legislation, where the details upon which much depends are more likely to be hammered out in the department than by the minister himself; in the case of delegated legislation, whose growth was one of the most publicised developments of the period, the minister's role was even more likely to be a fiction. And much, too, will depend on how things are in practice administered in the field and on the arrangements made for handling such business; here it is perhaps a rare minister who can find the time to master the detail involved. Not surprisingly historians have found it easier to deal with the roles of ministers and of 'pressure groups' since both are likely to spend much of their time explaining their intentions and wishes to the public, while civil servants normally have to make their influence felt behind the scenes and have less opportunity than, say, the leaders of the armed forces, of mobilising pressure groups of their own.

To say that the subject of the influence of the civil service and of civil servants is an important one is not to say that it is easy to handle. Indeed a writer who is himself clear about its importance may find the material largely intractable for this purpose. This appears to be the case of the American historian of the welfare state, Professor Bentley B. Gilbert. It is notable how heavily he has to rely upon the diaries of Sir George Newman, chief medical officer to the Ministry of Health from 1920 to 1935, not merely because of Newman's importance but also because there is no other high official in the field whose career has left comparable materials for study.[20]

Professor Gilbert himself believes that social policy is unique in the degree to which the basic decisions did not arise out of the clash of parties but from the work of those mostly closely involved with the execution of policy, and that this was true even of major pieces of legislation. 'In some major areas,' he writes, 'notably national health insurance, the administrators, the approved societies, deliberately kept themselves anonymous. The effect of all this was of course, that the critical decisions, although frequently highly political in content, were made by administrators.'[21] Yet in fact the approved societies and other non-official bodies were also much more articulate and their individual leaders easier to study in their personal role. When we come to civil servants, even Professor Gilbert's detailed analysis provides too little material for him to come to any ready-made conclusions.

He certainly believes that one of the obstacles to more far-reaching reform at a time when postwar opinion was still very malleable was to be found in the resistance of what he calls 'office-holders', who themselves cherished the values of an earlier period and saw little need for major changes to be made.[22] But the example he quotes is not of an official but of a minister, Hayes Fisher (Lord Downham), president of the Local Government Board from 1917 to 1918; and on the reforming side he gives the main prominence to Christopher (later Viscount) Addison whose long career did not suffer from lack of publicity whether from his own pen or from that of others.

It is true that Professor Gilbert does attribute a good deal of the responsibility for the failure to consolidate the government's activities in the health field at that time to the rivalry between Newman, then at the Board of Education and Arthur Newsholme whom he was to succeed at the new Ministry of Health.[23] He believes that the changes in staffing (including the elevation of Newman) which Addison made could with political support have done much to make the ministry a more important force in the period of postwar reconstruction and that it was the unexpected collapse and premature death of Sir Robert Morant that 'deprived Addison of the one person at his disposal capable of the task of reconstruction'. The fact that Morant's successor Sir William Robinson did not get on well with Newman was another blow.[24] But such judgements do not take one very far.

The only important clue to the extent of the civil service share in the making of social policy is in Professor Gilbert's treatment of the Anderson committee, which he calls a 'small only semi-official committee of seven civil servants under John Anderson', set up seemingly on the initiative of Horace Wilson immediately after the 1923 election but before Baldwin's resignation to look into ways of co-ordinating various welfare services. In the short run this committee's work laid the foundation for Neville Chamberlain's initiative on pensions after the return of the Conservatives to office in 1924; and in the long run it led to the carrying out of Wilson's particular pet scheme when the Unemployment Act of 1934 ended the competition between unemployment insurance and Poor Law relief. Since there is reason to believe that Baldwin had not approved (and perhaps was ignorant of) the creation of the committee and since it lacked a Treasury representative – despite the fact that finance was the very heart of the problem – it is understandable that Professor Gilbert thinks the committee to have had a somewhat irregular status.[25] But it is hard to see how a committee of civil servants including two permanent secretaries can be styled only 'semi-official', and one would need to know more of their contribution once the matter had come to ministerial and cabinet level. It may be that Professor Gilbert is less sensitive than a non-American would be to this borderline between the official and the ministerial to which a British historian would probably attach greater importance.

If one turns from the attempt to deal with relations between civil servants and ministers in individual departments and branches of policy to the central subject of most discussion – the role of the Treasury in the interwar years – the role of the civil servants concerned had many and by now quite visible ramifications.[26] In respect of financial policy proper there is little to suggest that the Chancellors of the period differed very profoundly in their assumptions from those of their advisers; certainly they did not differ according to party – the Socialist Philip Snowden was the most unbending Gladstonian of the lot. The battle to substitute for the old priorities of balanced budgets and the automatic check against inflation provided by the discipline of the gold standard, the new ideas about the management of national resources in the interests of maintaining full employment of which Keynes was the accredited exponent was waged during this period without provoking a major shift in economic thinking on the official side or in the machinery for its formulation; these changes were to happen only after the Second World War. What did happen from 1931 onwards was the introduction of a series of expedients including protective tariffs and a managed currency without the full acceptance of the collectivist philosophy underlying them.

It has been pointed out that most of the work of the Treasury was done in sections not concerned with high financial policy. In Mr Roseveare's words, 'the axis round which financial policy formed was an extraordinarily frail one, and it was insecurely geared to the machinery of government'.[27] Fisher himself claimed no expertise in the matter and left it largely to Hopkins. Hopkins did not see eye to eye with F. W. (later Sir Frederick) Leith-Ross, his deputy from 1925 to 1932, and when the latter was transferred in 1932 to the post of Chief Economic Adviser, the title proved a misnomer and Leith-Ross continued in fact to be mainly occupied with a relatively new aspect of Treasury work, relations with foreign governments and financial institutions. It has been suggested that one reason for the importance attached to the Bank of England and its advice was the weakness of the Treasury on this side. There is also the possibly significant fact that three civil servants from the finance side of the Treasury, two of them very senior, left it to join the Bank during the 1920s.[28]

What concerned Fisher more was the new co-ordinating role he wished to give the Treasury and the accompanying responsibility for the direction of the machinery of government as a whole. If Treasury control was to mean more than an Olympian exercise of the power of saying yea and nay, then its personnel would require direct experience within the spending departments. Treasury control would then imply ideally a partnership between the Treasury and the departments so that at each stage of a project the Treasury angle would be fully explained and understood. By 1930, when Fisher gave evidence to the Royal (Tomlin) Commission on the Civil Service, 'some of the fruits were already mature. His fellow Permanent Secretaries were apparently happy with the new order, liking the new mobility of the administrative grade and the ease of consultation with the Treasury.'[29] But just because Royal commissions provide so much obvious material for historians of government, it is important not to take statements made to them at their face value. We need both to ask whether there was not more friction than Fisher and his colleagues were prepared to admit, and whether the injection of Treasury thinking would seem in retrospect to have conduced to the national interest. And that demands a closer look at the subject matter of debate.[30]

One example already referred to is that of the Treasury's attitude towards colonial policy especially during the period when Leo Amery as Colonial Secretary was trying to move towards a more positive policy of promoting economic development in overseas territories.[31]

Of the friction between the Treasury and the Colonial Office during Amery's period as secretary of state there is ample evidence from both sides; indeed it is Amery's own articulateness – another diarist and writer of memoirs – that perhaps explains in part why we are better informed about the Treasury's role in this field of activity than in some others. While Amery regarded the Treasury as obstructionist, its officials had a poor opinion of him. Sir Otto Niemeyer, formerly Controller of Finance at the Treasury and now with the Bank of England described him to Montagu Norman as the 'Mad Mullah Minister'. And the opinion was general in the Treasury that the officials of the Colonial office were a poor lot hastily producing schemes for development without reckoning the cost; there is, ran one Minute, 'not a glimmering of financial sense in the place'.[32]

In Professor Drummond's view Amery was confused about the difference between 'Treasury control' and Treasury opinion. 'There is no evidence', in his view, 'that the Treasury actually obstructed where any policy had been definitely accepted – in statute, by cabinet, or through interdepartmental discussion. But when policies had not been settled, Treasury influence was consistently on the side of caution – minimum discretion to the spending departments, minimum assistance to the overseas Dominions and Colonies, maximum protection for the UK's taxpayers and bond-buyers'. But it was not just that in Professor Drummond's words, 'Amery was a sort of vulgar proto-Keynesian', believing that more investment overseas would generate employment and give higher prosperity in Britain and the rest of the empire.[33] Nor should too much be made of the fact that Churchill, the Treasury's ministerial head at the time, was anything but a Keynesian, being at this time an old-fashioned free-trader like his predecessor and successor, Philip Snowden. For the difference in attitude between the two departments antedated this particular set of antipathies.[34]

It is first necessary to see what Treasury control meant in the strict sense where the colonial empire was concerned. In principle colonies were expected to balance their budgets from their own resources and Treasury control in detail only came into the picture if they failed to do so and were forced to ask for grants-in-aid. Few colonies were in this position in the 1920s, but as the world situation worsened in the 1930s the number increased. It rose from seven in 1932 to fifteen in 1936.[35] In these circumstances the Treasury exercised control similar to that over the home departments, as was spelled out in a Colonial Office paper in 1936.[36] Annual estimates had to be submitted for approval as well as any new forms of expenditure except the most trivial, and the Treasury had to sanction any excess expenditure in sub-heads or in the total budget even if there was a corresponding increase in revenue. Sanction was also required for changes in the colony's pensionable establishment, and prior authority was needed for the writing off of losses of cash or stores. In addition, colonial loans, where these were used instead of grants-in-aid, required the Treasury's sanction. It was likely that loan proposals would be scrutinised with care, as the Treasury's general attitude in the period, as shown in relation to the Dominions as well, was that there should not be too much competition on the London money market which might reflect adversely on home investment and the balance of payments.[37] It is worth emphasising that Treasury control of a colony in deficit applied to its entire budget, not merely to that proportion for which it was receiving assistance. Although the Treasury was bound to relax its control immediately after a deficit loan had been paid off, or three years after a grant had been made, the rule was amended in practice since the Treasury often imposed conditions in respect of future budgeting even after detailed supervision was abandoned.

On the loans side the Treasury's intervention was even more important in respect of the relatively large sums called for by Amery's policy of positive development: the East African guaranteed loan of 1926 and the Colonial Development Fund of 1929. Although these were for specific purposes and not to help out with deficits and therefore did not entail full-scale Treasury intervention in the colonies concerned, the Treasury had the determining voice in saying what advances were to be made and upon what conditions – it was thus fully and necessarily involved in the policy-making process.

In its opposition to expenditure for purposes close to the heart of the 'imperial visionaries' (to use Professor Drummond's phrase) the Treasury's attitude was a consistent one. In this it was of course supported by a section of public and parliamentary opinion which had been voiced in the opposition to the Act of 1920 enabling the Board of Trade to guarantee part of the costs of what became the British Empire Exhibition at Wembley in 1924 and 1925. When the decision to prolong the Exhibition for a year came before the House of Commons and a supplementary estimate was asked for, Liberal members during a debate on 11 and 12 February 1925 advocated that any public money to be voted should be subject to full Treasury control. A further much larger supplementary estimate to meet part of the loss – on an exhibition visited by 22½ million people – some no doubt like the present writer visited it several times in their imperial enthusiasm – met with much criticism when presented to the House of Commons on 10 December 1925.

There was similar diffidence about using British funds to shore up the affairs of the Imperial Institute (the recipient of a Royal Charter in 1888), which was suffering from a withdrawal of financial support from the overseas territories. Advances were in fact made both to the Institute and to the Imperial Mineral Resources Bureau before (in 1925) the two institutions were amalgamated and a new formula for their financing worked out.[38]

The main target of the Treasury's hostility was, however, the Empire Marketing Board, which was the fruit of the Conservative Party's bad conscience about its repudiation of its commitment to Imperial Preference when Baldwin returned to power in October 1924. There was much opposition from Churchill and others to the plan for spending on the promotion of inter-imperial trade the 'Empire million', the amount by which it was estimated that the Dominions would have profitted from a preference scheme.[39] The constitution of the Empire Marketing Board which began operating in May 1926 was that of a committee representing both government departments and the Dominion governments.[40] The Australian Prime Minister, fearful of what would happen if the usual canons of Treasury control were applied, had protested against the submission of its estimates to the British Parliament and wanted an independent commission reporting to all the Dominion governments.[41] In fact Amery did succeed in making the grant a block one, with money unspent at the end of a fiscal year not returnable to the Treasury, and proceeded to spend it on a variety of research projects for the benefit of colonial agriculture and marketing as well as on campaigns for the purchase of more empire products. Its most notable achievement in the propaganda field was the use of the cinema film, and one by-product was the birth of the British documentary film industry.[42]

The Treasury from the beginning disliked the whole thing and above all the means by which it was financed; it used the worsening economic situation (after Amery's departure from office) to cut down on appropriations and to underspend where possible.[43]

The Treasury could also take advantage of the hostility to the Board expressed on economic grounds both by the out-and-out free traders and by the home agricultural lobby.[44] Attempts at the 1930 Imperial Conference to extend its activities and to make it a joint enterprise of the British and Commonwealth governments were torpedoed by the British delegation although it was now opened to Dominion contribution.[45] The Commonwealth governments did not feel that the British attitude made participation acceptable, and in the end the Treasury got its way and the Board was dissolved on 30 September 1933.[46]

It was with the handling of the Empire Marketing Board in

mind that the Treasury viewed Amery's proposed Colonial Development Act. A Treasury minute (to which Warren Fisher signified his agreement) dealt with the way in which the Empire Marketing Board carried over unspent surpluses to the following year: this, writes the author, 'will constitute a most inconvenient demand upon the Exchequer at some future time of stress and I think that such an arrangement ought to be stopped.'[47] 'Now,' runs a further Treasury minute, 'Mr. Amery wants to . . . abolish Treasury control and substitute the "block grant" system borrowed from the Empire Marketing Board with himself in sole control, unhampered, apparently, even by an advisory committee . . . The idea is so preposterous that it is hardly necessary to argue it seriously.'[48] The Treasury knew that in these objections it could count on parliamentary support since the Select Committee on Estimates had been critical of the financing of the Empire Marketing Board.[49] And it got its way with the new Labour government; Parliament was to vote an annual and varying sum to the Colonial Development Fund and unspent balances were to revert to the Treasury.[50]

Already able to deal in detail with matters of colonial expenditure appearing in the estimates of the Colonial Office itself or of the service departments, the Treasury held out against spending money for development even when it was pointed out that this might in the long run save money in the case of a deficitary colony like British Somaliland: 'The Treasury could not contemplate the provision of additional funds for a forward development policy . . . they would see no justification for continuing to incur expenditure on medical and other services for improving the conditions of the natives, which the natives do not really desire and for which they are unwilling to pay.'[51]

Encouraged in the pursuit of such economies by the financial stringency that set in after 1929, Fisher moved early in 1931 to acquire powers of supervision over all colonial finances, not only over those of the deficitary territories. Just as the 'natives' were to be saved from improvements they did not desire, so the officials of the colonial office were to be saved from their own incompetence; as one of Fisher's officials minuted:

> . . . I am told privately that they [the Colonial Office] would even welcome the support of the Treasury in fighting the battle of financial prudence . . . against profligate Ministers such as Mr. Amery and Governors such as Sir Edward Grigg. They

realise that an enquiry into their financial administration during the past few years would show them up badly.[52]

While this was for private consumption, Fisher's official explanation was that it was the prudence of the local colonial governments (which might have a non-official element) which was in doubt. Britain was expected to bail them out when they got into trouble, but unless they were grant-aided the Treasury had practically no official information about their finances: 'We do not know whether they are building or have built up reserves against a rainy day; and whether such reserves as exist are in easily realisable form, or whether they are invested in business'[53] The Colonial Office now agreed that the estimates of all colonies should be submitted to the Treasury,[54] and in this way the latter acquired more than a merely advisory role since it could claim that any activity that might render a colony liable to need a grant-in-aid should be subject to its investigation.

Treasury suspicion of the Colonial Office and of the Colonial Services did not much abate. When in 1935 the Colonial Office put to the Treasury a scheme for upgrading the hitherto relatively unimportant office of Treasurer in colonial administrations into the more responsible role of 'financial adviser', Hopkins, now Controller of the Finance and Supply Services Department, doubted whether any suitable men would be found in the Colonial Services. He advised (in this case unsuccessfully) that they should be drawn from either India (where the provincial governments had provided a model for the scheme) or from the United Kingdom itself.[55]

It is hardly necessary to go into greater detail respecting Treasury attitudes to particular items of expenditure overseas. The general picture is clear enough. In a period where Keynesian economics has proved to be an inadequate guide to promoting the country's economic health one is less tempted than might have been the case a few years ago to enlarge upon the failings of a generation dominated by classical theory. It is understandable enough that the Treasury should have wanted expenditure in colonial territories to be limited to items that could show a quick return in the shape of increased opportunities for British exports.[56] What is noteworthy in the present context is the quite overwhelming arrogance the Treasury mandarins showed in expressing their views. Sarcasm flowed from the pens of composers of minutes:

Mr. Amery's financial philosophy is based on the assumptions that idle funds are available in the market for Colonial investments, and that the Exchequer has surplus cash for subsidies to attract them into enterprises which offer no early return. From these assumptions it follows that if Mr. Amery is given a free hand, the land will flow with milk and honey.[57]

It is hardly surprising that in other aspects of governmental activity the interventions of Fisher's Treasury were not altogether welcome. Defence is of course the most difficult of all subjects for an economy-minded Treasury, since except in the event of war (which it is the object of most defence spending to avoid) it is hard to assess the returns on money spent. Defence estimates have therefore been the familiar battle-ground between economising chancellors and their colleagues in the service departments; and in this the interwar period was no exception. The subject is too large to deal with here in any depth, and it is necessary to limit the discussion to one example.

The chosen example, the fate of the Singapore base, also serves to highlight one particular reason which had strengthened the hands of the Treasury in dealing with defence preparations – the inability of the armed services and their spokesmen to agree upon the technical issues involved.[58] The argument over whether big guns or aircraft were the proper foundation of the defences of the Singapore base was only one of the issues in British defence policy between the wars in which the intrusion of a new element, an independent air force, into the old army-navy argument complicated the situation for the planners and lent weight to the Treasury view that decisions should be postponed until full agreement could be reached. Just as the colonial office was suspect of wishing to squander the taxpayers' money in pursuit of imaginary ideas of 'development', so the armed services were thought of as always desirous of over-insuring. In addition, the creation of a major base such as that announced at the 1921 Imperial Conference and confirmed by the British government in February 1922 involved commitments to expenditure over a period of years and was difficult to fit into the Treasury's preference for neatly balancing annual budgets.[59]

If one looks at the Treasury's role over the whole period from the proposal to build the base until the fall of Singapore in February 1942, two things stand out. The first, and perhaps the less important, is the insistence maintained into the period of great danger after the outbreak of the war in Europe that no authority could be delegated to the men on the spot, that the Treasury must decide upon the correct levels of expenditure even at the purely local level, and that none of the correct time-consuming procedures for the authorisation of expenditure could be by-passed. The second feature of the story is the ignoring by the Treasury of the conventional textbook assumptions about Treasury control, namely that the Treasury should not be concerned with the substance of departmental policy but only with its financial aspects. Fisher's mandarins were as self-confident of their capacity to deal in grave matters of strategic policy as they were in their ability to decide whether the Somalis wanted medical services.

When the Singapore proposal was originally made, the Controller of Supply Services, Sir George Barstow, stated his objections in a minute that went far beyond the realm of finance, although admittedly it concluded that it would be financially ruinous to build a base that could hold out until the arrival of a fleet from Britain.[60] Britain, he argued, should congratulate herself on her distance from Japan and keep her fleet to look after the home waters. (The fears for the security of the Dominions or of Britain's colonial possessions were ignored.) In another document, Barstow dismissed as 'an almost impossible hypothesis' the idea of a Japanese attack in the British empire in reliance on American neutrality.[61] In yet another paper he said that he could see no reason why Britain should not be friends with Japan even if the Anglo-Japanese alliance were abrogated.[62]

Efforts to get the decision to build the base reversed were made by the Treasury at every opportunity. In February 1923 Barstow argued that the outcome of the Washington Conference, the debt settlement with the United States and Britain's current financial position all pointed to cancellation.[63] Warren Fisher himself added his voice to the debate: 'the question here is political on the largest scale and the sea-faring man is not an oracle about such a topic. The expert is a good servant, but the last person to have the final word.'[64] It does not seem to have occurred to him that the Inland Revenue was hardly a better training ground than naval service for someone purporting to make judgements on such issues.

The Labour government's decision in 1924 to suspend work on the base was preceded by further arguments from Barstow.[65] The Baldwin government resumed the work but the return of Labour to office in 1929 gave the Treasury a new opportunity to intervene, and when the work was slowed down by the new government, the Treasury argued in favour of total cancellation of the project despite the cost of compensation to the contractors.[66]

In 1930 the Treasury argued that the London Naval Conference had led to such an easing of tension with Japan that the Singapore base was no longer required.[67] Fisher again produced his own strategic appreciation: 'You are', he wrote to Snowden,

> aware of my views about the Singapore base. I never could see any justification for it: Japan is not going to attack the British Empire single-handed let alone if aggression by her were to bring in the U.S.A. on the British side; and as regards Singapore itself, it is not a white man's country and the demoralizing effect of the clime on ships' crew is a factor of real importance to take into account.[68]

Although Fisher's confidence in his strategic judgement was unimpaired, the Treasury was somewhat worried lest if the work be cancelled altogether, the Dominions which had contributed to the project might ask for their money back; to stop might then prove more expensive than to go on.[69] The Treasury suggested a compromise by which the existing contract for a graving dock should be honoured but no additional expenditure entered into.[70] And it was ultimately agreed to follow another Treasury suggestion that the work on the dock should be spun out till 1937.[71]

While this decision, approved by the Imperial Conference in 1930, marked the end of the Treasury's opposition in principle to the building of the base, it did not mean that intervention on financial grounds in respect of its proposed defences would be abandoned. In 1925 the Treasury had already been involved in the guns versus planes controversy and had argued against any combination of the two methods as more costly than plumping for one of them.[72] In 1929 the Treasury argued in favour of aircraft as being cheaper than guns, but the Labour government's fundamental opposition to the whole idea of the base was not going to help a change. So the Treasury found itself in the position it had hoped to avoid of supporting an air component as part of a defence scheme based primarily on guns. In the end it found itself unable to prevent the air ministry sending out an experimental squadron of torpedo-carrying aircraft.[73]

By 1932 when the inter-service controversy came to a head, the Treasury's strategists found themselves back on the side of the guns: 'It appears probable that as a reliable deterrent, the gun will, in the long run, be cheaper than the aeroplane would be.'[74] In support of its new position the Treasury now invested its energies in opposing plans to build a second aerodrome near the base.[75] In the end, however, the air staff got its way; indeed one high official in the Treasury had already accepted the force of their argument.[76]

The Treasury's venture into defence planning thus landed it with the worst of all worlds. The Singapore programme went ahead as the political situation worsened; there was heavy expenditure on fixed heavy guns while supplementary air defences were also tried out. What could be argued was that the Treasury was largely responsible for the decision to give the main weight to the guns; by 1934 the basic pattern was fixed. The fact that the guns pointed seawards and the ultimate assault came from the land was something which the Treasury in its wisdom did not foresee at this juncture any more than did the service chiefs of whose judgement it was so doubtful.

In the late 1930s, as the possibility of an attack became closer, the unfortunate soldiers responsible for its defence did what they could in the face of the indifference of the civil authorities and of the inflexible rules of the Treasury. Clearly, it was thought, the citizens should do something for their own defence. But this meant raising local levies; and the inflexible rule was that these could only be paid for out of money raised locally which in a colony like Singapore meant getting the assent of the 'unofficial members' of the local legislature. Efforts to get the home government to see how inappropriate such a principle could be in the case of a base intended as a vital part of the defence of the entire empire proved unavailing.[77]

It is obvious that in a brief essay of this kind it would be inappropriate to draw too many conclusions; many areas of great importance for the general topic have not been touched on at all. But the evidence does at least suggest that accounts of policy-making that limit themselves to the role of ministers ignore much of what actually went on. The anonymity of the civil service may or may not be a valuable convention of the constitution; it is one that the historian of modern Britain accepts at his peril.

Notes

1. See, e.g. *The Diplomatic Diaries of Oliver Harvey, 1937–40*, ed. John Harvey (London, 1970); *The Diaries of Sir Alexander Cadogan, 1938–45*, ed. David Dilks

(London, 1971); *The Killearn Diaries 1934–46*, ed. Trefor Evans (London, 1972).

2. Neither Charles Mowat in his *Britain between the Wars* (London, 1955) nor W. N. Medlicott in his *Contemporary England, 1914–1964* (London, 1967) deal with the topic. In his *English History, 1914–1945* (Oxford, 1965) A. J. P. Taylor does allude to it but only to assert that there is no evidence that the powerful civil servants of the period were more influential than some of their famous predecessors.

3. It is perhaps significant of the professional historians' attitude that in the lists of office-holders given in the Royal Historical Society's *Chronology of British History*, 2nd ed. (1961) one can find the obscurest Welsh bishops but not the names of the permanent heads of the great departments of state.

4. The position at this time is usefully depicted in the classic work by H. E. Dale, *The Higher Civil Service of Great Britain* (O.U.P., 1961). See also D. N. Chester and F. M. G. Wills on *The Organization of British Central Government*, 1914–1964, 2nd ed. (1968).

5. See G. K. Fry, *Statesmen in Disguise, The Changing Role of the Administrative Class of the British Home Civil Service, 1853–1966* (London, 1969) pp. 56 ff.

6. Ibid., pp. 52–6; see also Henry Roseveare, *The Treasury* (1969) Chapter 8.

7. Some of the literature on this matter is referred to in a long footnote by Fry, op. cit., pp. 52 ff.

8. Z. S. Steiner, *The Foreign Office and Foreign Policy, 1898–1914* (Cambridge, 1969) p. 171.

9. K. Middlemas and J. Barnes, *Baldwin* (London, 1969) p. 344. Here and elsewhere in this essay I am drawing on material from the unpublished Volume II of my book, *Imperial Sunset*. I am indebted to the Ford Foundation and the Social Science Research Council for assistance during the research for this work. I am also grateful to my two research assistants over this period, Miss J. F. Maitland-Jones and Mrs Mary Brown (née George).

10. See Ann Bridge (Lady O'Malley), *Permission to Resign* (London, 1971). This book contains a personal description of Fisher of some interest since he remains one of the least well-known of the major figures of the period.

11. David Carlton, *MacDonald versus Henderson: The Foreign Policy of the Second Labour Government* (London, 1970) p. 23.

12. This is again touched upon in the footnote by Fry referred to supra., n. 7. In so far as the advocates of rearmament in the 1930s were also pressing for a reorganisation of the government machinery dealing with defence, Fisher's opposition was of course an important factor. See, e.g., B. H. Liddell Hart, *Memoirs*, vol. I (1965) p. 321.

13. See Stephen Roskill, *Hankey, Man of Secrets*, 3 vols (1970–4).

14. It is interesting to note that after exercising so much influence behind the scenes during more than three decades, Hankey made little impact as a Minister from September 1939 to March 1942.

15. Wilson retired under the age limit rule in 1942, his successor Sir Richard Hopkins was two years his senior. A nice Churchillian touch at the expense of someone widely regarded as the chief appeaser!

16. Sir John Wheeler-Bennett, *John Anderson, Viscount Waverley* (1962).

17. Hopkins is not mentioned at all by either Mowat or Taylor and only once by Medlicott.

18. See Ann Trotter, 'The Dominions and Imperial Defence: Hankey's Tour in 1934', *Journal of Imperial and Commonwealth History*, vol. 2, no. 3 (May 1974).

19. See in particular on this subject Ian M. Drummond, *Imperial Economic*

Policy 1917–1939 (London, 1974); also his earlier study, *British Economic Policy and the Empire 1919–1939* (London, 1972).

20. Bentley B. Gilbert, *British Social Policy, 1914–1939* (London, 1970).

21. Gilbert, op. cit., p. 307.

22. Ibid., pp. 121–2.

23. Ibid., p. 99.

24. Ibid., pp. 133–4.

25. Ibid., pp. 242–3.

26. The best account is that in Roseveare, op. cit., pp. 258 ff.

27. Ibid., p. 271.

28. Ibid., p. 254.

29. Ibid., p. 253.

30. What we clearly require for the interwar period are books as good as one which we have for one aspect of the Treasury's role in the mid-Victorian era. See Maurice Wright, *Treasury Control of the Civil Service, 1854–1874* (Oxford, 1969).

31. Here I have profitted from the work by Professor Drummond referred to in note 19 but see also my review of his general thesis and approach in *Government and Opposition*, vol. 10, no. 10 (1974).

32. Drummond, *Imperial Economic Policy*, pp. 127–9.

33. Ibid., p. 127.

34. It seems fair to assume that the officials at the Treasury were not subjected in this respect to any dissuasion by Churchill during Amery's period of office, although we must await Mr Martin Gilbert's volume on these years for a proper account of Churchill in his capacity as Chancellor of the Exchequer. It is clear that Churchill's 'imperialism' had no economic content to it, and that it is easy to understand why Amery did not find him an ally in his schemes. 'I have always said', wrote the latter in August 1929, 'that the key to Winston is that he is a mid-Victorian, steeped in the politics of his father's period, and unable ever to get the modern point of view'. Quoted by Robert Rhodes James in *Churchill Revised: A Critical Assessment* (New York, 1969) p. 100.

32. See E. A. Brett, 'Development Policy in East Africa between the Wars' (London University, unpublished Ph.D. thesis, 1966) p. 101; P.R.O. T. 161/826/S.36937/1, minute of 31 Jul 1936.

36. Colonial Office Misc. Paper 460.8, Jan 1936, P.R.O. T.161/826/S.36937/1.

37. Amery who (on 1 July 1925) became the first Secretary of State for the Dominions as well as retaining his title as Secretary of State for the Colonies was outraged by the Treasury attitude on this score as well. See Amery to Baldwin, 6 Jun 1925 in Baldwin Papers, vol. 193, Imp. 9, p. 136; of P.R.O./CAB.23/50 mtg 28(25). The new Committee on Civil Research set up on 13 June 1925 was supposed to handle this subject. Middlemas and Barnes, op. cit., p. 313.

38. Cmd 2355 (1925).

39. Baldwin Papers, vol. 93, Imp. 9, pp. 96 ff. Cf. L. Amery, *My Political Life* vol. II (1953) p. 346. The struggles with Churchill and others over the Empire Marketing Board are fully recounted in Amery's unpublished diaries; I am grateful to the Rt Hon. Julian Amery for giving me access to this important source for the history of the period.

40. Cmd 3372 (1929).

41. P.R.O., C.P.112 (1926); Baldwin Papers, vol. 93, Imp. 24, pp. 233 ff., 321–2.

42. When the Empire Marketing Board was finally destroyed its first and only secretary, Sir Stephen Tallents, succeeded in saving the film unit by having it transferred to the Post Office. J. M. Lee, 'The Dissolution of the Empire Marketing Board, 1933; Reflections on a Diary', *Journal of Imperial and Commonwealth History*, vol. 1 (1972).

43. P.R.O., CAB.32/117. Committee on Economic Consultation and Co-operation (Ottawa Conference, 1933).

44. See, e.g., the debate in the House of Lords, 18 Jul 1927.

45. The question can be followed in the papers of the 1930 Imperial Conference; see in particular C.P. 366 (1930); CAB.32/79;85;100;117.

46. Op. cit., p. 355.

47. P.R.O., T.161/615/S.29573/1.

48. Minute of 4 Jan 1929, ibid., 33978.

49. *Second Report of the Select Committee on Estimates* (H.C. 71,114 of 1928).

50. Even so the Treasury attempted to cut down on expenditure on development by charging to the fund expenditure which should properly have been included in the Colonial Office or Empire Marketing Board estimates. Sir Basil Blackett, Chairman of the Colonial Development Advisory Committee to Sir Warren Fisher, 30 Sep 1929, P.R.O., T.161/579/S.34609/04.

51. Treasury Memorandum for Middle East Standing Official Committee (1931), P.R.O., T.161/538/S.36565/2. It is an interesting reflection on the way things have changed that it was under a Labour government that these remarks about the 'natives' not needing medical services were made in an official paper.

52. Minute of 8 Apr 1931, P.R.O., T.161/493/S.36290. Sir Edward Grigg (1st Baron Altrincham) was governor of Kenya from 1925 to 1930.

53. Sir Warren Fisher to Sir Samuel Wilson, 14 Apr 1931, P.R.O., T.161.493/S.36290. Wilson was permanent under-secretary at the Colonial Office from 1925 to 1933.

54. Wilson to Fisher, 28 Oct 1931, ibid.

55. Memorandum by Sir R. Hopkins (1935) P.R.O., T.161/757/S.37417.

56. 'The scheme for constructing 110 miles of railway in rapidly developing Tanganyika, at a total cost of £565,000 (involving construction orders in this country of £278,000) . . . is clearly more advantageous to this country than the 4 schemes . . . in poor and stagnant Antigua for constructing concrete houses for peasants, laying concrete drains in villages, removal of leper asylum and inauguration of a sanitary campaign, costing altogether £31,000 . . .' Memorandum of 18 Jun 1931, P.R.O., T.161/485/S.34609. This followed an earlier warning to the Colonial Development Advisory Committee against spending money on health schemes in the West Indies which were unlikely to give Britain a return in the shape of increased exports. A. P. Waterfield to Sir Basil Blackett, 25 Nov 1930, P.R.O., T.161/297/S.34650.

57. Minute of 7 Jan 1929, P.R.O., T.161/291/S.33978.

58. The reflections that follow owe much to the book by S. Woodburn Kirkby, *Singapore: The Chain of Disaster* (London, 1971).

59. See in general on the Singapore question, S. Roskill, *Naval Policy between the Wars*, vol. I (London, 1968).

60. Memorandum by Sir George Barstow, 15 Jun 1921, P.R.O., T.161/800/S.18917/1.

61. Reservation by the Treasury Representative to the Overseas Defence Committee, ibid.

62. Barstow to Col. S. H. Wilson (secretary of the Overseas Defence Committee), ibid.

63. Minute by Barstow, 20 Feb 1923, ibid.

64. Note by Sir Warren Fisher, same date, ibid.

65. Memoranda by Barstow, 26 Feb and 1 Mar 1924, P.R.O., T.161/800/S.18917/2.

66. Memoranda by A. P. Waterfield, 11 and 16 Jul 1929, P.R.O., T.161/800/S.18917/6.

67. Memorandum by Waterfield, 12 May 1950, ibid.

68. Minute by Sir Warren Fisher for Chancellor of the Exchequer, 12 May 1930, ibid.

69. Minute by Mr Fraser, 8 Mar 1929, P.R.O., T.161/800/S.18917/6. Treasury brief (prepared Sep 1930) for Imperial Conference, ibid., S.18917/8.

70. Memorandum by Waterfield to War Office, 25 Sep 1930, P.R.O., T.161/800/S.18917/8.

71. Memorandum by Mr Upcott, 2 Oct 1930 with note by Snowden, 9 Oct 1930, ibid., S.18917/9.

72. Minute for Sir G. Barstow, 1 Jan 1925, P.R.O., T.161/800/S.18917/3.

73. Minute by Waterfield, 24 Jul 1929, P.R.O., T.161/800/S.18917/6 and Air Ministry's notes on the Treasury's view, 20 Dec 1929, and other documents in P.R.O., T.161/201/S.18917/014.

74. Minute by Mr Upcott P.R.O., T.161/560/18917/016/1.

75. Treasury memorandum by Mr Grieve, 5 Apr 1933, approved by Sir Warren Fisher, P.R.O., T.161/560/S.18917/016/2.

76. Memorandum by Sir E. Strohmenger, 11 Apr 1933, ibid.

77. General Percival paper on 'the volunteer vote', 20 Oct 1936; Brigadier Studd to General Dobbie, 24 Nov 1937, Imperial War Museum, Percival papers, Boxes 39/40.

10 The Press and the Party System between the Wars

COLIN SEYMOUR-URE

J. A. Spender, worthy and rational editor of the *Westminster Gazette*, 'the sea-green incorruptible', found himself disputing government policy with the owner of a mass circulation paper. The man undertook to prove his paper's line correct. He sent for the circulation figures and pointed triumphantly to the rise that began when his line was started. Spender was numbed. 'I found it impossible to persuade him that there was any gap in his reasoning.'[1]

Therein lay the difference between the old journalism and the new; the solid, late-Victorian press and the twentieth-century popular press. The one was highly political and linked financially to the party system; the other was broader in its range and based in the market economy. Between the two world wars the press continued to go through important changes. They brought with them equally important changes in the relationship of the press and the party system.

Newspapers and parties have always been closely involved. Many of their functions (organising opinion, articulating ideas) are compatible. At one extreme, British newspapers in the nineteenth century had been the clients of political parties. After the Second World War politicians would become, at the other extreme, clients of the newspapers – pressing peerages upon them where earlier, in return for peerages, they extracted large sums of money. Between the wars the press progressed from one extreme towards the other. Considering also the fluidity of the political parties, it is not surprising that the period was characterised by a 'dislocation' of the press and the party system. Beaverbrook and Rothermere, possessing papers, could not capture the Conservative party: Oswald Mosley, launching the New Party, could not capture a Paper.

Where press and parties are close, one finds strong organisational ties, a balance between the electoral strength of parties and their respective shares of circulation, and a high degree of loyalty to party policies and leaders. This essay seeks to explore the decline in such links and the developments in the press that may have contributed to it.

The view across the toastrack was much the same in 1939 as in 1919. The number of London-based morning papers fell only from eleven to nine; and one of the deaths, the *Morning Post*, came as late as 1937. There were four deaths in all, as Table 10.1 shows. But these were partly offset by two births. In 1921 the *Westminster Gazette* became a morning paper, after an influential history as an evening paper, and in 1930 the Communist party founded the *Daily Worker*. The *Westminster Gazette* survived only until 1928. The *Daily Chronicle*, long the most popular Liberal paper, amalgamated with the *Daily News* in 1930 into the *News Chronicle*. Those two and the *Morning Post*, whose readership was said to drop each day by the number of deaths announced in its columns, were the deaths of political importance. The death of the *Daily Graphic*, which merged with the *Daily Sketch* in 1926, was insignificant (though it deserves recognition as the first daily pictorial paper, founded in 1890).

The simple continuity of names and numbers conceals long-term changes briefly checked by the war. The overall trend was towards a set of dominant national newspapers, squeezing out the provincials; whereas before the war the nationals were more accurately described as 'metropolitan' and the provincials flourished.

Four separate elements in the trend can be distinguished. First was the sheer decline in the number of provincial mornings – from forty-three in 1919 to twenty-five in 1939 (Table 10.2). Already in 1928 *The Economist* could comment: 'Unless assisted by the earnings of an associated evening paper, secure in its appeal to 'racing and football' readers, a provincial daily is, broadly speaking, no longer a very profitable asset.'[2] Evening papers, as the remark suggests, were less vulnerable. Even so, there was a drop from about ninety to seventy-seven. The result was to reduce competition rather than to leave many more towns without a daily paper

TABLE 10.1

Metropolitan Morning, Evening and Sunday Newspapers, 1919–39

	1 2		3	
Morning	9 0 1 2 3 4 5 6 7 8 9 0 1 2 3 4 5 6 7 8 9			
	+ +			

Morning Post (1772)
The Times (1785)
Daily News (1846) —————————(*News Chron.* 1930)—————
Daily Telegraph (1855)
Daily Chronicle (1869)
Daily Graphic (1890)
Daily Mail (1896)
Daily Express (1900)
Daily Mirror (1903)
Daily Sketch (1908)
Westminster Gazette (1921)

Daily Worker (1930)————

	1 2		3	
Evening	9 0 1 2 3 4 5 6 7 8 9 0 1 2 3 4 5 6 7 8 9			
	+ +			

Globe (1803)
Evening Standard (1827)
Pall Mall Gazette (1865)
Evening News (1881)
Star (1887)
Westminster Gazette (1893)

	1 2		3	
Sunday	9 0 1 2 3 4 5 6 7 8 9 0 1 2 3 4 5 6 7 8 9			
	+ +			

Observer (1791)
Weekly Dispatch (1801) ————(Renamed *Sun. Dispatch* 1928)————
Sunday Times (1822)
Lloyds Weekly News (1842) —(*Sun. News*)————
News of the World (1843)
Reynold's News (1850)
Sunday Referee (1877)
The People (1881)
Sunday Herald (1915) ————(*Sun. Graphic*)————
Sunday Pictorial (1915)
Sunday Express (1918)
Sunday Illustrated (1921)
Sunday Worker (1925)

Sources: Various

altogether. (That came after the Second World War.) In 1921 fifteen towns outside London had more than one morning paper; by
1938 there were only seven, and in two of them, Sheffield and
Newcastle, both papers were in the same ownership. If morning
and evening papers are taken together, the drop was from thirty-
three towns to twenty-one.

TABLE 10.2   *Number of Provincial Morning and Evening Newspapers*

	Morning				Evening			
1921	31	2	8	41	75	4	10	89
1925	27	2	7	36	72	4	9	85
1930	24	1	6	31	71	2	9	82
1935	22	1	6	29	68	2	9	79
1939	18	1	6	25	66	2	9	77

Source: Royal Commission on the Press 1947–9

The second element was the growth of newspaper chains, linking provincials with each other and – more important to the present argument – with the national dailies. By 1939 ten of the
twenty-five provincial mornings belonged either to the Berry brothers or the Pearson/Rowntree Westminster Press, and one more
belonged to another chain. In 1921 only five out of forty-one had
belonged to chains. By 1934 40 per cent of provincial evenings
were in chains too, compared with 8 per cent in 1921.

By 1939 the chains had in fact started to decline. Initially, they
were given impetus by the energies of the Berrys (who became
Lords Kemsley and Camrose) and by the death in 1922 of Lord
Northcliffe, whose brother, Lord Rothermere, sold some of
Northcliffe's properties and bought new ones. By 1929 half the
London mornings were similarly linked, over half the national and
provincial Sundays, and 45 per cent of the daily and Sunday press
as a whole. Thereafter the focus shifted away from the London
mornings so that only two were in chains by 1939; and the proportion of provincials dropped as overcapitalisation and competitive pressure led the owners to rationalise their holdings.[3]

Some notable provincial dailies remained independent
throughout the period – the *Birmingham Post, Yorkshire Post* and

Manchester Guardian; and in Bristol local resentment prompted the foundation of an evening paper to rival the local chain product. In general, however, the twinkling shoal of provincial papers was trawled by the press barons and neatly parcelled on the slab.

Thirdly, the provincial press suffered in circulation. Before the Audit Bureau of Circulations was set up in 1931, figures were unreliable and difficult to get.[4] But the totals in Table 10.3 would have to be seriously in error for their impact to be lost. Clearly the London mornings expanded hugely in the process of becoming national papers. In twenty years their circulation nearly doubled. The growth of Manchester as a centre for printing northern editions, pioneered by Northcliffe with the *Daily Mail* in 1900, made this possible. By contrast the London evening press remained static and the provincials dropped slightly. Figures for the provincial mornings seem particularly scarce. The 1947 Royal Commission on the Press estimated their circulation in 1937 at 1,600,000.[5] Given that the number of mornings had dropped from 1920 by one-third but the number of evenings by only one-tenth, it is possible that the mornings' share of the combined 1920 circulation was as high as three million. The penetration of the provincial mornings in the community at that date would have been well over half that of the London papers; while in 1937 it was an insignificant sixth or seventh. Yet even at the later date the nationals did not dominate every area. In the Northeast, for example, well under half the families were taking a national newspaper in 1935.[6]

TABLE 10.3   *Daily Press: Total Circulations*

	Metropolitan		Provincial	Total
	Morning ('000)	*Evening* ('000)	*Morning & Evening* ('000)	('000)
1920	5,430	1,940	7,300	14,670
1925	7,440	1,980	7,080	16,500
1930	8,650	2,030	7,270	17,950
1935	9,390	1,830	6,960	18,180
1939	10,570	1,900	6,990	19,460

Source: N. Kaldor and R. Silverman, *A Statistical Analysis of Advertising Expenditure and of the Revenue of the Press.*

The circulation figures for individual papers (which are highly

tentative for 1921) are given in Table 10.4. These figures fluctu-
ated much more than we have come to expect since 1945, and very
dramatic differences could be made by changes in price. The *Daily
Telegraph* while it cost two pence dwindled from 180,000 in 1918 to
90,000 in 1929 but then shot to 175,000 in a year upon reduction to
a penny; and by 1939 it was close to three-quarters of a million.
The Times at three pence was down to 113,000 in 1921 but was up
to 192,000 two years later at a penny-halfpenny. The *Morning
Post*'s price dropped to a penny in 1927 and its circulation went
from 80,000 to 104,000 in a year. The contrast for most papers between 1921 and 1939 is great, and with it comes the provincials'
eclipse. A 'quality' provincial morning paper (such as the *Manchester Guardian* and the *Yorkshire Post*) might sell anything between 25,000 and 50,000 in 1921. This did not look completely
ridiculous beside *The Times* or *Morning Post*; and 'populars' like the
Daily Dispatch (Manchester, 400,000) and *Glasgow Daily Mail*

TABLE 10.4   *Circulation of Metropolitan Morning Newspapers, 1921–39*

	1921 ('000)	1925 ('000)	1930 ('000)	1935 ('000)	1939 ('000)
Morning Post (1772)	50	70	132	120	—
The Times (1785)	113	190	186	183	204
Daily News (1846)	300	570	1,452	1,345	1,299
Daily Telegraph (1855)	180	125	90*	461	737
Daily Chronicle (1869)	661	949	—	—	—
Daily Mail (1896)	1,533	1,720	1,845	1,719	1,533
Daily Express (1900)	579	850	1,693	1,911	2,546
Daily Mirror (1903)	1,003	964	1,072	950	1,571
Daily Sketch (1908)	835	850	926	750	750
Daily Herald (1912)	211	350	1,119	2,000	1,850
Westminster Gazette (1921)	—	200	—	—	—
Daily Worker (1930)	—	—	?	?	100†

Omitted: Daily Graphic (1890–1926)

* In December 1930 the price was halved and circulation immediately rose to
175,000.

† 150,000 on Saturdays.

Note: Rounded figures are approximates.

Sources: A. P. Wadsworth, *Newspaper Circulations 1800–1954*; P. E. P., *Report on the
British Press*; Royal Commission on the Press 1947–49; W. A. Belson, *The British
Press* (mimeo, n.d.)

(203,000) could compare with the *Daily News* or *Daily Express*. By 1939 that was all over. Only among the Sundays did the provincials hold their own, with giants like the *Sunday Chronicle* and *Empire News* (both of Manchester) maintaining circulations well over a million.

The last change in the pattern of the press was the rapid decline of the London evening papers. In 1900 there had been almost as many of these (nine) as of morning papers (ten). At the end of the war there were still six, selling well over one-third as many as the morning papers. Two of them, however, the *Pall Mall Gazette* and *Westminster Gazette*, were 'clubland' papers with matchstick circulations in the twenty-thousands but a quite disproportionate political influence.[7] These lost their function with the end of the Edwardian era (and improved public transport). By the mid-1920s only the *Star, Evening Standard* and *Evening News* (Northcliffe's first venture) remained.

It can thus be seen that the interwar period was a stage in the change from a press consisting before 1914 in a large number of metropolitan morning and evening papers and a very large number of provincial morning and evening papers, to a small number of national morning papers and a small number of provincial morning and evening papers after 1945.

This development had several implications for the party system. Firstly, it meant that there was decreasing party competition in the provincial press. As A. P. Wadsworth of the *Manchester Guardian* reflected, 'The party political spirit was less keen than it had been when every large town had to have its Tory and its Liberal papers who fought and scratched each other like the papers of Eatanswill.'[8] Secondly, regardless of interparty competition there was less scope for the expression of regional particularism in the parties. National papers were interested in national politics; in parish pumps only if they spewed up dirty water.

Thirdly, at the metropolitan level the shrivelling of the evening press and the modest decline in the mornings after 1930 reduced the opportunity for the reflection of nuances of debate inside the parties about policy and personalities. Neal Blewett, in his exhaustive study of the 1910 general elections, was able to line up no less than seventeen metropolitan dailies behind the parties.[9] A comparable study of the 1935 election would have ten national dailies (if the *Daily Worker* is included) but might find it incongruous to include the three London evenings. On the Conservative side a specific example was the death of the *Morning Post*.

This was an individualistic voice on the right wing of the party. It had been a spokesman of opinion against the India Bill. In 1930 it had flirted with Beaverbrook's Empire Free Trade policy; the editor, H. A. Gwynne, tried to bring Beaverbrook and Baldwin together, while confiding that he personally felt closer to Beaverbrook's view of the issue.[10] The paper's idiosyncracy was illustrated both in the quip that no cause could be regarded as completely lost until the *Morning Post* took it up, and, more ominously, in the infamous series of articles about the Jewish world conspiracy, as demonstrated by the (forged) 'Protocols of the Elders of Zion'. During the General Strike the *British Gazette* was printed on its presses. But these presses were sold soon afterwards because of continuing financial losses, and the paper was then printed under contract.

Of more significance, however, was the decline of the Liberal press. Before the war it was already numerically smaller than the Conservative press since it could count on three London morning papers as opposed to seven and two evening papers against four; and it could claim only half the circulation.[11] By 1930 the Conservatives still had six morning and two evening papers while the Liberals had one of each. The successive amalgamations of the Liberal mornings are shown in Figure 10.1. At the end of the war the rival wings of the Liberal party each had their spokesmen. But after 1930 only one large-circulation paper, the *News Chronicle*, remained for the whole party whose philosophy made a virtue of diversity and argument. (The *Manchester Guardian* had a national reputation but remained essentially a provincial paper, with a circulation of 40,000.)

Yet this decline of the Liberal press, though lamentable, accurately mirrored the decline of the Liberal party. It did not constitute a dislocation of the relationship between the press and the party system except inasmuch as the compensating growth of the Labour party was unaccompanied by a corresponding development of a Labour press. Indeed, Labour could only claim one paper – the *Daily Herald* – which was a great success in the 1930s and for a few years was the highest circulation daily. The beginning of the radicalisation of the *Daily Mirror* started in 1935; and the *Daily Worker* with a circulation somewhat more comparable to other papers in the 1930s than later, added strength to the left-wing press. But in the 1920s the *Daily Herald* had been very weak and the *Daily Worker* non-existent. The left-wing press thus lagged in its growth well behind the Labour party. The party was

more conscious than ever, particularly after the experience of the
Zinoviev letter scare in the 1924 election campaign, of being up

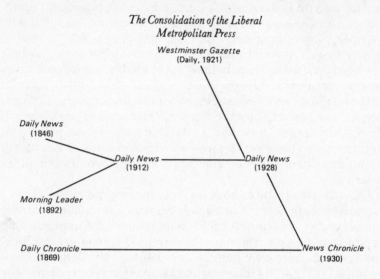

*The Consolidation of the Liberal
Metropolitan Press*

against an overwhelmingly hostile press.[12] At least in pre-1914
two-party days, the 1925 *Labour Year Book* grumbled, 'the false-
hoods and misrepresentations of one party were promptly ex-
posed and refuted in the national organs of the other.' Now there
was no such balance; and to make matters worse the right-wing
press was not even loyally and consistently Conservative but
under 'purely capitalistic control'.[13] In the 1920s, then, Labour
was the party that could most reasonably complain of under-
representation; while in the 1930s the shift of party support
among the electorate was broadly balanced by the decline of the
Liberal press and the rise of Labour. The dislocation corrected
itself. Within the parties, on the other hand, the developments
already described above produced a press less finely tuned to echo
the movement of opinion and personalities.

The changing pattern of the press also involved different forms
of ownership, the result of which was a major loss of party control.
Before 1914 'party ownership' had generally meant ownership by
a wealthy individual or syndicate (which might possibly include
party leaders) or by nominees through whom subsidies were
channelled.[14] The Cadbury family, for example, bought the *Daily
News* in 1901 and Lloyd George sat on its board for some years.

George Newnes founded the *Westminster Gazette* in 1893 specifically to provide a vehicle for E. T. Cook and J. A. Spender, whose
Pall Mall Gazette had just been sold over their heads to an ambitious Conservative, W. W. Astor.[15] In 1911 Max Aitken paid
£40,000 for the Conservative *Globe*; but only £15,000 was his own
money – the rest came from party funds. At that time at least one
Conservative morning, the *Standard* (1857–1917), was also receiving regular Conservative subsidies.

Such practices continued into the 1920s. An outstanding
example was Lloyd George's ownership of the *Daily Chronicle*.
Towards the end of the war Lloyd George, aware of his isolated
position, determined to ensure himself a mouthpiece by acquiring
a newspaper. The *Daily Chronicle* had already been identified with
him for many years through his friendship with the editor, Robert
Donald; but latterly it had become somewhat critical. In 1918 Sir
Henry Dalziel, acting as Lloyd George's agent, purchased the
paper with a large portion of the Lloyd George Fund. For a time
Lloyd George's son Gwilym acted as manager, but in November
1926 there was a reshuffle. Lloyd George sold most of his interest
(at a profit of at least £1¼ million) to two Liberal businessmen, Sir
David Yule and Sir Thomas Catto. Lord Reading was made
chairman and Lloyd George retained political control until he decided to sell the paper in 1928.[16]

Lloyd George was also involved in some of the various schemes
for the future of *The Times* which were canvassed when the fatal
nature of Northcliffe's illness became clear in 1922.[17] *The Times*,
Lloyd George thought, could be fashioned into an ideal
instrument for the pursuit of his postwar policies and centre
party plans. His political secretary, Grigg, was close to
Northcliffe's associates; and his parliamentary secretary, David
Davies, also actively canvassed a proposal under which Lloyd
George would have become editor and managing director. In
the event, of course, ownership passed largely to the Astor
family.

Another good example was the purchase of the *Morning Post* in
1924 by a Conservative syndicate including the Duke of Nor-
thumberland, Sir Percy Bates (chairman of Cunard) and Major
J. S. Courtauld, M.P.[18] The previous owners were the Borth-
wick family, one of whom (as Lord Glenesk,) became the first
newspaper peer (he died in 1908). This sale was widely assumed
to put the paper in the pocket of the Conservative party – an assumption which the editor, H. A. Gwynne, strongly resented.

'You surely must know', he wrote to Beaverbrook after a paragraph to that effect appeared in the *Evening Standard*, 'that I rescued the *Morning Post* from the Conservative Party. And as for the close relations with the Conservative Central Office, I think you would find if you enquired there, that they regard the *Morning Post* as a thorn in their side.' Moreover, he had 'never had any pressure of any kind put upon me by any single Director in this Company. We made the decision quite clear between ourselves when they took over . . .'[19] The new owners cut overheads and halved the price, pushing up circulation quite successfully.

The classic case of a paper owned by a party corporately, rather than by a wealthy oligarchy, was the *Daily Herald* between 1922 and 1929. The paper had been founded in 1912 and survived only as a weekly during the war. In 1919 Ernest Bevin became a director and through him union donations were acquired. In 1922 the T.U.C. and the National Executive Committee of the Labour party agreed to take the paper over officially. Sales increased steadily (from 200,000 in 1923 to 363,000 by the General Strike), but only once, in the first six months of 1924, was a profit made.[20] By 1929 the T.U.C. had sunk over half a million pounds into the paper, and Congress voted to enter an arrangement with J. S. Elias of Odhams. Odhams bought 51 per cent of the shares; the T.U.C. kept 49 per cent. Political control remained with the T.U.C. directors alone, hence in 1931 the paper stuck with the party and not with the leaders who joined the National government.[21]

The conversion of the *Westminster Gazette* to a morning paper in 1921 is the last example of control in a party interest.[22] The disappearance of the economic and social conditions that made the 'clubland' evening papers viable confronted the owning syndicate (of which Lord Cowdray was by now the chief member) with the choice of cutting its losses and closing down or trying to exploit the opportunities open to a competitive morning paper. Cowdray invested perhaps £750,000 in building up circulation to a quarter of a million or more – and had in return the satisfaction of indulging his antipathy to Lloyd George. But he could not make the paper profitable, and in 1928 it amalgamated with the *Daily News*.

In the 1920s parties and syndicates were thus prepared to go on subsidising papers as before. In the 1930s, however, the practice declined. The foundation of the *Daily Worker* is the only case comparable to those quoted. In 1925 the *Sunday Worker* was founded.

On 1 January 1930 this was converted into a daily, partly as a protest against the 'betrayal' of the *Daily Herald* to the capitalist Odhams group. The paper attracted little advertising and called regularly on its readers for financial help, which totalled £9000 in the first two years. But it achieved a circulation of 100,000 by 1939 – 150,000 on Saturdays.[23] The Liberal party, as has been shown, had no one willing to keep other than the *News Chronicle* and the evening *Star* going in the 1930s. Indeed in 1934 Frances Stevenson recorded in her diary that Walter Layton, one of the controllers of the *News Chronicle*, believed the Liberal party had missed the boat and was 'a complete washout'. 'Layton and indeed all the management of the *News Chronicle* are inclined to go Labour.' Aylmer Vallance, the editor, was said to be thinking of 'a combination and understanding with the *Herald* on a progressive policy'. Layton had also had discussions at this time with Elias about jointly extending the *News Chronicle* group, but nothing came of them.[24]

The Labour movement, we have seen, had also not been willing to extend its subsidy to the *Daily Herald* indefinitely. The *Morning Post* could find no new supporters when it tottered again in 1937. Lord Lloyd, a member of Churchill's anti-India-Bill lobby and an opponent of appeasement, pleaded with Chamberlain not to let 'this great conservative organ sell out'.[25] Chamberlain was unsympathetic and evidently said he had no use for independent Conservative criticism. An approach by the paper's manager to Lord Camrose, owner of the *Daily Telegraph*, kept alive the possibility of survival – and the *Morning Post* was in fact published separately for some months after Camrose bought it. Eventually, however, the papers were combined. Camrose was unwilling to continue two separate publications that would inevitably have come to resemble each other quite closely.[26]

By 1939 the party leaders had lost control over the finances of the press – and therefore over press personnel and policies. (The Labour party never found *Daily Herald* policy easy to manage.) This development occurred at the time when the number of newspapers was decreasing and circulations were soaring. The new breed of owners and managers might have partisan opinions; but they were not party men.

Since established parties found it difficult to own or direct newspapers after 1930, new parties and groups not surprisingly found it virtually impossible. No longer could a grand design or a new career be launched by founding or buying in to a paper. 'I know the man for you,' Bonar Law said to R. D. Blumenfeld, impoverished controller of the *Daily Express* in 1910. 'Max Aitken is enormously rich. He knows nothing about newspapers and is not interested in them. But he wants to have a big political career, and he'll be glad of a paper which will back him.'[27] Oswald Mosley was to have no such luck.

After the foundation of the *Daily Herald* in 1912, no new daily newspaper was started up to 1939, apart from the *Daily Worker* (whose economic situation makes it a marginal case). The *Westminster Gazette* was of course already appearing daily before 1921, as an evening paper. In the twenty-five years before 1912 new papers were commonplace; no less than thirteen metropolitan mornings were launched between 1890 and 1914. Some, like the veteran journalist W. T. Stead's *Daily Paper*, which lasted thirty-two issues, merely tickled the founder's fancy. Others were more substantial: Franklin Thomasson's Liberal *Tribune* (1906–8) was started more or less as an obligation imposed by his father's will and lost £300,000 in less than two years.[28] Licence to enter the industry was more often than not licence to fail: only four of the thirteen survived the war. Sunday papers alone proved a practical proposition after 1914: six were founded between 1915 and 1925. Only two expired within three years or so, though Beaverbrook spent £2 millions on the *Sunday Express* before it became profitable.[29] Between the wars buying in to an existing daily paper was a rather more practical proposition than creating a new one. Before 1914 there had been some spectacular examples, like C. A. Pearson's purchase of the *Standard* in 1904 to promote the campaign inside the Conservative party for tariff reform. The outcome of Bonar Law's advice to Blumenfeld was a quick trip to Monte Carlo where Aitken signed a cheque for £25,000, the start of his association with the *Daily Express*. As has already been seen, the best postwar example to match those takeovers was Lloyd George's purchase of the *Daily Chronicle*. Although strictly speaking that happened before the war ended, the transfer of ownership took place on 5 October 1918.[30] The Labour Party's official takeover of the *Daily Herald* should properly be regarded as 'buying in', though it was not the result of party leaders looking around for a likely property.[31] In the same way the Conservative syndicate that bought the *Morning Post* in 1924 did so more as a salvage operation than in any desire to launch new initiatives.

Ownership changes are not always easy to trace, but among London morning papers at least twelve took place between 1918 and 1939. That figure excludes amalgamations (i.e. the death of one paper through absorption by another, even if the name was retained somewhere in the title) and changes following inheritance. All except two took place in the 1920s, and altogether only seven papers were involved. Apart from the cases just quoted, none can be regarded as a purchase by politicians 'buying in' to the industry. They were predominantly commercial decisions like Rothermere's disposal of his *Daily Mirror* shares in 1931 (he thought the paper had no future and floated his shares off in blocks on the stock exchange);[32] and like Lord Burnham's sale of the *Daily Telegraph* to the Berry and Iliffe interests in 1928 (Burnham lacked cash to put the paper on a sound footing). Only Major John Astor's purchase of *The Times* in 1922 should perhaps be added to the list of those buying in. His motives took a party political form, in the negative sense that he deliberately wanted to keep *The Times* from becoming the tool of party politicians like Lloyd George. His view is typified by the well-known arrangement made about any future sale, which was to be conditional on the approval of a bland group of non-party figures like the Lord Chief Justice and the president of the Institute of Chartered Accountants.[33]

One more purchase can be added to that list from the field of London evening papers. After he left the *Daily Chronicle* when it passed to Lloyd George, its editor, Robert Donald, bought the failing *Globe* for £40,000. He hoped to build it up gradually into an independent and progressive paper. The venture was a disaster – a perfect example of fighting the next war on the principles of the last. In retrospect a seedy quality was added by the involvement of the speculator Clarence Hatry, who may have seen newspaper ownership as a way of fulfilling his ambition to procure a baronetcy. In 1921 the paper was amalgamated with the *Pall Mall Gazette*.

With those few exceptions, none of them in the second half of the interwar period, 'buying in' was not in fact a method used by politicians anxious to acquire a mouthpiece. What could they do instead? The next best thing to a daily was a weekly. Mosley's New Party sought to found one and the National Labour party to buy one. The New Party's frustrating attempts to launch *Action* are well evoked in the diaries of Harold Nicolson, who edited it for its brief life from 8 October to 31 December 1931.[34] The first issue sold 160,000 copies and the last barely 15,000 – though by then the party itself had been swamped. In the October general election twenty-two of its twenty-four candidates lost their deposits. As one would expect from Nicolson, *Action* was 'reflective, intellectually subtle, journalistically rather amateurish: it attempted to reconcile propaganda for a political party with a faint air of distaste for all party politics. . .' After the election Mosley claimed that Rothermere wished to place 'the whole of the Harmsworth Press at his disposal'.[35] Earlier, however, the New Party had faced what Beaverbrook described as 'a conspiracy of silence in the newspapers, except for the particular newspapers I am connected with'. Indeed, Beaverbrook thought that the party might have been saved by 'brilliant journalistic support'.[36] His own reaction to its formation in March 1931 had been friendly. In response to a letter from Mosley requesting publicity, he replied: 'I will see that your Manifesto gets as much publicity as possible'; though Beaverbrook's own priorities were reflected in the next sentence – 'We have struck a bad day on account of the excitement over Moore-Brabazon'.[37] Brabazon had that day (to the embarrassment of the Conservative leadership) chosen to announce his withdrawal from the contest for the Conservative nomination in the St George's Westminster by-election, in which Beaverbrook's own political movement, the Empire Crusade, was putting up a candidate.[38] Mosley's strength was in party meetings; even so, the absence of wide press support at the most favourable time for his party's prospects was bound to damage him.

After the formation of the National government in 1931 the National Labour Party was in desperate need of propaganda to counter Labour hostility. Robert Donald, whose career after he left the *Daily Chronicle* seems to have been a sequence of miscalculations, was invited by Ramsay MacDonald to be chairman of the party's publicity committee. First a fortnightly *News-Letter* was founded. Then in 1932 a weekly magazine was secured – *Everyman*, which 'for many years had been stimulating popular interest in books and in intellectual pursuits generally'.[39] Donald became editor. The material sounded unpromising and the paper had little success.

Such endeavours look pathetic against the bounding circulations of the big dailies in the 1930s. This growth was the logical continuation of the trends set in motion at the turn of the century. To a reader then 'the daily newspaper of his choice had the intimate quality of a personality.'[40] Daily papers were of small circulation and limited to the upper and middle classes. The success of the *Daily Mail* lay in expanding into the lower middle classes. By the time it was founded (1896) these had the purchasing power, education and leisure to buy a daily paper (they had been buying

Sunday papers for years). They could not yet afford one penny. But at the same time branded consumer goods were expanding, and for these a mass circulation newspaper was an ideal advertising medium. Advertising revenue enabled Northcliffe to sell the *Daily Mail* for a halfpenny (and to bill it as 'A Penny Newspaper for One Halfpenny'). The paper exploited new subjects – fashion, cookery, social gossip, sports like bicycling – which appealed to women and to those who, moving upwards in the social scale, were conservative by nature but did not want a totally political, still less a rigidly partisan paper. Northcliffe was interested in profits, moreover; the *Daily Mail* was the first daily paper in which the public could buy shares. The paper's economic basis was thus linked firmly to circulation; and the higher the circulation (assuming elastic advertising revenue) the healthier the profit.

Northcliffe cut the knot of political subsidy that so often joined papers to parties. Instead, he wove a cat's cradle of advertising subsidies. This did not matter while the market for readers was expanding. Nor was it a bar to partisanship. Up to the First World War there was still room for the *Daily Mail, Daily News, Daily Chronicle, Daily Express* and *Morning Leader*, all 'popular' papers selling at a halfpenny, to compete against each other while all survived, supporting between them the different factions of two parties. After the war, however, this became increasingly difficult, both for those papers and for 'heavy' ones like *The Times* and *Morning Post*. Already in 1914 Northcliffe had declared that London could not support *The Times*, the *Morning Post*, and the *Daily Telegraph* as well. (One might add the *Standard*, which died in 1917, to the list.)[41] The *Morning Post*, so the *Daily Mail* scoffed on 15 June 1928, was nothing but 'a parasite in the advertising business'. Readers, and therefore advertising revenue, began to be won at the expense of other papers. The costs of competition rose, and those least able to afford them were hit hardest.

The death of the *Daily Chronicle* is a perfect example of the results. Contrary to the view of the 1947 Royal Commission on the Press, which has found its way into the literature, the paper's failure did not lie 'purely in its financial entanglements'.[42] Certainly the paper had been bought by its new owners, the Inveresk Paper Company, at an inflated price in 1928; and much effort (including an attempt to lure away Beverley Baxter, editor of the *Daily Express*) went into its modernisation of make-up and style. But the real explanation for the failure was the revamped *Daily Herald*. This came out on 17 March 1930, a few days after the new *Daily*

Chronicle, with twenty pages instead of ten and Ramsay MacDonald starting the presses. The *Daily Chronicle* was simply 'torpedoed flat'.[43] Newsagents were left with thousands of unsold copies. The *Daily Herald* sold a million with its first number. Ten weeks later the *Daily Chronicle* was merged with the *Daily News*.

As with the *Daily Chronicle*, the formation of the newspaper chains, which brought certain economies of scale, had in many cases also involved grossly inflated capitalisation. To get a return, big dividends were needed – which meant big circulation again. Economic pressures therefore all worked towards concentration of ownership and a reduction in the number of newspapers. At the same time they confirmed the 'depoliticisation' that had started with the original attempt to attract a new readership. Politics became subordinate. 'With a few notable exceptions', *The Economist* noted halfway through the interwar period, 'the British Press consists no longer of "organs of opinion"'. The use of apostrophes is significant. Party papers contributed to the live discourse of politics and were an integral part of the system; for the new popular papers an 'organ' analogy was inappropriate. 'The largest circulations develop an opportunist politics of their own which cuts across the schemes of all parties,' wrote J. A. Spender sourly in 1925. 'Their allegiances and their loyalties are quite temporary, and the politician who claims their support is liable to a swift reminder that the newspaper has more important things to think about.'[45]

Nothing illustrates the subordination of politics better than the extremes to which the popular papers went to win circulation in the late 1920s and 1930s. The selling point was the free gift; the newspaper was the wrapping. Free gifts, free insurance and prize competitions were the main methods.[46] Free insurance had been started in the war by the *Daily Chronicle*, which offered 'registered readers' insurance against Zeppelin raids. The original purpose was to make circulation steadier by holding readers to a regular order. The method could be used equally well to increase readership, and *The Economist* estimated that 56 per cent of gross profits were spent in the process.[47] By the late 1930s as many as three-quarters of the readers of the popular press were 'registered' – and insured against anything from the collapse of a grandstand to the birth of twins. The *Daily Mail* had paid out £1,000,000 by 1928. Ghoulish publicity surrounded train disasters.

Prize competitions had been a staple of the early days of Newnes and Northcliffe in the late nineteenth century. 'Entries' for what were usually forecasting games like football pools had to be accompanied by a coupon. Newsagents sold coupons by the dozen, neatly clipped and sometimes already filled in, for a modest fee plus the cost of the unwanted papers. The *Sunday Express* calculated that in the thirty-five weeks of the football season up to £3 millions worth of unread waste paper was probably bought.

In 1928 a legal decision ruled out many of the competitions as lotteries. The focus then shifted to free gifts. When Elias determined in 1930 to push the *Daily Herald* circulation up to 2 millions, the other popular papers had no option but to join in or watch readers and advertising drain away. The *Daily Herald, Daily Express, Daily Mail* and *News Chronicle* recruited some 50,000 canvassers, who moved through city streets like locusts, crunching registered readers and leaving a litter of free cameras, mangles and flannel trousers behind them. A whole Welsh family, it was rumoured, could be clothed from head to foot for the price of eight weeks reading of the *Daily Express*. In 1933 a barrage of sixteen-volume sets of Dickens hit *Daily Herald* readers. The other papers met the challenge. But at a cost: the *Daily Express* had to sell at ten shillings apiece 124,000 sets that had cost fourteen-and-fourpence each to produce.

The whole business seemed ludicrous viewed from the editorial chair of a Spender or a Gwynne. Where was the high political mission of the press, the rational, intellectual ideal behind the nineteenth-century notion of 'public opinion'? No wonder the founders of the *Daily Worker* felt that the *Daily Herald* had been 'sold out' by the Labour movement, for Elias was one of the ringleaders in these developments.

Circulations were obviously not built by these methods alone. But the kind of content which attracted readers was in the tradition established by Northcliffe in the *Daily Mail*, and it put a premium on brightness, liveliness – anything that would entertain. The newspaper developed a broad social function, as distinct from a narrowly political one. As the number of readers increased, the content had to become more total and miscellaneous. This required a completely different kind of editorial direction from pre-war days. Editors became technicians, not trenchant political essayists. Had he and his like been put in charge of a really popular paper, Spender freely conceded in 1927, they 'could have been relied upon to kill it in about a fortnight'.[48] To Gwynne, Beaverbrook wrote reflectively on the death

of the *Morning Post*: 'Journalism has become a difficult and tire-
some business now – not in the least like the journalism of twenty
years ago. Other qualities enter into the production of newspapers
that are best displayed not by those who have been taught to write
well and edit wisely, but by those who have got business ability,
and capacity for economical and vigorous industrial direction.'[49]
Beaverbrook's own young men at the *Daily Express* – the 'young
Eaglets' like Arthur Christiansen, Frank Owen and Dick
Plummer – typified the new qualities. The *Daily Express*, a self-
congratulatory article proclaimed when the circulation reached 2
millions in 1933, was 'in great measure, an achievement of
youth. . . ; sprawling all over the delicate mechanism of the commercial side of the papers and extracting brilliant results from
it; pulling the beards of statesmen more than twice their age;
questioning, exploring, innovating and achieving'.[50]

In 1935 'youth' was also about to bring tabloid journalism to
Britain in the shape of the *Daily Mirror*. The impetus came from
Cecil King, Northcliffe's nephew, who was advertising director;
from Guy Bartholomew, the editor, and from Hugh Cudlipp,
aged twenty-two, the features editor. Like most of Fleet Street's
innovations the idea came from America, on the advice of the advertising agency, J. Walter Thompson. The now familiar *Daily
Mirror* style and interests were built up, with an increasing radicalism and challenge to conventional wisdom.[51] The *Daily Mirror*
was slow to fall into line behind Baldwin over the abdication ('Tell
us the Facts, Mr Baldwin'), and it pursued an uncompromising
campaign against appeasement. In the war and in the later 1940s
it was to capture the mood of the working class better than any
other paper. Its steady growth in circulation in the late 1930s –
without much need for the sales methods of the other papers –
was, for the working class, a repetition of the *Daily Mail's* expansion into the lower middle classes in the Edwardian era. This was
the last great market; and it was tapped with the same dependence on advertising revenue and the same stress on a range of
values and interests geared to entertainment that characterised
the non-tabloid techniques of the popular papers.

The emphasis in the press on entertainment may also have
reflected the competitive position of the whole industry between
the wars. Newspapers increasingly had to compete for the money
and time of readers against the cinema and the B.B.C. The paper-
back book was established in the 1930s – and significantly it was
with the 'Penguin Special', a topical survey of some problem of the

moment, that Allen Lane made his first impact in 1937, more than with reprinted fiction. Lastly there was the growth of pictorial journalism, turned to best account in Stefan Lorant's *Picture Post* (1938). Greater physical mobility, and the growth of spectator sports like greyhound racing, must also have eaten into the time people would spend reading newspapers, as well as helping to define their range of interests. It was not surprising that short articles, big headlines, and plenty of pictures made a successful formula for attracting them.

The 'depoliticised' popular press by no means lost all interest in politics. To some extent the change was a growth of interest in other subjects more than a loss of interest in politics. There was, furthermore, nothing in it that was inconsistent with strong party loyalty. But that loyalty had rested before the war on the politician's ability to *command* a paper and ultimately to get rid of a recalcitrant editor, as the Cadburys ditched A. G. Gardiner from the *Daily News* in 1918 and Lloyd George ditched Donald from the *Daily Chronicle* in the same year. Now the loyalty rested only on sentiment. Even the readers of the *Daily Herald*, whose policy remained in the clutches of the T.U.C., had been wooed by Elias with free gifts and a non-political appeal. If partisanship and good newspaper management clashed, partisanship would go – unless the proprietor had a party goal; and that, nowadays, was not something the parties themselves could control.

In the 'depoliticised' papers, partisanship had become precarious and therefore unpredictable. The implications are brought out by considering the politicians' obsession with responsibility. The popular papers, complained Spender, an apologist for the old system, concentrated in 'the hands of a few individuals' who were responsible to nobody but themselves 'a power which was a serious rival to Parliament, and upon which in the last resort Parliament depends'.[52] Lloyd George wrote of Northcliffe: 'He owed no allegiance to any party, so that every genuine party man deplored his paper. Most of them bought it and read what was in it and then damned it.'[53] Baldwin, in probably the most famous jibe of all against the press barons, attacked Rothermere and Beaverbrook in 1931 for aiming in their Empire Free Trade movement at 'power without responsibility – the prerogative of the harlot throughout the ages'.[54]

Lloyd George's remark holds the key to the politicians' attitude. The newspaper proprietors were unreliable. They could not be bought. They were untrammelled by party machinery and the

fine adjustments of policy that bring concerted action. Not all of
them had political goals. William Harrison bought the *Daily
Chronicle* in 1928 explicitly to assure an outlet for his paper mills'
production. Guy Bartholomew was non-political. Others were
quietly conformist. John Astor, though a Conservative M.P. from
1922 until after the Second World War, was teased by his relations for owning *The Times* but not actually reading it.[55] Lord
Burnham and his successors at the *Daily Telegraph* had no extrava-
gant ambitions. Nor did Elias. Between the wars Rothermere and
Beaverbrook were the two who, like Northcliffe in 1914–18, pursued personal political careers at odds with party orthodoxies,
and it would have been surprising if the party leaders had not
fallen out with them.

The initiatives of Beaverbrook and Rothermere are too well
known to need detailed analysis. What it is essential to note in the
present context, however, is that each went so far as to promote
parliamentary candidates. At the height of their ambitions they
joined forces in 1930, somewhat uncomfortably, in the movement
for Empire Free Trade, which briefly threatened Baldwin's position as Conservative leader. Their papers were not merely
detached from the old parties but were turned directly against
them as the instrument of new ones. This was perfectly consistent
with the history both of newspapers and of political parties, but
obviously that did not make them any more acceptable to Baldwin.

A characteristic episode of Rothermere's, in which Northcliffe,
too, was involved, was the anti-waste campaign after the war. As
well as articles nosing out unnecessary government expenditure,
their papers divided M.P.s into 'waste M.P.s' and 'anti-waste
M.P.s'. They highlighted lists of Members who voted for 'squan-
dering estimates', thereby provoking an attempt to have the articles declared in contempt of Parliament.[56] At the Dover by-
election in January 1921 Rothermere backed Sir Thomas Polson
as an anti-waste candidate, his only opponent being the Conservative, John Astor. Polson described himself as an 'independent anti-waste candidate, the friend of every working man, and
every working woman, the friend of the farmer and farm worker
and of the great middle-classes who have been so hard-hit by the
squander-mania of the present Government.'[60] Horatio Bot-
tomley wrote an article in the *Daily Mirror* called 'Dover's chance
to make history'. Polson won convincingly – 56 per cent of the
votes and a majority of 3130. He announced that he would aim to

abolish the ministries of Shipping, Munitions, Food and Health. But on the break-up of the coalition at the next general election he lost the seat to Astor, who also had a kind of revenge in buying *The Times*. The anti-waste campaign petered out.

Empire Free Trade was a much more solid movement.[61] In 1929 Beaverbrook launched his campaign for creating out of the empire a single economic unit protected by a tariff wall, within which the Dominions would gain a market advantage, further raw materials and food while Britain gained a similar market for manufactured goods. Beaverbrook hoped to convert the Conservative party to the idea, and he started giving support to by-election candidates who endorsed it. By the beginning of 1930 he was clear that Baldwin would never allow any kind of Empire Free Trade group to exist inside the party. Beaverbrook therefore declared war on all parliamentary candidates who opposed his scheme. The Empire Crusade was launched. 'I want Empire Free Trade,' he wrote to Gwynne, who had urged the folly of breaking with the Conservatives. 'I don't care if it comes from one party or another. If no party gives it I am for trying to take it from the public.'[57] Rothermere was proceeding on similar lines. In June 1930 he issued his famous letter: 'I cannot make it too abundantly clear that under no circumstances whatsoever will I support Mr Baldwin unless I know exactly what his policy is going to be, unless I have complete guarantees that such policy will be carried out if his party achieves office, and unless I am acquainted with the names of at least eight or ten of his most prominent colleagues in the next Ministry.'[58] Baldwin turned this to advantage. At a public meeting in Caxton Hall he read it out. Then he commented: 'A more preposterous and insolent demand was never made on the leader of any political party. I repudiate it with contempt, and I will fight that attempt at domination to the end.'[59] In October 1930, however, the Crusade candidate beat the official Conservative nominee in the Paddington South by-election. In alliance with Rothermere's United Empire Party, Beaverbrook's Crusade contested four more by-elections before the economic crisis and the National government eclipsed it. Even without that, the movement's failure was assured by the defeat in March 1931 of its candidate, Sir Ernest Potter, in the hard fought by-election of St George's, Westminster, which was regarded as a test case of Baldwin's leadership of the Conservative Party.

The Empire Free Trade campaign is the classic case in the period of the attempt by press barons to wield independent power.

They used their papers to by-pass organised parties or, at most, as a substitute or nucleus for new party organisations. The Communist Party hoped, obviously, to grow with the *Daily Worker*, and the New Party with *Action*. But in those cases movement and paper would grow together, feeding each other resources and strength. The press barons, in contrast, already possessed an instrument linking themselves to the millions of their readers. It had won them on one basis, largely non-political; and now it was to be turned deliberately to create a movement – or the semblance of one – which had no spontaneity or foundations but was constructed from the top downwards. The press barons' political style was populist. The leaders of established institutions – in Parliament, party and the traditional press (if Spender is a guide) – saw them as a threat. They had no geographical, social or economic constituency. Their constituency was an inchoate mass of readers, with whom they were linked in fact not even by the empathy of the mass orator and his surging audience, but from whom they claimed to draw strength and legitimacy. Spender, for all his distaste, admitted that Northcliffe was 'the only completely convinced democrat that I ever knew. He did really believe that things ought to be decided by the mass opinion about them, and to find out what that was . . . seemed to him not only profitable but right and wise.'[62] Yet the definition of mass opinion was really the barons' own. Their leadership ignored intermediaries and was free from the restraints of collective membership. Their instrument, with the new style of popular journalism, was ideal for preaching a populist gospel. Short articles and pungent prose favoured assertion more than argument, with no room for the elaborate syntax of exposition and qualification. Their gospel itself had populist elements. Empire Free Trade was in essence a simple idea. 'I have made up my mind that I am for Empire Free Trade,' wrote Beaverbrook. 'No damned economists are going to put me off.'[63] It was offered as a total solution to Britain's economic problems. It rejected present institutions and policies in favour of old ideas and the old empire. The total and simplist elements coincided well with the total appeal and superficial nature of the popular newspaper. Even the national penetration of the papers gave the movement an appearance of national importance.

With Beaverbrook and Rothermere the dislocation of the press and party system came close to the actual displacement of party by newspaper and of legitimate party leaders by populist proprietors. There were populist elements in the developing style of

Daily Mirror politics in the late 1930s, too ('the people and the *Daily Mirror* versus the politicians'). *The Times*, too, was later criticised in its own official history for following public opinion over appeasement instead of recognising that, unlike party politicians who had to take the electorate into account, a paper should face the issues on their merits alone. But *The Times* in fact had been sticking to party orthodoxy too closely; and neither Geoffrey Dawson nor those who made policy on the *Daily Mirror* had any particular ambitions of their own.

After the Second World War the press and the parties came back into phase. The party system settled down and the press lined up beside it, taking few initiatives and reflecting fairly accurately the jostle of policy and personalities. Yet the period of interwar dislocation carried a lesson which would become highly relevant in any future realignment or upheaval of the parties. The roles of parties and of the media of communications are so closely linked in a democracy that any serious dislocation throws in question the capacity of the former to project their ideas and leaders; and, by corollary, it challenges the right of those who control the latter to deviate from orthodoxy. Between the wars the parties progressively lost direct control of the press and, in the spectacular case of the press barons, failed to accomodate the men who did. The politicians eventually won. But the basis of press/party relations would not be the same again.

Notes

1. J. A. Spender, *The Public Life*, 2 vols (London, Cassell, 1925) vol. II, p. 108.

2. *The Economist*, 10 Nov 1928.

3. The history of the chains is succinctly described in the Royal Commission on the Press, 1947–9, *Report* (London, H.M.S.O., 1949) Cmd 7700, Chapter 7 and Appendix IV; and also in Political and Economic Planning, *Report on the British Press* (London, 1938) pp. 95–105. The latter is a useful source on the interwar press generally.

4. See N. Kaldor and R. Silverman, *A Statistical Analysis of Advertising Expenditure and of the Revenue of the Press* (London, C.U.P., 1948) p. 84.

5. Op. cit., p. 195.

6. P.E.P., op. cit. p. 237, quoting Incorporated Society of British Advertisers survey of 1935.

7. J. A. Spender edited the *Westminster Gazette* from 1896 to 1921. He remarked in his memoirs: '. . .Such papers caught the politicians when they were assembled in the House of Commons, and gave the serious reader something to think about in his leisure hours – in the clubs when his working day was over, and at home in the evenings.' *Life, Journalism and Politics* 2 vols (London, Cassell, 1927) vol. II, p. 134. The last vestiges of the clubland press can still be discerned in the

Evening Standard's 'Londoner's Diary', which projects a sophisticated literary/social/political life style foreign (except in his imagination) to the swaying commuter on the Orpington train.

8. A. P. Wadsworth, *Newspaper Circulations 1800–1954* (Manchester Statistical Society, 1955) p. 27.

9. Neal Blewett, *The Peers, the Parties and the People* (London, Macmillan, 1972) p. 301.

10. Beaverbrook papers, Gwynne to Beaverbrook, 22 Feb 1930.

11. Blewett, op. cit., p. 301.

12. On the Zinoviev letter, see Lewis Chester *et al.*, *The Zinoviev Letter* (London, Heinemann, 1967).

13. *The Labour Year Book 1925* (London, Labour Publications Dept) p. 352.

14. See A. J. P. Taylor, *Beaverbrook* (London, Hamish Hamilton, 1972) pp. 61–2, for interesting light on party subsidies.

15. Viscount Camrose, *British Newspapers and their Controllers* (London, Cassell, 1947) p. 7.

16. On this episode see A. J. P. Taylor, op. cit., pp. 157–8; Frank Owen, *Tempestuous Journey* (London, Hutchinson, 1954) pp. 686–7; Camrose, op. cit.; H. A. Taylor, *Robert Donald* (London, Stanley Paul, 1934); Thomas Jones, *Lloyd George*, London (O.U.P., 1951) p. 61–2, 223; Donald McCormick, *The Mask of Merlin* (London, Macdonald, 1963) p. 233; Sir Charles Mallet, *Mr Lloyd George: A Biography* (London, E. Benn, 1930) p. 286–7.

17. *History of the Times* (London, *The Times*, 1948) vol. IV, Part 2, pp. 684–721. Northcliffe died on 14 August 1922.

18. Wilfrid Hindle, *The Morning Post, 1772–1937* (London, Geo. Routledge, 1937) p. 239–40. Bates became Lord Hurcomb. He died in 1946 when about to embark in the *Queen Elisabeth* for her maiden voyage as a passenger liner.

19. Beaverbrook papers, Gwynne to Beaverbrook, 14 May 1925.

20. Labour Party, *Report of 24th Annual Conference*, p. 42.

21. R. J. Minney, *Viscount Southwood* (London, Odhams, 1954) pp. 223–6, 237; Hamilton Fyfe, *Sixty Years of Fleet Street* (London, W. H. Allen, 1949) pp. 192–5.

22. The history of the *Westminster Gazette* is well analysed by J. A. Spender in his *Life, Journalism and Politics*, vol. II, Chapter 30. See also Wilson Harris, *J. A. Spender* (London, Cassell, 1946).

23. P.E.P., op. cit., p. 106. Cf. William Rust, *The Story of the Daily Worker* (London, People's Press Printing Society, 1949) pp. 12–14. A wholesalers' boycott, which lasted until 1942, made distribution difficult and early printing necessary. The paper was on sale in London at 8.00 p.m. the day before the dated issue.

24. A. J. P. Taylor (ed.), *Lloyd George: a Diary by Frances Stevenson* (London, Hutchinson, 1971) p. 260.

25. F. R. Gannon, quoting an undisclosed source, in *The British Press and Germany 1936–1939* (Oxford, Clarendon Press, 1971) p. 49.

26. Lord Burnham, *Peterborough Court* (London, Cassell, 1955) p. 116–8.

27. A. J. P. Taylor, *Beaverbrook*, p. 53.

28. Philip Gibbs, *The Pageant of the Years* (London, Heinemann, 1946) pp. 56–62.

29. A. J. P. Taylor, *Beaverbrook*, p. 175.

30. *History of the Times*, vol. iv, Part 2, p. 1077.

31. Ernest Bevin did in fact look around for a paper before the *Daily Herald* was secured. He tried to get hold of the *People*. Minney, op. cit., p. 228–9.

32. Maurice Edelman, *The Mirror* (London, Hamish Hamilton, 1966) pp. 19–20; Hugh Cudlipp, *Publish and Be Damned* (London, Dakers, 1953) p. 274.

33. The arrangement is given in full in *History of The Times*, vol, iv, pp. 790–1.

34. Nigel Nicolson (ed.), *Harold Nicolson: Diaries and Letters 1930–39* (London, Collins Fontana, 1969) pp. 75–97.

35. *Ibid.*, pp. 84, 95.

36. Beaverbrook to Nicolson, 25 June 1931, in ibid., p. 77.

37. Beaverbrook archives, Beaverbrook to Mosley 28 Feb 1931.

38. For an account of the by-election see Gillian Peele, St. George's and the Empire Crusade', in Chris Cook and John Ramsden, *By-Elections in British Politics* (London, Macmillan, 1973) pp. 79–108.

39. H. A. Taylor, op. cit., p. 259.

40. *The Economist*, 3 Nov 1928.

41. *The Times*, op. cit., p. 1129.

42. Op. cit., p. 66.

43. The phrase generally used in Fleet Street. Minney, op. cit., p. 240. See also Fyfe, op. cit., pp. 190–1.

44. 3 Nov 1928.

45. *The Public Life*, vol. ii, p. 104.

46. P.E.P., op. cit., pp. 86–90.

47. 17 Nov 1928.

48. *Life, Journalism and Politics*, p. 136.

49. Beaverbrook papers, Beaverbrook to Gwynne, 5 Oct 1937.

50. Arthur Christiansen, *Headlines all my Life* London, Heinemann, 1961) pp. 93–4.

51. Edelman, op. cit., Chapter 2.

52. *The Public Life*, vol. ii, p. 114.

53. David Lloyd George, *The Truth about the Peace Treaties* 2 vols (London, Gollancz, 1938) vol. i, p. 266.

54. Edelman, op. cit., p. 19.

55. Michael Astor, *Tribal Feeling* (London, John Murray, 1963) p. 146.

56. 8 Dec 1920, 135 H. C. Debates, c. 2116–9, c. 2226–8, c. 2406–7.

60. Edelman, op. cit., p. 17.

61. See A. J. P. Taylor, *Beaverbrook*, Chapters 11–13, Cf. Gillian Peele, op. cit.

57. Beaverbrook papers, Beaverbrook to Gwynne, 19 Feb 1930.

58. Edelman, op. cit., pp. 18–19.

59. loc. cit.

62. Quoted in Harold Herd, *The March of Journalism* (London, Allen and Unwin, 1952) p. 249.

63. Beaverbrook papers, Beaverbrook to Gwynne, 28 Jan 1930.

Index

259